Simply Good Food

New Basics for Today's Cook

SIMPLY GO

OD FOOD

NEW BASICS FOR TODAY'S COOK

Katie Stewart
and
Caroline Young

M
MACMILLAN

First published 1994 by Macmillan Reference Books

a division of Macmillan Publishers Limited
Cavaye Place London SW10 9PG
and Basingstoke

Associated companies throughout the world

ISBN 0 333 59841 5

9 8 7 6 5 4 3 2 1

A CIP catalogue record for this book is available from the British Library

Typeset by Spottiswoode Ballantyne
Printed and bound in Great Britain
by Mackays of Chatham PLC, Chatham, Kent

Contents

INTRODUCTION

Good Food

This is a book that I have wanted to write for a long time but I needed a partner, someone who understood food and enjoyed cooking as much as I did. Caroline Young came to my rescue. We both have years of experience in the food industry and have worked together preparing recipes and photographs for *Woman's Journal* magazine for the last six years, so we know each other's style well. During our working sessions we have shared ideas, swapped recipes and learned from each other. Cooking is much more fun when there is someone else interested in the end result and when a conversation can spark off a whole train of new thought. We decided our book should take a fresh look at everything. There have been so many changes: we have less time to cook but there are more foods to choose from, there are fashionable trends like the ill-fated *nouvelle cuisine* and more permanent ones like the importance of a healthy diet, and how many of us don't have at least one vegetarian in the family now? We started with a blank sheet of paper, ready for anything.

There is nothing to beat good home cooking. However simple, something freshly cooked is always better tasting, better looking and better for you. The trouble is, there are so many other demands on everyone's time. We both have jobs and cook for our families. Our friends, just like everyone else, want recipes that are quick to prepare but put on a good appearance. It's been something of a challenge but we got there, and as you turn the pages you will find no recipes that are overly long or complicated. In fact, there are many almost instant ideas.

We are committed to a healthy eating style but not in a boring or intense way. Good healthy menus can be achieved with small changes and some additions to your store cupboard. For health and speed and simply good food, there are pasta dishes, wonderful salads with delicious dressings, surprisingly good grain recipes and many vegetarian dishes that are so appetizing that they'll be enjoyed by non-vegetarians too. Even so, we are not averse to adding a spoonful of double cream or an extra knob of butter where it is justified by the end result.

For inexperienced cooks there is plenty of detail in the useful How to Cook Perfect . . . outlines; this is where you will find all those really useful little tips and hints that nobody ever tells you. For the ambitious cook there are boxes of specialist information, on those interesting new products you see in the supermarket but haven't necessarily got to grips with yet – olive oil, fromage frais, sun-dried tomatoes, fresh ginger and how to make your own wonderful pesto, for instance.

Our recipes are presented in a clear and simple style. Please follow them as we say, at least for the first time. We have included the use of modern equipment like a food processor whenever it suits, but you'll find the 'by hand' method too. We've referred to the microwave, which is indicated by the use of the symbol M, but only when we think it's an asset, saves time and where the end result is as good as when cooked conventionally. Please read the note on Microwave Know-how referring to wattages of different ovens. A good quality heavy frying pan with a non-stick finish and a lid is something we have found indispensable, for risotto, stir-fries and many simple simmered and braised dishes. The recipes include unusual and exciting flavours with spices, flavoured oils and vinegars and exotic sauces to make recipes interesting. To measure accurately throughout we used the standard measuring set of spoons and all our measurements are level. You'll find sets of measuring spoons in any supermarket or cookshop, and it really is worth using them to get the flavour just right. We give both metric and imperial measures but please always stick to one or the other. We use size 2 eggs in our recipes. We have indicated vegetarian recipes with a V symbol. Particularly strict vegetarians may wish to choose alternative ingredients.

This is an up-to-date cookbook for everyone, but that doesn't mean to say that we have ignored traditional recipes – we simply took a second look at them. Now some have a new twist, others have quicker mixing or cooking methods or use newer ingredients. Traditional recipes can only survive if they adapt to modern kitchens; this way we can keep them alive. Our choice of recipe content is wide: there are easy recipes for weekday suppers, fun recipes for weekends, recipes for dinner parties and special occasions. If you have trouble deciding what to choose, turn to the Good Ideas for instant help.

We both hope you get as much pleasure reading and cooking from *Simply Good Food* as we did writing and cooking and eating our way through it. This is our offering for today's good cook.

Katie Stewart
Caroline Young

Microwave Know-how

The microwave oven is a valuable member of your kitchen team of appliances and has many uses other than those we have suggested. The manufacturer's handbook and microwave cookbooks are excellent sources of ideas.

Microwave ovens vary in wattage and it is important to know the wattage of your model to get good cooking results. It should be stated on the oven itself or in the oven handbook. If in doubt, contact the manufacturer.

Microwave cooking in our recipes is indicated by the symbol M and, unless otherwise stated, is on HIGH/100%. Cooking times are for 650-watt ovens. For lower wattage ovens, add on about 20 seconds per minute. For higher wattage ovens, deduct about 10 seconds per minute. If unsure, always err on the safe side and cook for less time, test the result and cook for a little longer if needed.

CHAPTER ONE

Soups and Starters

Soups

These days homemade soups need not be time-consuming or expensive – it is the skilled combination of ingredients and gentle cooking that is important. Bring out your prettiest soup bowls to serve any of them as a first course, or choose one of the heartier soups to serve with warm crusty bread and a simple salad for a satisfying light meal.

HOW TO MAKE BETTER SOUPS

- ❦ The smaller the vegetables are cut, the quicker they will cook.
- ❦ Lightly frying ingredients such as onion, garlic, leeks and celery before adding liquid brings out their natural sweetness and flavour.
- ❦ Gentle simmering brings out the flavour of the ingredients; keep the saucepan covered to avoid evaporation.
- ❦ When a recipe includes milk, always reheat the soup gently just to serving temperature – boiling will spoil the texture and flavour.
- ❦ The seasoning of a soup can be best judged when it is fully cooked. Check cold soups again after chilling.
- ❦ Soups thicken as they cool. When reheating, do not add extra liquid because a soup will thin again with heating. For chilled soups, a little extra cream, stock or milk may be needed to achieve the right consistency.
- ❦ Some soups, especially vegetable ones, taste even better the day after making. Cook quickly to room temperature, then cover and chill. Bring to serving temperature over a low heat, stirring frequently.

Jerusalem Artichoke Soup

SERVES 4 AS A MAIN DISH SOUP, 6 AS A STARTER [V]

450 g/1 lb Jerusalem artichokes
1 medium onion
4 sticks celery
50 g/2 oz butter
600 ml/1 pint vegetable stock
600 ml/1 pint milk
freshly milled pepper
25 g/1 oz fresh breadcrumbs
25 g/1 oz chopped hazelnuts

Using a stiff-bristled brush, scrub the artichokes and trim the stems. Drop into a large pan of boiling water, return to the boil, then reduce the heat to a gentle simmer for 5 minutes. Drain and leave to cool slightly while preparing the other vegetables.

Peel and thinly slice the onion. Finely chop the celery, discarding any leaves. Slice the artichokes. Melt 25 g/1 oz of the butter in a large saucepan. Add the vegetables, cover, and cook over a low heat for 20 minutes or until very soft but not browned. Stir in half the stock.

Purée until smooth. Return to the saucepan and add the remaining stock. Bring to the boil. Stir in the milk and bring slowly to serving temperature over a low heat.

Meanwhile, melt the remaining butter in a frying pan. Stir in the breadcrumbs and hazelnuts. Cook over a high heat, stirring constantly, until crisp and golden brown.

Serve the soup in warm bowls, topped with a spoonful of the crisp nutty crumbs.

Parsnip and Peanut Butter Soup

SERVES 4 AS A MAIN DISH SOUP, 6 AS A STARTER [V]

Peel and finely chop the onion. Trim and finely chop the celery. Peel and crush the garlic. Pare and thinly slice the parsnips.

Heat the oil in a large saucepan. Add the onion, celery and garlic. Cover and cook over a low heat for about 10 minutes, or until soft but not browned. Stir in the chilli powder. Add the parsnips and stock and bring to the boil. Cover, reduce the heat to a gentle simmer, and cook for 20–25 minutes, until the parsnips are quite tender.

Purée until smooth. Return the soup to the saucepan and add the peanut butter, soy sauce and lemon juice. Stir over a low heat until the peanut butter has dissolved. Add the milk and heat to serving temperature.

Ladle the soup into warmed bowls. Top each serving with a spoonful of smetana or Greek-style yogurt and sprinkle with a pinch of paprika.

- 1 medium onion
- 3 celery sticks
- 2 cloves of garlic
- 450 g/1 lb parsnips
- 30 ml/2 tablespoons olive oil
- 5 ml/1 teaspoon chilli powder
- 300 ml/½ pint vegetable stock
- 60 ml/4 tablespoons crunchy peanut butter
- 30 ml/2 tablespoons dark soy sauce
- 10 ml/2 teaspoons lemon juice
- 600 ml/1 pint milk
- 150 ml/¼ pint smetana or Greek-style yogurt
- paprika

Chestnut and Carrot Soup

SERVES 4 AS A MAIN DISH SOUP, 6 AS A STARTER [V]

Peel and finely chop the onion and ginger. Peel and chop the carrots. Drain the chestnuts.

Heat the butter in a large saucepan. Stir in the onion and ginger. Cover and cook over a low heat, stirring frequently, until the onion is soft but not brown. Add the carrots and chestnuts.

Add the stock and bring to the boil. Lower the heat and simmer, covered, for 20 minutes or until the vegetables are quite tender.

- 1 medium onion
- 2.5 cm/1 inch fresh ginger
- 700 g/1½ lb carrots
- 1 (350 g) can whole peeled chestnuts
- 25 g/1 oz butter
- 900 ml/1½ pints vegetable stock
- salt and freshly milled pepper
- 150 ml/¼ pint soured cream

Purée the soup in a blender or processor until smooth. Return to the saucepan and season to taste. Heat gently to serving temperature.

Ladle into warmed soup bowls and serve topped with a spoonful of soured cream.

Bean and Vegetable Broth

SERVES 6 AS A MAIN DISH SOUP, 8 AS A STARTER [V]

2 medium onions
2 cloves of garlic
2 red peppers
4 medium carrots
15 ml/tablespoon olive oil
1½ litres/3 pints vegetable stock
100 g/4 oz green beans
1 (432 g) can cannellini beans
50 g/2 oz small 'soup' pasta
salt and freshly milled pepper
few leaves of chard, spinach or Chinese leaves
90 ml/6 tablespoons extra virgin olive oil
50 g/2 oz grated Parmesan

Peel and finely chop the onions. Peel and crush the garlic. Halve, de-seed and dice the peppers. Peel and finely dice the carrots.

Heat the oil in a large saucepan. Add the onions and cook, covered, over a low heat until softened but not brown. Stir in the garlic, peppers, carrots and half the stock. Bring to the boil, then cover the pan and reduce the heat to a gentle simmer. Cook for 10 minutes, until the vegetables are just tender.

Trim the green beans and cut into 1 cm/½ inch pieces. Add to the pan with the remaining stock. Bring to the boil, then reduce the heat to a simmer for 5 minutes.

Tip the cannellini beans into a strainer and rinse under cold water. Add to the soup with the pasta and continue cooking, uncovered, until the pasta is just tender – about 5 minutes. Season to taste.

Wash and pull the midribs away from the chard, spinach or Chinese leaves, then roll the leaves into a bundle and shred across into ribbons. Place a portion in each warmed soup bowl and spoon in the soup. Add a tablespoon of olive oil and a sprinkling of Parmesan to each bowl.

SOUP KNOW-HOW

Puréed soups Soups may be puréed in a food mill, a blender or processor or worked through a sieve. Each method will give a slightly different result. Use a sieve if you wish to remove any threads from celery or possibly tough skins of beans or tomatoes. A blender will make a very smooth soup, a processor will give a slightly less smooth result due to the shape of the container. For the best result, ladle the vegetables into the processor using a slotted spoon, adding just a little of the stock. Purée and return to the pan.

Chunky soups If two-thirds of the soup is blended or processed until smooth, then the remainder added and very briefly processed with one or two quick bursts of power, a very pleasing thick and slightly chunky texture will be obtained.

Storing soups Don't waste space in the fridge or freezer storing large containers of soup, store them in a condensed form. Completely cook the soups, using the minimum of liquid. Purée if wished, then chill or freeze the resultant thick mixture. To serve, thaw if frozen, stir in liquid to make a serving consistency and gently heat.

Stocks Gone are the days of the old-fashioned stock pot – we use chilled stock from the supermarket or good-quality cubes. Both chilled stocks and cubes vary, and the choice will depend on your personal taste. Vegetable stock cubes are ideal for light soups such as fish as well as for vegetable-based soups. Combine a vegetable cube with either a chicken or a beef cube for a light-flavoured poultry or meat stock.

SOUP GARNISHES

- Reserve a little of one of the soup ingredients – watercress leaves, herbs, leeks, carrots – to finely chop or grate and sprinkle on top of the soup.
- Thinly slice and fry a few button mushrooms to float on top of cream of mushroom soup.
- A spoonful of double cream swirled over a soup looks very appetizing. Alternatively choose soured cream, Greek-style yogurt or smetana.
- A small knob of flavoured butter (see pages 30–1) – parsley, lemon or herb – stirred into vegetable or bean soups just before serving looks pretty and adds richness.
- Pass round a bowl of grated Cheddar or Parmesan when serving soups such as minestrone, mixed vegetable or onion.
- Scatter a pinch of paprika, coarsely ground black pepper or herb-flavoured pepper over a pale-coloured soup.
- Coarsely chop some toasted nuts and sprinkle over a puréed vegetable soup – hazelnuts with Jerusalem artichoke soup, walnuts with leek and potato soup.
- Stir a spoonful of pesto into minestrone or tomato soup.
- Very finely chop a small amount of red, green and yellow peppers and sprinkle over pale green soups such as cream of leek or chilled avocado.
- Top cream of tomato soup with a small swirl of garlic-flavoured mayonnaise.
- Swirl a little mango chutney into double or soured cream, Greek-style yogurt or smetana and spoon on top of curry-flavoured soups such as mulligatawny.

Black Bean Soup

SERVES 4 AS A MAIN DISH SOUP, 6 AS A STARTER

1 large onion
2 large green peppers
2 cloves of garlic
15 ml/1 tablespoon olive oil
1 (432 g) can black-eyed beans
1 litre/$1^3/_4$ pints vegetable stock
100 g/4 oz smoked streaky bacon
15 ml/1 tablespoon sherry vinegar
salt and freshly milled pepper

Peel and very finely chop the onion. Quarter the peppers, removing and discarding the stem and seeds. Finely chop the flesh. Peel and crush the garlic. Heat the oil in a large saucepan and add the onion. Cover and cook over medium heat until very soft and translucent but not brown. Stir in the chopped peppers and garlic.

Tip the beans into a sieve and rinse under cold running water. Add to the saucepan with the stock. Bring just to the boil then reduce the heat to medium. Cover the pan and gently cook for 15 minutes.

Meanwhile, finely chop the bacon, discarding any rinds. Place in a large frying pan and cook over a medium high heat until crisp and golden brown. Add the bacon to the soup, together with any bacon fat in the pan.

Stir in the sherry vinegar. Season to taste – remember the bacon may be salty. Ladle into warmed soup bowls.

Leek and Butter Bean Soup

SERVES 4 AS A MAIN DISH SOUP; INCREASE THE CREAM TO 300 ML/$^1/_2$ PINT TO SERVE 6 AS A STARTER

V

4 leeks
2 medium onions
2 cloves of garlic
40 g/$1^1/_2$ oz butter
grated nutmeg
1 (439 g) can butter beans
900 ml/$1^1/_2$ pints vegetable stock
150 ml/$^1/_4$ pint single cream
freshly milled pepper

Trim, split and wash the leeks. Very finely shred about a teacupful of the tender green stems and set aside for the garnish. Finely slice the remaining leeks. Peel, halve and thinly slice the onions. Peel and crush the garlic.

Melt 25 g/1 oz of the butter in a large saucepan. Add the leeks, onions, garlic and a grating of nutmeg. Cover and cook over a low heat for about 20 minutes, or until very soft but not browned.

Tip the butter beans into a strainer and rinse under cold water. Add to the saucepan along with 300 ml/

½ pint of the stock. Bring to the boil, cover and reduce the heat to a gentle simmer for 5 minutes.

Purée until smooth. Return the soup to the saucepan and stir in the remaining stock and the cream. Season to taste with pepper and reheat for serving.

Meanwhile, melt the remaining butter in a small frying pan and add the reserved green leek shreds. Quickly cook over a high heat, stirring constantly, until just tender.

Serve the soup in warm bowls topped with the green leek shreds.

Leek, Scallop and Watercress Soup

SERVES 4 AS A MAIN DISH SOUP

- 2 medium onions
- 4 leeks
- 225 g/8 oz potato
- 1 bunch watercress
- 50 g/2 oz butter
- salt and freshly milled pepper
- grated nutmeg
- 600 ml/1 pint vegetable stock
- 6–8 fresh scallops
- 150 ml/¼ pint single cream
- paprika
- chopped fresh parsley

Peel, halve and thinly slice the onions. Trim, split and wash the leeks, then shred all the white and some of the tender green stems. Peel and chop the potato. Wash the watercress and pick off the green leafy tops.

Melt half the butter in a large saucepan. Add the onion, leeks, potato, a seasoning of freshly milled pepper and a grating of nutmeg. Cover and gently stew the vegetables over a low heat for 20 minutes or until very soft.

Add the watercress and cook for a moment to wilt the leaves. Purée the vegetable mixture and return to the saucepan. Stir in the vegetable stock.

Melt the remaining butter in a frying pan. Slice the scallops thickly. Add them to the hot butter and fry for 1–2 minutes until the flesh has firmed up and they are tinged with brown. Stir the cream into the scallops then turn the scallops and cream into the soup.

Gently reheat the soup and check for seasoning. Ladle into soup bowls, and dust each serving with paprika and a scattering of finely chopped parsley.

CROÛTONS AND OTHER CRUNCHY BITS

Croûtons can be all shapes and sizes, not just neat little cubes. Make chunky 1 cm/½ inch cubes to serve with thick main dish soups, tiny elegant ones to serve with thinner starter soups. 'Pulled bread' is irregularly shaped *croûtons* – instead of dicing the bread, simply pull apart a thick slice of bread into small pieces. Whichever shape or size, quickly fry *croûtons* in oil, stirring constantly, until light golden brown. Lift out of the pan and drain on kitchen paper. Serve freshly cooked or cool and store in an airtight container. For extra flavour add garlic to the cooking oil or sprinkle the freshly cooked *croûtons* with fresh or dried herbs, or paprika.

A topping of crunchy crumbs adds texture to a very smooth soup. Fry fresh breadcrumbs in oil until just golden brown, stirring constantly. A crushed clove of garlic added to the oil will flavour the crumbs.

Garlic toasts are even quicker than *croûtons*. Spread chunky slices of bread with garlic or herbed butter and grill, buttered-side only, until golden brown. Serve piping hot.

For 'Italian-style' toasts combine olive oil and crushed cloves of garlic. Spread on bread slices and grill until golden.

Cheese toasts traditionally are floated on top of French onion soup but go well with bean and vegetable main-dish soups too. Blend together grated cheese and a little butter to a spreading consistency. Spread on slices of bread and grill until golden brown and bubbling. The butter could be garlic- or herb-flavoured, or add a little mild or hot mustard to taste.

Vegetable Chowder

Illustrated on Plate One

SERVES 4 AS A MAIN DISH SOUP, 6 AS A STARTER [V]

- 1 medium onion
- 225 g/8 oz potatoes
- 225 g/8 oz carrots
- 50 g/2 oz butter
- 30 ml/2 tablespoons plain flour
- 1.1 litres/2 pints vegetable stock
- 1 (326 g) can sweetcorn with peppers
- salt and freshly milled pepper
- 100 g/4 oz grated mature Cheddar

Peel and finely chop the onion. Peel and dice the potatoes and carrots.

Heat the butter in a large saucepan. Add the onion and cook over a low heat, stirring frequently, until soft but not brown. Stir in the flour and gradually add the stock.

Add the potatoes and carrots. Bring to the boil, then lower the heat, cover with the pan lid and simmer, for 20–30 minutes, until the vegetables are quite tender.

Drain the sweetcorn and add to the soup. Season to taste. Heat a minute or two longer, then ladle into warmed soup bowls. Serve topped with the grated cheese.

Fresh Tomato Soup with Tarragon

SERVES 4 AS A MAIN DISH SOUP, 6 AS A STARTER V

900 g/2 lb ripe tomatoes
1 medium onion
3 medium carrots
1–2 cloves of garlic
1 orange
45 ml/3 tablespoons olive oil
5 ml/1 teaspoon caster sugar
30 ml/2 tablespoons chopped fresh tarragon leaves
salt and freshly milled pepper
15 ml/1 tablespoon tomato purée
450 ml/$^3/_4$ pint vegetable stock
4 pieces of sun-dried tomatoes in oil
150 ml/$^1/_4$ pint thick Greek-style yogurt

Wash the tomatoes and cut out the stem ends. Slice the tomatoes thickly. Peel and finely chop the onion. Pare and finely dice or grate the carrots. Peel and crush the garlic. Pare 2 pieces of rind from the orange, squeeze the juice and reserve.

Heat the olive oil in a large saucepan. Add the onion and sprinkle with the sugar. Cook gently, stirring frequently, until the onion is softened and pale golden brown – this adds flavour. Add the garlic and stir into the mixture.

Add the tomatoes, carrots, orange rind, tarragon and a good seasoning of salt and pepper. Cover with the pan lid and let the vegetables simmer gently for about 40 minutes to draw the juices.

Mix the tomato purée and reserved orange juice with the stock and stir into the vegetables. Re-cover and cook gently for 20–30 minutes, by which time all the vegetables should be tender.

Meanwhile, finely chop the sun-dried tomatoes and mix with a little of their oil. Lift the strips of orange peel out of the soup. Purée the soup until smooth, return to the saucepan and reheat to serving temperature.

Ladle into warmed soup bowls. Top each serving with a spoonful of Greek-style yogurt and a little chopped sun-dried tomatoes and oil.

Celery and Stilton Soup

SERVES 2–3 AS A MAIN DISH SOUP, 4 AS A STARTER V

1 medium onion
1 head of celery
1 large potato
(175–225 g/6–8 oz)
600 ml/1 pint vegetable stock
100 g/4 oz Stilton
300 ml/½ pint single cream
salt and freshly milled pepper
paprika

Peel and finely chop the onion. Separate the celery stalks, reserving the leaves. Scrub the stalks well and chop finely. Peel and dice the potato.

Place the vegetables in a large saucepan and add the stock. Bring to the boil, then lower the heat and simmer, covered, for 20–30 minutes, until the vegetables are quite tender.

Purée the soup mixture in a blender or processor. Return one-third of the soup to the blender with the cheese. Process until just smooth, then add to the remainder of the soup in the saucepan. Add the cream and stir until well blended.

Taste for seasoning (remember Stilton is naturally salty) and gently reheat. Do not allow to boil.

Ladle into warmed soup bowls, sprinkle with paprika and add a celery leaf garnish.

Chilled Courgette Soup with Tomato Salsa

SERVES 4 AS A MAIN DISH SOUP, 6 AS A STARTER V

700 g/1½ lb baby courgettes
1 bunch spring onions
600 ml/1 pint vegetable stock
300 ml/½ pint Greek-style yogurt
salt and freshly milled pepper

Wash, trim and roughly chop the courgettes. Trim the spring onions and chop. Place the vegetables in a saucepan and add the stock. Bring just to the boil, then cover and simmer gently until the courgettes are quite soft. Cool to room temperature.

Spoon the vegetables and stock into a food processor or blender. Add three-quarters of the yogurt and buzz until smooth. Season with salt and pepper. Pour into a bowl, cover and refrigerate until well chilled – several hours or overnight.

Meanwhile, make the Tomato Salsa. Slash the stem end of the tomato with a knife and cover with boiling water for 2–3 minutes. Drain and skin. Cut into quarters, remove and discard the stem, core and seeds. Chop the tomato flesh into small cubes. Peel the onion and finely chop. Place both in a small bowl and stir in the vinegar and olive oil. Season to taste and allow to stand for several hours or overnight to allow the flavours to mellow.

To serve, stir the soup and spoon into chilled soup bowls. Top each serving with a spoonful of the remaining yogurt and the Tomato Salsa.

1 large ripe tomato
1 small red onion
15 ml/1 tablespoon red wine vinegar
15 ml/1 tablespoon olive oil

Iced Avocado Soup with Pepper Salsa

SERVES 6 AS A STARTER **V**

Halve the avocados lengthwise and remove the stones. Scoop out the flesh with a spoon and put into a blender or food processor. Add half the chilled stock and the lemon juice and buzz until smooth.

Pour the soup into a bowl and stir in the remaining stock and the cream. Season with salt and pepper. Cover tightly with clingfilm and refrigerate until well chilled.

Meanwhile make the Pepper Salsa. Quarter the peppers, removing and discarding the stem, seeds and any white membrane. Cut the flesh into tiny dice and place in a small serving bowl. Stir in the chives, oil and vinegar and lightly season. Cover and chill until needed.

Serve the soup in well-chilled bowls – glass would be very pretty. Add a spoonful of the Pepper Salsa to each bowl and pass around the remainder to be added at the table.

2 large ripe avocados
900 ml/1½ pints chilled vegetable stock
juice of 1 lemon
150 ml/¼ pint single cream
salt and freshly milled pepper
1 small red pepper
1 small yellow pepper
60 ml/4 tablespoons chopped fresh chives
10 ml/2 teaspoons olive oil
10 ml/2 teaspoons white wine vinegar

Starters

The best ideas are always the simple ones – starters should be tempting, not filling. Small and attractively presented combinations of colour, texture and flavour is what you should aim for. Fresh fruits with seafood, smoked salmon with hot potato salad – the list can be endless and need not involve any cooking!

AVOCADOS

When possible, buy avocados several days before you wish to serve them, as they are frequently sold under-ripe. Leave at room temperature for about 36 hours. You can tell when one is ready to eat by the 'feel' – the fruit should give to gentle pressure when cradled in the hand. At this stage it is perfect to eat in the half shell or cut for a salad. For dips or spreads, it should feel very soft all over.

Ideally avocados should be prepared just before serving. Cut an avocado in half horizontally. Gently twist to separate the two halves. To remove a difficult stone, hold one half of the fruit cupped in your hand and hit the stone firmly with a sharp knife. Lift up the knife – with the stone attached.

To retain the brilliant green colour just under the skin, gently pull the skin off rather than peeling with a knife. Brushing with lemon juice will help preserve the creamy colour.

Crunchy Mushrooms with a Choice of Dips

SERVES 4 V

For the Mustard Dip
150 ml/$^1/_4$ pint fromage frais
15 ml/1 level tablespoon wholegrain mustard
2–3 spring onions

For the Garlic Dip
150 ml/$^1/_4$ pint mayonnaise
1–2 cloves of garlic
30 ml/2 tablespoons chopped fresh parsley

450 g/1 lb button mushrooms
1 egg
30 ml/2 tablespoons oil
100–175 g/4–6 oz fresh white breadcrumbs
15 ml/1 level tablespoon paprika
salt and freshly milled pepper

Make the dips ahead of time.

For the Mustard Dip, in a small bowl whisk together the fromage frais, mustard and a seasoning of salt and pepper. Trim and finely chop the spring onions and stir in. Cover and chill for at least 1 hour.

For the Garlic Dip, spoon the mayonnaise into a small bowl and whisk in 1–2 teaspoons of warm water to thin it to a dipping consistency. Peel and crush the garlic and stir in, with a good seasoning of salt and pepper and the chopped parsley. Cover and chill for at least 1 hour.

Heat the oven to 190°C/375°F/gas mark 5.

Wipe the mushrooms and trim the stalks level with the caps. Lightly mix the egg with the oil in a shallow plate. Spread the breadcrumbs on a large sheet of greaseproof paper and sprinkle over the paprika. Lightly mix together.

Roll each mushroom first in the beaten egg and then in the breadcrumbs. Arrange the mushrooms on oiled baking sheets so that they do not touch. Bake for 20 minutes. Serve very hot with the dips.

Grilled Avocados with Prawns

SERVES 4

350 g/12 oz cooked and peeled king prawns
45 ml/3 level tablespoons mayonnaise
salt and freshly milled black pepper
75 g/3 oz Gruyère
2 ripe avocados

Dry the prawns on kitchen paper to remove any moisture, then place in a bowl. Add the mayonnaise and a seasoning of salt and pepper. Lightly turn to coat the prawns with the dressing. Using a cheese slice, very thinly slice the cheese, or grate coarsely.

Heat the grill to high and set the grill rack about 7.5 cm/3 inches from the heat. Slice each avocado lengthwise, twist the halves to separate, then remove the stones. Cutting a tiny sliver from the base of a wobbly avocado will encourage it to sit level.

Spoon some prawns into each avocado hollow and top with the cheese. Set under the grill until the cheese has melted and the prawns are heated through. Serve piping hot.

Strawberries and Cucumber in a Mint Dressing

SERVES 4

V

30 ml/2 tablespoons chopped fresh mint
5 ml/1 level teaspoon caster sugar
salt and freshly milled pepper
30 ml/2 tablespoons raspberry vinegar
60 ml/4 tablespoons grapeseed oil
½ a cucumber
225 g/8 oz ripe strawberries

In a mixing bowl pound the chopped mint with the sugar, using a wooden spoon, to draw out the flavouring oils. Add a seasoning of salt and pepper and the vinegar and stir to dissolve the seasonings. Stir in the oil and taste – the flavouring should be sweet-sour. Slice the cucumber very thinly, add to the dressing and marinate for 1 hour.

Slice the strawberries on to individual serving plates, add the cucumber slices and spoon over the mint dressing.

SIMPLE COMBINATIONS

Asparagus Vinaigrette [V] Serve freshly cooked, well-drained asparagus drizzled with Fresh Herb Vinaigrette (page 50). 700–900 g (1½–2 lb) of cooked asparagus will serve 4–6.

Minted Grapefruit [V] Arrange fresh grapefruit segments in individual dishes and drizzle over a little green crème-de-menthe. Allow 1 grapefruit per person.

Pesto Pasta Cook 3–4 pieces of fresh ravioli per serving, according to the packet directions. Drain well and arrange on warm plates. With a fork, whisk together equal quantities of pesto, olive oil and lemon juice (about 15 ml/1 tablespoon of each for 2 servings). Spoon over the warm pasta and serve immediately.

Orange and Sweet Onion Salad [V] Arrange peeled and thinly sliced oranges and mild red onions on individual flat plates. Spoon over Vinaigrette Dressing made with sherry vinegar (page 38), and top with pitted black olives. *Illustrated on Plate One.*

Pears and Parma Ham Quarter, peel and core a ripe pear per serving. Arrange on flat plates with lightly rolled slices of Parma ham (2 per serving). Spoon over a little Fresh Herb Vinaigrette (page 50) made with mint. Serve immediately, garnished with a mint sprig.

Prawns and Grapefruit Alternate fresh pink grapefruit segments and peeled, cooked prawns in a circle on individual plates. Allow 1 grapefruit and 100 g (4 oz) prawns for 2 servings. Stir a little fresh lemon juice into mayonnaise to soften its consistency slightly and spoon into the centre of the plate. Sprinkle with finely chopped fresh chives or parsley and serve immediately.

Melon and Berries [V] Cut and peel very thin wedges from 2 or more different coloured melons. Arrange on individual plates and add a few fresh strawberries or raspberries. Serve topped with a spoonful of soured cream seasoned to taste with salt and freshly milled black pepper.

Mozzarella and Anchovy Croûtes

SERVES 4

1 (50 g) can anchovies
50 g/2 oz soft butter
2 cloves of garlic
olive oil
freshly milled pepper
45 ml/3 tablespoons chopped fresh parsley
2 large ripe tomatoes
1 baguette French bread
150 g (5 oz) mozzarella

Drain the anchovies, reserving the oil. Measure the butter into a bowl. Peel and chop the garlic, add to the butter and beat with a wooden spoon until soft and creamy.

Measure the anchovy oil and make up to 30 ml/2 tablespoons with olive oil if needed. Add to the butter with a good seasoning of pepper and the parsley and beat until well blended in.

Slice the tomatoes. Cut the baton diagonally into 8 thick oval slices and place on a baking sheet. Spread one side of each slice with the seasoned butter and arrange the tomato slices on top.

Drain the mozzarella on kitchen paper and cut into very thin slices. Arrange over the tomatoes and top with the anchovies. If not serving immediately, cover and chill until serving time.

Heat the oven to 190°C/375°F/gas mark 5.

Bake the *croûtes* for 10 minutes or until bubbling hot. Serve very hot.

Gingered Pineapple with Chive Cheese

SERVES 4 V

- 2.5 cm/1 inch fresh ginger
- 15 ml/1 tablespoon clear honey
- 4 thick fresh pineapple slices
- 175 g/6 oz curd cheese
- 15–30 ml/1–2 tablespoons soured cream
- salt and freshly milled pepper
- 15 ml/1 tablespoon chopped fresh chives
- 15 ml/1 tablespoon fresh lemon juice
- 45 ml/3 tablespoons grapeseed oil
- whole chives for garnish

Cut away the brown skin of the ginger and finely grate the flesh. Place in a shallow dish with the honey and add the pineapple slices. Chill the fruit for at least 1 hour, turning occasionally – the honey will form a syrup.

Mix the curd cheese with enough soured cream to give a soft consistency. Season with salt and pepper and stir in the chopped chives. Arrange the pineapple slices on individual serving plates and neatly spoon the cheese on top. Stir the lemon juice and oil into the honey syrup and season to taste. Spoon over the pineapple and cheese and garnish each plate with 2 or 3 whole chives.

BUYING AND STORING SMOKED SALMON

Smoked salmon can be ordered direct from the smokers and sent by mail order to anywhere in the country. You can also buy top-quality smoked salmon in any supermarket or speciality food store.

For a special occasion it's well worth considering a whole side of smoked salmon. Allow time to shop around a bit as you may have to order it specially. You will probably be able to order it ready sliced but if you like to slice it yourself the right knife – a Granton – helps. It has a long blade with a scalloped (not serrated) edge. Take wafer thin slices, the width of your hand, from the top of the fish through to the skin, working from the tail towards the head. The slices should be so thin you can see the knife blade through them. Fold the left-over skin back over the fish in between times to keep it moist. Well wrapped and refrigerated, a side will stay fresh for up to 2 weeks.

Vacuum-packed pre-sliced smoked salmon is the most popular buy. Stored in the refrigerator unopened, it will keep well for 2–3 weeks. Take note of the 'use-by' date. Once opened, use quickly. Smoked salmon pieces or trimmings are useful for sandwiches or for making paté. They are more likely to be available direct from the smokehouse because they are the offcuts from whole sides. You can get them by post if not locally.

For the best flavour, smoked salmon should be served at room temperature. Once separated into slices it quickly dries out, so keep it well covered until just before serving.

SMOKED SALMON SPECIALS

Smoked salmon is too delicious to be eaten just with lemon wedges. Serve the following suggestions in small portions as starters, or more generously sized as a light meal.

Serve thinly sliced smoked salmon with . . .

- Hot potato salad. Cook baby potatoes until just tender and drain well. Toss with lemon or garlic mayonnaise and serve immediately.
- Cold, very lightly cooked scrambled eggs. The eggs should be very creamy. Sprinkle with finely chopped chives or tarragon.
- Wedges of ripe dessert pear and avocado. Spoon over a little oil and vinegar dressing and serve immediately.
- A neat spoonful of taramasalata or smoked salmon paté from the delicatessen counter. Add lemon wedges and a pretty lettuce leaf.
- Hot creamy scrambled eggs. Arrange the smoked salmon on plates and slip into a just-warm oven to warm through while scrambling the eggs. Gently heat a little double cream. Add the hot eggs to the plates and trickle over a spoonful of warm cream. Season with freshly milled pepper and serve immediately.

CHAPTER TWO

Vegetables

Vegetables deserve more appreciation, as with little effort they make colourful side dishes. Sometimes just a glaze, a herb butter or a sprinkling of something crunchy is all that's needed to bring out their natural flavours and enhance the textures. Add one or two additional ingredients and you have a warming main dish.

POTATOES

Perfect Roast Potatoes

The ultimate roast potato should be crisp and golden brown on the outside, soft and fluffy on the inside. For perfect results just follow these simple guidelines:

- Always choose a main crop potato. All are good for roasting – Maris Piper or Désirée are the very best.
- Traditionally roast potatoes are peeled, but they may be just scrubbed if preferred. Leave small potatoes whole, cutting larger ones to a similar size.
- Place in a large pan and cover with cold water. Add a teaspoon of salt. Quickly bring up to the boil, then drain immediately.
- Potatoes for roasting must be dry – either return them to the pan and shake just above the heat for a few moments, or dry on a clean teatowel.
- Pour 30–45 ml/2–3 tablespoons oil into a roasting tin large enough to hold the potatoes in a single layer. Place in the hot oven for a few minutes to heat up. Add the dried potatoes and turn to coat with the hot oil.
- A high temperature and short cooking time gives the best results: at 220°C/425°F/gas mark 7 they will be cooked in 50–60 minutes. If cooking with the joint, place the potatoes above the meat. When the meat is cooked, remove it from the oven, increase the oven temperature to 220°C/425°F/gas mark 7 and cook the potatoes for a further 15–20 minutes to crisp them.
- Lift the cooked potatoes out of the tin with a slotted spoon and drain them on kitchen paper. Sprinkle with sea salt and serve immediately.
- If you have to delay serving them, keep them hot uncovered to avoid softening the crisp finish.

Fantail Potatoes

- Choose small even-sized main crop potatoes. Peel or scrub and dry well. Cut in thin slices two-thirds of the way through (like garlic bread) and turn in the hot oil as for roast potatoes, finishing with the cut side uppermost. Sprinkle with a little sea salt and cook as for roast potatoes.

Quilted Potatoes

- Scrub medium or large main crop potatoes and dry well. Cut in half horizontally to give an oval cut surface. Score this surface into diamonds and brush with oil. Sprinkle with sea salt and place cut side uppermost in a roasting tin. Cook as for roast potatoes.

Paprika Wedges

- Peel or scrub medium or large main crop potatoes and dry well. Cut lengthwise into long wedges. Brush the cut surfaces with oil and sprinkle with sea salt and paprika. Cook as for roast potatoes. *Illustrated on Plate Two.*

Oven-baked New Potatoes

- Scrub or peel small even-sized new crop potatoes. Place in a shallow casserole and sprinkle with olive oil. Cover with a lid and shake the dish to coat the potatoes with the oil. Cook, covered, at 190°C/375°F/gas mark 5 for 30–40 minutes, or until tender when pierced with a fork. Sprinkle with sea salt and serve immediately.

Garlicky New Potatoes

- Scrub or peel small even-sized new crop potatoes and place in a shallow casserole.

Separate the cloves of a whole head of garlic but do not peel. Add to the potatoes together with a spoonful or two of olive oil. Cover and shake to coat the potatoes and garlic with oil. Cover and cook at 190°C/375°F/gas mark 5 for 30–40 minutes or until the potatoes are tender when pierced with a fork. Serve the garlic with the potatoes. It will have cooked to a mild creamy consistency and can be easily removed from the papery skins.

Aubergine and Potato Gratin

SERVES 3–4 AS A MAIN DISH [V]

- 1 large onion
- 2 cloves of garlic
- 2 medium aubergines
- 30 ml/2 tablespoons olive oil
- 1 (397 g) can chopped tomatoes
- 15 ml/1 tablespoon tomato purée
- 5 ml/1 level teaspoon caster sugar
- 5 ml/1 teaspoon red wine vinegar
- salt and freshly milled pepper
- 150 ml/¼ pint vegetable stock
- 700 g/1½ lb potatoes
- 25 g/1 oz butter
- 30 ml/2 level tablespoons plain flour
- 450 ml/¾ pint milk
- freshly grated nutmeg
- 100 g/4 oz grated mozzarella
- 30 ml/2 level tablespoons grated Parmesan
- 2 eggs

Peel and finely chop the onion, and peel and crush the garlic. Leaving the aubergines unpeeled, cut them into large cubes. Heat the oil in a medium saucepan, add the onion and cook over a low heat to soften. Add the garlic and stir. Stir in the aubergines, then add the tomatoes, tomato purée, sugar, vinegar, salt and pepper and the stock. Bring to a simmer, cover with the pan lid and cook gently for 40 minutes to make a rich vegetable sauce.

Meanwhile, peel the potatoes and cut in 0.5 cm/¼ inch slices. Tip them into a large pan of cold water and bring just to the boil. Simmer for 5–6 minutes until barely tender, then drain well.

Spoon half the vegetable sauce over the base of a 1.7 litre/3 pint baking dish. Cover with half the potato slices. Top with the rest of the vegetable sauce and finally add the remaining potato slices in an even layer. Set aside while making the cheese topping.

Heat the oven to 190°C/375°F/gas mark 5.

Melt the butter in a medium saucepan, stir in the flour, and cook, stirring, for 1 minute. Gradually add the milk, stirring constantly, to make a smooth thin sauce. Bring to a simmer and cook, stirring, 2–3 minutes. Off the heat season with salt, pepper and a pinch of nutmeg. Add the mozzarella and Parmesan and stir until melted.

Let the sauce cool for 5 minutes, then beat in the eggs. Pour evenly over the aubergine and potato layers. Set in the heated oven and bake for 30–40 minutes until bubbling hot and golden brown.

ADDING ZIP TO VEGETABLES

Vegetables don't have to be second-class citizens when just a simple addition or two can make them extra special. Quickly cook and well drain any vegetable and then add your chosen additions. Always serve vegetables freshly cooked and piping hot.

- Introduce crunch with slivered toasted almonds or brazil nuts; crisply grilled bacon bits; crunchy fried breadcrumbs or *croûtons*.
- Add colour with onion rings fried until golden brown; golden seedless raisins; finely chopped fresh herbs; a dusting of toasted oatmeal; freshly grated Parmesan.
- Boost natural fresh flavours with freshly milled pepper and sea salt added after cooking; a sprinkling of caster sugar; freshly grated nutmeg.
- Add a pretty glaze with a drizzle of extra virgin olive oil; melted Flavoured Butters (pages 30–1); hot melted butter flavoured with finely grated lemon or orange peel.
- For something different sprinkle with flavoured or nut oils – hazelnut, walnut, sesame, chilli or garlic. Or combine hot melted butter with a little concentrated curry sauce. Just a dash of balsamic vinegar will intensify natural flavours.

Potato Cheese Pan-fry

SERVES 2 AS A MAIN DISH

350 g/12 oz potatoes
1 large onion
100 g/4 oz smoked back bacon rashers
15 ml/1 tablespoon olive oil
salt and freshly milled pepper
5 ml/1 teaspoon chopped fresh sage
100 g/4 oz Cheshire cheese

Scrub the potatoes and cut into 1 cm/½ inch dice. Add to a saucepan of cold salted water and bring just to the boil. Simmer for 2 minutes, then drain thoroughly.

Meanwhile, peel and slice the onion. Trim and chop the bacon. Heat the oil in a 25 cm/10 inch frying pan. Add the onion and bacon and cook gently for about 5 minutes, to draw the fat from the bacon.

Add the potatoes and stir the mixture for a moment.

Season with salt and pepper and add the sage. Stir to blend all the ingredients. Cover the pan with a lid and cook gently over a low heat for 15 minutes, or until the potatoes are tender.

Remove the pan lid. Lightly stir in the cheese, broken into small pieces, and heat uncovered for a further 5 minutes. Serve immediately.

Parsnip and Gruyère Bake

SERVES 3–4 V

- 900 g/2 lb small parsnips
- 1 medium onion
- 65 g/2½ oz butter
- salt and freshly milled pepper
- 30 ml/2 level tablespoons plain flour
- 300 ml/½ pint milk
- 150 ml/¼ pint double cream
- 75 g/3 oz grated Gruyère
- freshly grated nutmeg
- 50 g/2 oz fresh breadcrumbs
- 25 g/1 oz finely chopped almonds

Peel and thinly slice the parsnips. Peel and finely chop the onion. Add the parsnips to a large pan of cold water and bring to the boil. Remove the pan from the heat, cover and leave to stand 5 minutes. Drain well.

Heat 25 g/1 oz of the butter in a small pan, add the onion and cook gently until soft. Take the pan off the heat.

Arrange one-third of the parsnip slices of a buttered 1.7 litre/3 pint baking dish. Spoon over half the softened onion and season with salt and pepper. Cover with another third of the parsnip slices, the rest of the onion and seasoning. Finally top with the remaining parsnip slices.

Heat the oven to 190°C/375°F/gas mark 5.

Melt 25 g/1 oz of the butter in a saucepan, stir in the flour and cook over a low heat, stirring, for 1 minute. Remove from the heat. Combine the milk and cream. Gradually stir into the flour and butter, beating well to make a smooth thin sauce. Bring just to the boil, then simmer for 2–3 minutes, stirring constantly, until the sauce is smooth and thickened. Remove from the heat and season with salt, pepper and a pinch of nutmeg. Add the cheese and stir until it has melted. Pour the sauce evenly over the layers of parsnip.

Melt the remaining 15 g/½ oz butter, add the

breadcrumbs and chopped almonds and mix with a fork. Sprinkle over the parsnip bake. Set in the heated oven and bake for 30 minutes until bubbling hot and golden brown.

Vegetable Ragoût with Toasted Goat's Cheese

SERVES 4 AS A MAIN DISH V

1 large onion
2 cloves of garlic
60 ml/4 tablespoons olive oil
1 small aubergine
350 g/12 oz young courgettes
150 ml/¼ pint vegetable stock
1 (432 g) can chick peas
150 ml/¼ pint double cream
30 ml/2 tablespoons prepared pesto (or see page 118)
salt and freshly milled pepper
8 thin slices French bread
25 g/1 oz garlic butter
150 g/6 oz goat's cheese

Peel the onion, slice thinly and separate into rings. Peel and crush the garlic. Heat 15 ml/1 tablespoon of the olive oil in a 25 cm/10 inch frying pan (use one that has a lid) or a shallow flameproof casserole. Add the onion rings. Cover and cook gently for about 5 minutes, until soft. Remove the lid of the pan and let the onions brown – this takes about 5 minutes. Add the garlic and stir. Dice the aubergine into 2.5 cm/1 inch cubes and thinly slice the courgettes.

Add the remaining oil, the aubergine and the courgettes to the onion in the pan. Cook, stirring, for 5 minutes. Add the vegetable stock, cover, and simmer for about 15 minutes, until the vegetables are tender.

Drain and rinse the chick peas and add to the pan. Combine the cream with the pesto and stir in, along with a seasoning of salt and pepper. Cook for a few minutes to heat through.

Meanwhile spread one side of each slice of bread with garlic butter. Cut the goat's cheese into 4 slices and place a slice on each piece of bread. Arrange, cheese-side uppermost, on top of the vegetable ragoût and place under a heated grill until golden brown. Serve immediately.

BEST COOKING METHODS

Cooking times are only a guide; your own preference is important. Vegetables cooked until just tender crisp look delicious and have the best flavour.

In a covered saucepan Use as little water as possible – about 2.5 cm/1 inch of boiling salted water is enough. Add the prepared vegetables and cook over a medium heat, covered with the pan lid to hold in the steam. Leafy green vegetables contain a lot of water – after washing them, simply shake off excess moisture and place in the pan without any additional water.

Steaming Steamed vegetables retain their natural bright colours and lose very few of their nutrients. As the vegetables are not immersed in the water it is possible to cook more than one variety at the same time. Simply cook those needing the longer cooking time, such as potatoes, for a few minutes before adding the rest, such as cabbage.

Use a purpose-designed steamer pan or a collapsible stainless steel steamer basket that will fit into a standard-sized saucepan. The boiling water in the base pan shouldn't reach the bottom of the steamer. Add the prepared vegetables and cook covered with the pan lid. If the water needs topping up, always add boiling water.

Roasting Slow cooking root vegetables are ideal for roasting in the oven. Leave smaller vegetables such as onions whole and cut larger vegetables into even-sized chunks. If the vegetables are mixed, add those needing less time part-way through the cooking. Heat the oven to 190°C/375°F/gas mark 5, placing a suitably sized roasting tin in the oven to heat up. Spoon 30–45 ml/2–3 tablespoons olive oil into the hot pan, add the vegetables and stir to coat with the oil. Season with coarse salt and freshly milled pepper and roast for 45–60 minutes or until the vegetables are tender.

Grilling Grilling brings out the natural sweetness and intense flavour of certain vegetables, especially those of Mediterranean origin. Quarter and de-seed peppers. Slice aubergines or courgettes thickly, or cut aubergines lengthwise and score the flesh in a criss-cross pattern. Cut large mild or red onions in thick slices. Preheat the grill. Arrange the vegetables on the grill rack and brush lightly with olive oil. Place about 7.5 cm/3 inches from the grill and cook until tender and beginning to char, turning once and brushing again with oil. Serve hot or cold.

Stir-frying This extremely quick method of cooking keeps the vegetables crunchy and brightly coloured. It is important to prepare all the vegetables before the cooking is started. Prepare the vegetables, cutting each variety to a similar small size to ensure even cooking. Heat a wok or large frying pan over a medium high heat. When it is hot add a little oil and swirl it around to coat the pan. Add the vegetables that take the longest time to cook and fry, stirring constantly, for a minute or two. Continue to add the other ingredients, stirring and shaking the pan constantly. To complete the cooking add a spoonful or two of water, stock or a suitable glaze and continue to cook until the liquid has evaporated or, in the case of a glaze, thickened and coated the vegetables. Always serve stir-fried vegetables immediately to enjoy their just-cooked crispness.

Microwave Vegetables cooked by this very quick method virtually cook in their own steam. Root vegetables need 15–30 ml/1–2 tablespoons of water or stock, leaf vegetables the water still clinging to them after washing. Cook in a covered container on HIGH/100% power, following the time chart in the oven cookbook. Allow root vegetables to stand a minute or two after cooking before draining and serving.

White Bean and Vegetable Chilli

SERVES 4 AS A MAIN DISH **V**

2 medium onions
2 cloves of garlic
1 green chilli
30 ml/2 tablespoons olive oil
2 medium carrots
225 g/8 oz sweet potatoes
2 red peppers
1 (432 g) can cannellini beans
10 ml/2 level teaspoons chilli powder
5 ml/1 level teaspoon ground cumin
1 (326 g) can whole kernel sweetcorn
1 (397 g) can chopped tomatoes
salt and freshly milled pepper
30 ml/2 tablespoons chopped fresh parsley
150 ml/¼ pint vegetable stock
5 ml/1 teaspoon soft brown sugar
30 ml/2 level tablespoons tomato purée
300 ml/½ pint thick Greek-style yogurt
100–175 (4–6 oz) grated Cheddar

Peel and finely chop the onions. Peel and crush the garlic. Halve the chilli lengthwise and remove the seeds. Finely chop the flesh.

Heat the oil in a large flameproof casserole, add the onion and fry gently to soften. Stir in the garlic and chilli and cook for a few moments more.

Meanwhile, peel and dice the carrots and sweet potatoes. Halve, de-seed and coarsely cut up the peppers. Drain and rinse the cannellini beans.

Stir the chilli powder, cumin and beans into the hot onion mixture. Add the prepared vegetables, sweetcorn and tomatoes. Season with salt and pepper and stir in the chopped parsley. Combine the stock, sugar and tomato purée and add to the casserole.

Bring to a simmer, then turn the heat to low, cover with the casserole lid and cook gently for 25–30 minutes.

Serve the vegetable chilli in deep plates, topped with spoonfuls of yogurt, and pass the grated cheese at the table.

HOW TO COOK BETTER VEGETABLES

- Use vegetables seasonally – they will be in prime condition and the taste is better.
- Buy vegetables that are fresh – look for shiny skins and crisp leaves. Remember, small *is* beautiful.
- Buy in small quantities and cook soon afterwards. Remove any plastic packaging to avoid condensation. Root vegetables, especially potatoes, should be kept in a cool, dark and dry place. They are best stored in a box covered with a newspaper. Other vegetables may be kept in the salad drawer of the fridge.
- Scrubbing or scraping vegetables rather than peeling them retains the goodness just under the skin. Cook vegetables in their skins whenever you can.
- The new 'mini' or 'baby' vegetables make pretty presentations especially on a mixed platter or for a vegetable garnish. They are particularly good steamed or added to a stir-fry.

Fresh Pear, Ham and Cabbage Stir-fry

SERVES 2 AS A MAIN DISH

½ a head Savoy cabbage (approximately 350 g/12 oz)
2 firm Conference pears
100 g/4 oz sliced ham
5 ml/1 teaspoon caraway seeds
45 ml/3 tablespoons grapeseed oil
75 ml/3 fl oz vegetable stock
freshly milled pepper

Cut the cabbage into wedges and slice away the hard stalk. Place the cabbage pieces cut side down on a chopping board and cut across into fine shreds. Peel the pears, quarter, and cut out the cores. Slice lengthwise. Finely shred the ham.

Set a wok or a 25 cm/10 inch frying pan over a medium high heat. Add the caraway seeds and toast for a moment, then tip out on to a plate. Heat 30 ml/2 tablespoons oil in the pan and add the pear slices. Stir-fry for 2–3 minutes until just tender, then remove to a plate.

Add the remaining oil to the pan with the cabbage shreds. Turn and stir until the colour comes up bright green and the shreds are glossy (the volume of the cabbage reduces as it cooks).

Add the vegetable stock. Add the pear slices, ham shreds, toasted seeds and a seasoning of pepper. Cook for 2–3 minutes, then serve immediately.

VEGETABLE PROTEINS

Tofu

This is a curd made from the pressed purée of soya beans by a process similar to making cheese. Nutritionally, it is an excellent addition to our diet: low in fat and calories, it is a rich source of protein and calcium. It is especially useful in a vegetarian diet, where it can be used in place of eggs, milk and cheeses.

Tofu has been used in Oriental cookery for over 2,000 years and is now widely available in supermarkets and Oriental stores. Look for it among the cheeses and store it in the refrigerator.

Tofu can be bought in various forms. Original tofu is a white, slightly spongy block with a bland flavour. It can be added to casseroles or curries (it readily absorbs other flavours) or it can be marinated. It can also be bought ready marinated or smoked, both of which have distinctive flavours – cut into cubes and add to stir-fries and salads or cook as kebabs. Silken tofu is suitable for making dips, sauces or desserts such as cheesecakes.

Quorn

Compared with tofu, quorn is a very new food. Vegetable in origin, it is harvested from a member of the mushroom family. Low in fat and calories, it is a good source of protein and fibre: 225 g/8 oz will serve 3–4 people depending on the other ingredients in the dish. Although it has the taste and texture of meat or poultry, it is approved for vegetarians.

Originally sold ready prepared in convenience dishes, it can now be found in a plain form in the meat section of supermarkets. Already cooked, it needs minutes to heat through in a sauce or a casserole, can be stir-fried or grilled, and will quickly absorb the flavours of a marinade.

Smoked Tofu and Vegetable Stir-fry

SERVES 2 AS A MAIN DISH [V]

- 1 (220 g) pack smoked tofu
- 2 cloves of garlic
- 2.5 cm/1 inch fresh ginger
- 60 ml/4 tablespoons soy sauce
- 45 ml/3 tablespoons dry sherry
- 1 bunch (6–8) spring onions
- 100 g/4 oz mangetout
- 1 small yellow pepper
- 1 (227 g) can bamboo shoots

Cut the tofu into 2.5 cm/1 inch cubes and place in a shallow dish. Peel and crush the garlic. Peel and very finely chop the ginger. Combine the garlic, ginger, soy sauce and sherry and pour over the tofu. Stir gently to coat the tofu on all sides with the marinade. Leave for 1 hour.

Meanwhile, trim and diagonally slice the spring onions. Top and tail the mangetout. Quarter the pepper, discarding the stem, seeds and any pith. Cut into thin slices. Drain the bamboo shoots and finely shred the Chinese leaves.

Drain the tofu, reserving the marinade. Heat the oil in a wok or a large frying pan. Add the tofu and cook, stirring, over a high heat for 2 minutes. Add the onions, mangetout and pepper. Continue to cook, stirring frequently, for 2–3 minutes, until the pepper is just slightly soft.

Stir the cornflour into 30 ml/2 tablespoons cold water and add to the marinade. Add to the wok with the bamboo shoots and Chinese leaves. Continue to cook, stirring, until the sauce thickens and glazes the stir-fry – about 1 minute.

Serve immediately with Chinese egg noodles or rice.

- 1/4 head of Chinese leaves
- 15 ml/1 tablespoon grapeseed oil
- 10 ml/2 level teaspoons cornflour

Courgette Moulds with Mustard Vinaigrette

SERVES 6 AS A MAIN DISH V

Wash and trim the courgettes, leaving them unpeeled. Take one courgette and slice lengthwise into 12 fine strips (a swivel potato peeler gives the best results). Soften the strips by placing them in a colander and pouring on boiling water from the kettle. Press the strips dry in absorbent kitchen paper.

Lightly oil 6 individual moulds (about 150 ml/1/4 pint size) and line each one with 2 softened courgette strips. Set aside while preparing the filling.

Cut the remaining courgettes up coarsely. Peel and finely chop the onion. Heat the grapeseed oil in a frying pan (use one that has a lid), add the onion, and soften over a low heat – do not allow it to brown. Add the courgettes, cover, and cook gently until they are barely tender – about 10 minutes. Let the mixture cool slightly.

Strip the basil leaves from the stems. Reserve 6 leaves for a garnish and add the remainder to the courgette mixture.

- 450 g/1 lb courgettes
- 1 medium onion
- 45 ml/3 tablespoons grapeseed oil
- 15 g/1/2 oz fresh basil leaves
- 225 g/8 oz curd cheese
- 2 eggs
- 50 g/2 oz fresh white breadcrumbs
- salt and freshly milled pepper
- 25 g/1 oz grated Parmesan
- 15 ml/1 tablespoon wholegrain mustard
- 30 ml/2 tablespoons white wine vinegar
- 90 ml/6 tablespoons olive oil

Turn the curd cheese into a food processor. Add the eggs and process briefly to blend, then add the courgettes, any juices from the pan, the breadcrumbs, a seasoning of salt and pepper and the Parmesan. Cover and blend to a coarse purée. Spoon the mixture into the prepared moulds.

Heat the oven to 180°C/350°F/gas mark 4.

Set the filled moulds in a deep roasting pan and add boiling water to come about 2.5 cm/1 inch up the sides. Cover with kitchen foil, lightly tucking it under the edge of the tin. Set in the preheated oven and bake for 20 minutes.

Meanwhile, make the vinaigrette by whisking together the mustard, vinegar, oil and a good seasoning of salt and pepper in a small bowl.

Remove the roasting tin from the oven and allow to cool for 5–10 minutes, then loosen the sides of the moulds with a palette knife and unmould on to warm (not hot) plates. Serve warm, with the dressing spooned over and garnished with the reserved whole basil leaves.

FLAVOURED BUTTERS

Butter is a flavour catalyst – combine it with fresh chopped herbs or some tangy-tasting ingredient and the result can be used to perk up hot vegetables or pasta, to slice over grilled steaks or baked potatoes, or to spread on hot breads, with delectable results.

Basic method Let the chilled butter warm to room temperature. A food processor will combine the mixture effortlessly. Just place the diced butter with the other ingredients in the processor and buzz until combined, scraping down the sides of the bowl at least once. To make by hand, cream the butter in a bowl, then beat in the remaining ingredients. Spoon the flavoured butter into a ramekin dish and use immediately or cover and chill until firm. Alternatively, turn the butter on to a square of greaseproof paper or foil, roll into a thick sausage, twist the ends like a cracker and chill – the butter can then be sliced for serving. Tightly covered, a flavoured butter will keep for 2–3 weeks in the refrigerator or several months in the freezer.

Blue Cheese Butter Combine 50 g/2 oz butter, 50 g/2 oz cream cheese, 75 g/3 oz Roquefort or Stilton, and some freshly milled pepper.

❦ Slice on to grilled steak or hamburgers before serving.
❦ Toss with hot drained pasta.

- Slip a slice into a split baked potato.
- Spread on toast, grill, and serve with soup or salad.

Anchovy Butter Combine 100 g /4 oz butter with the contents of a 50 g/2 oz can anchovies, drained and chopped, 15 ml/1 tablespoon chopped fresh parsley and 1 clove of garlic, peeled and crushed.

- Spread on hot toasted French bread slices and serve with drinks.
- Spread on toast and top with a poached egg for tea.

Garlic and Herb Butter Combine 100 g/4 oz butter with 15 ml/1 tablespoon chopped fresh parsley, 2 cloves of garlic, peeled and crushed, and freshly milled pepper.

- Spread in a slashed French loaf for garlic bread.
- Add to piping hot boiled new potatoes.
- Spread on top of tomato halves before grilling or baking.
- Add slices to smokies or trout fillets before grilling.

Lemon and Parsley Butter Combine 100 g/4 oz butter, the grated rind of 1/2 a lemon, 30–45 ml/2–3 tablespoons chopped fresh parsley and freshly milled pepper.

- Stir a nut into vegetable soup.
- Add flakes to scrambled eggs.
- Slice on to grilled or poached fish fillets.
- Substitute tarragon for parsley and spread between the skin and flesh of a chicken breast (or whole bird) before roasting.

Mixed Mustard Butter Combine 100 g/4 oz butter, 30 ml/2 tablespoons whole-grain mustard, 15 ml/1 tablespoon Dijon mustard and freshly milled pepper.

- Spread on bread for roast ham, beef or chicken sandwiches.
- Heat with peeled prawns until bubbling hot and serve on toast (or with hot rice) and lemon wedges.
- Slice over grilled pork chops.
- Spread on gammon rashers before grilling.

Onion Butter Finely chop 1 small onion and sauté in 15 ml/1 tablespoon olive oil with a pinch of sugar until golden, then cool. Combine with 100 g/4 oz butter, 30 ml/2 tablespoons chopped fresh parsley, 15 ml/1 tablespoon Dijon mustard and freshly milled pepper.

- Fork into freshly cooked rice and serve with grilled sausages.
- Beat into mashed potatoes.
- Gently toss with hot, well-drained cauliflower florets.
- Use to butter bread for cheese sandwiches.

VEGETABLE SIDE DISHES

Carrots with Orange and Ginger [V] Scrub or scrape 450 g/1 lb new carrots and cut lengthwise into thin sticks. Place in a large frying pan (use one that has a lid) and add 200 ml/7 fl oz orange juice, 5 ml/1 level teaspoon caster sugar, 5 ml/1 level teaspoon ground ginger and 25 g/1 oz butter. Cover and simmer for 15 minutes or until the carrots are just tender, then remove the pan lid and simmer until the liquid has almost evaporated and the carrots remain in a shiny butter glaze. Serves 4. *Illustrated on Plate Two.*

Corn Fritters [V] Sift 50 g/2 oz plain flour and a pinch of salt into a medium mixing bowl. Add 1 egg and the contents of a 198 g can creamed-style sweetcorn. Using a wooden spoon, stir to a soft batter. Warm a heavy frying pan over a moderate heat. Add 15 ml/1 tablespoon oil and when thoroughly heated, drop dessertspoonfuls of the batter on to the hot surface – not too close or they will run together. Fry until the fritters are golden on the underside, then flip them over to cook the second side. Drain on kitchen paper and transfer to a baking tray. Cook the remaining batter, adding more oil to the pan as needed – the batter should make about 12 corn fritters. As they are cooked, keep the fritters warm, uncovered, in a warm oven (110°C/225°F/gas mark ¼). Serves 4.

Baked Tomatoes in Olive Oil and Herbs [V] Heat the oven to 190°C/375°F/gas mark 5. Put 6 cloves of garlic into a small saucepan. Cover with cold water and bring to the boil. Draw off the heat and leave to stand, covered. Meanwhile, rinse 12 medium tomatoes and, with a vegetable knife, cut out the stem ends. Slice a deep cross into the rounded sides. Arrange, cut sides up, in a baking dish. Drain, peel and mash the garlic cloves with 5 ml/1 level teaspoon caster sugar and a seasoning of salt and pepper to make a sweet garlic purée. Push the garlic mixture into the tomato cuts. Drizzle the tomatoes with 45 ml/3 tablespoons olive oil. Set in the heated oven and bake for 15–20 minutes. Serves 6.

Sweet Potatoes with Brown Sugar and Butter [V] Scrub 700–900 g/1½–2 lb sweet potatoes and, if very large, cut into large chunks. Bring to the boil in water to cover and simmer for 15–20 minutes until tender. Drain, lift off the skins and slice the potatoes thickly. Heat the oven to 180°C/350°F/gas mark 4. Layer the potato slices in a buttered dish, sprinkling them with 30 ml/2 tablespoons soft brown sugar, ½ level teaspoon ground cinnamon and 25 g/1 oz butter cut in flakes. Set in the heated oven and bake for 20–25 minutes, until the potatoes are hot and glazed. Serves 4.

Glazed Courgettes with Lemon [V] Rinse 450 g/1 lb small courgettes and cut across into thick diagonal slices. Peel 1 medium onion and slice thinly, then separate the slices into rings. Melt 25 g/1 oz butter in a large frying pan. Add the onion rings and sprinkle with 15 ml/1 level tablespoon caster sugar. Fry gently for a few minutes to soften. Add the courgette slices and stir them into the hot onion and butter. Thinly slice 1 lemon and add to the pan. With a spatula or fish slice, stir and turn the courgette slices over a moderate heat until they are glazed and golden – about 10 minutes. Season with salt and freshly milled pepper. Serves 4.

Leeks with Smetana and Parmesan [V] Trim 450 g/1 lb small leeks and cut off the green leaves about 2.5 cm/1 inch above the white stems. Rinse thoroughly in cold water. Arrange the leeks in a large frying pan (use one that has a lid) and add 150 ml/¼ pint vegetable stock. Bring to a simmer, cover with the pan lid and cook for 10 minutes or until tender. Evenly spoon over 150 ml/¼ pint smetana and sprinkle with 15–30 ml/1–2 tablespoons grated Parmesan. Place under a heated grill until bubbling and golden brown – protect the handle of the frying pan with double thickness foil, if necessary. Serves 4.

Cauliflower with Spiced Yogurt [V] Separate 1 medium cauliflower into florets. Add to boiling salted water and simmer for 8 minutes until tender, then drain. Meanwhile peel and thinly slice 1 large onion. Heat 5 ml/1 teaspoon oil in a large frying pan, add the onion and sprinkle with 5 ml/1 level teaspoon caster sugar. Cook over a medium heat until soft and golden brown, stirring occasionally. In a small bowl combine 150 ml/5 fl oz natural yogurt, 5 ml/1 level teaspoon cornflower and 10–15 ml/2–3 teaspoons curry paste. Add to the onion and cook, stirring, until slightly thickened and bubbling hot. Spoon over the freshly cooked cauliflower. Serves 4.

Potato and Onion Galette [V] Butter a 20.5 cm/8 inch diameter, 2.5 cm/1 inch deep sponge cake tin thoroughly. Sprinkle the buttered tin with 5 ml/1 level teaspoon caster sugar and set aside. Heat the oven to 190°C/375°F/gas mark 5. Peel and thinly slice 900 g/2 lb potatoes – this is most quickly done in a food processor. Peel 1 medium onion, then cut in thin slices, keeping them intact. Arrange the onion slices on the base of the prepared tin – remember that the base will eventually become the top. Arrange layers of potato slices to fill the tin. Add 25 g/1 oz butter, cut in flakes and a seasoning of salt and freshly milled pepper to the layers. Press down gently. Cover with a square of buttered foil, set in the heated oven and bake for 45 minutes or until the potatoes are tender. Turn the galette out on to a warm ovenproof serving plate and place under a hot grill for a few minutes to caramelize the surface. Cut in wedges for serving. Serves 6.

Red Cabbage with Apple and Orange [V] Cut a small (or ½ a large) red cabbage into wedges and cut away the white core. Finely shred across the leaves. Peel 1 medium onion and thinly slice. Peel, quarter and slice 1 large cooking apple. Heat the oven to 180°C/350°F/gas mark 4. Heat 15 ml/1 tablespoon oil in a roomy flameproof casserole and add the onion. Cook over a medium low heat until soft but not brown. Add the cabbage, apple, finely grated rind of 1 orange and 150 ml/¼ pint orange juice, 30 ml/2 tablespoons red wine vinegar, 50 g/2 oz caster sugar, 50 g/2 oz seedless raisins and a seasoning of salt and pepper. Bring just to the boil. Cover and place in the oven. Cook for 1½ hours, stirring occasionally, until the cabbage is quite soft and the liquid has evaporated. Stir well before serving. Serves 4–6. *Illustrated on Plate Two.*

THE SWEET TASTE OF GARLIC

Garlic takes on a new, more gentle flavour when you bake or roast it. The taste is sweeter, mellow and less intense, and the flesh inside the papery skins softens to a smooth purée.

Baked Garlic Heat the oven to 160°C/325°F/gas mark 3. Break open a head of garlic and separate out the cloves. Enclose the garlic cloves in a square of kitchen foil to make a baggy parcel – pull up the corners and twist together to hold it closed. Set the parcel on the oven shelf and bake for 40 minutes (pop it in the oven when you are baking something else). Carefully open the foil and gently press the cloves – they should feel quite soft.

Serve the baked garlic cloves hot – they are particularly good with roast chicken or with cold meats. To eat, simply press each clove with a fork to squeeze out the soft flesh. They are also good spread on hot buttered French bread or jacket potatoes.

Alternatively, you can let the baked cloves cool, close the foil again and store the parcel in the refrigerator to keep on hand for a supply of mild sweet garlic to use in recipes. Use the same amount as raw garlic cloves in a recipe – the flavour will be milder. Baked garlic will keep for around 2 weeks in the refrigerator.

Roasted Garlic This is currently very fashionable, but roasting at too high a temperature will scorch the garlic and make it taste bitter. Rub whole heads of garlic with olive oil and add to the pan of roasting vegetables – potatoes or mixed root vegetables (see page 25) – about 20 minutes towards the end of their cooking time. Serve hot as in the baked garlic recipe.

CHAPTER THREE

Salads and Salad Dressings

Put a little extra thought into making salads and you will be rewarded with colour, crunch and zingy fresh flavours. Here are warm salads, great main dish salads and superb dressings, as well as a new look for some old favourites.

OILS

Our cooking methods are changing as we become more health-conscious, and the use of oils in place of animal fats in cooking has grown. Now that we have all been made aware of the benefits of the Mediterranean style of diet, which includes the use of cholesterol-free olive oil, the popularity of olive oil has soared and the choice on the supermarket shelves has blossomed. There is also a bewildering variety of other oils in the shops today. For the best cooking results we should choose the right oil not only for the way we want to use it but also for its individual flavour.

Olive Oil

Very much the flavour of the moment, but if you are confused about which is what, read on. In simple terms the grades of olive oil run as follows:

Virgin olive oil comes from the first 'cold' pressing. Most olive oil producers use a heat system which gives more oil. The traditional 'cold' pressing yields a much reduced quantity of far higher quality.

Extra virgin olive oils are more expensive and have individual tastes and aromas – from light and aromatic to fruity and pungent. An estate-bottled extra virgin olive oil is the finest because the oil is pressed from selected olives and is unblended, rather like a château-bottled wine. Classy estate-bottled oils are expensive, and are frequently found in wine merchants because it's often the wine growers who produce them. The colour of extra virgin olive oils can vary from gold to an intense green.

Commercial extra virgin olive oils are blended from several estates for a consistent flavour. These will have brand names or supermarket own labels.

Pure olive oil is produced from subsequent heavier pressings of the olive pulp and this is blended with a proportion of virgin oil for flavour – the proportion of one to the other will be reflected in the price you pay for your bottle of olive oil.

Olive oil has an indefinite shelf life kept in a cool dark cupboard, so there is no reason why the serious cook can't have at least two different types on the go at one time. Extra virgin oils are the ones to use when the flavour really counts – in simple dressings with a squeeze of lemon juice, to drizzle over *crostini* or *antipasti.* Use less expensive olive oil to make more robust dressings, for grilling, frying and roasting and general cooking purposes.

Grapeseed, Corn, Sunflower, Soya and Groundnut (Peanut) Oils

These are pleasantly light, general-purpose oils with varying degrees of flavour. Choose one to use in stir-fries, marinades, dressings and baking. A specific type, such as grapeseed, is a pure oil and has a better taste than the blended or mixed oils. Yet again, price is a guide – blended oils, including those labelled salad or vegetable oil, are generally at the cheaper end of the market.

Nut Oils

For flavour, the most interesting oils are those obtained from nuts. Nut oils are generally used in 'cold' recipes or are added at the very last minute to hot foods, as heat can destroy their flavour and aroma.

Walnut and hazelnut oils have very pronounced flavours – a little goes a long way. They both make wonderful salad dressings if you add a tablespoon of either oil to the olive (not extra virgin) or mild-flavoured oil used in the recipe.

Sesame oil is widely used in Oriental cookery, principally as a flavouring oil sprinkled over a fully cooked dish just before serving. There are two kinds: the paler oil has a more delicate flavour than the dark (toasted) sesame oil, which should be used very sparingly – drizzle over bulgar wheat pilaffs and salads (pages 134 and 136), for instance.

Buy any of these special oils in small bottles, as they are used in very small quantities and don't keep longer than about 6 months once opened. Keep in a cool dark cupboard.

Spinach with Mushrooms and Feta Cheese

SERVES 2 AS A MAIN DISH

- 100 g/4 oz small leaf spinach
- 2 eggs
- 100 g/4 oz feta cheese
- 500 g/2 oz button mushrooms
- 50 g/2 oz smoked streaky bacon rashers
- Creamy Poppy Seed Dressing (see page 50)

Rinse the spinach in several changes of cold water to remove any grit. Drain and dry in a teatowel. Place in a large salad bowl.

Place the eggs in a pan of cold water and bring to the boil. Simmer for 5 minutes, then plunge into cold water. Peel and quarter. Break the cheese into small chunks. Wipe and slice the mushrooms. Remove any rind from the bacon and cut into 2.5 cm/1 inch pieces. Fry until crisp.

Spoon 30 ml/2 tablespoons Creamy Poppy Seed Dressing over the spinach and lightly toss together. Serve immediately, topped with the bacon, eggs, cheese and mushrooms.

VINEGAR – THE SUBTLE SEASONING

A selection of good wine vinegars is among the most useful seasonings we have in our kitchens. An important ingredient in salad dressings, used discreetly vinegar adds a subtle sharpness and character that will lift up the flavour of a dish – a dash of wine vinegar adds zest to a gravy; a spoonful stirred in towards the end of cooking will perk up a casserole and cut through any fatty taste; in a marinade it will help tenderize meat and, in the right recipe, wine vinegar will make the flavour of a soup sparkle (see Black Bean Soup, page 6).

Wine vinegar is made from soured wine. There are thin characterless wine vinegars and good matured ones – you soon learn the difference. Good vinegars are more expensive but you need to use less of them. Among the very best are those manufactured using the traditional Orléans method, which produces a full-bodied flavour. But, whichever brand you buy, you will find that red and white wine vinegar are two essential kitchen basics.

Use white wine vinegar in dressings for green or delicately flavoured salads (page 41) and red wine vinegar for simple tomato salads or grilled peppers (page 25).

Balsamic vinegar, once a treasured Italian holiday souvenir, is now easier to find in our shops. The authentic version is made only in Modena in northern Italy. It is aged in wood for at least 10 years and has a rich brown colour. The flavour is wonderful – aromatic, slightly sweet yet mildly tart too.

Use in small quantities: a spoonful added to your favourite oil and vinegar dressing for a richer taste, a splash in pan gravies to bring out the flavour of a steak, sprinkled straight from the bottle on to steamed vegetables, or in Couscous Salad with Grilled Vegetables (see pages 140–1).

Cider vinegar is made from soured cider. It has a mild but noticeable apple aroma and flavour and is slightly sweet. It is popular in the new 'California-style' of cooking, where light-flavoured meats and fish are combined with fruit and vegetables in quickly cooked recipes.

Try it in recipes in place of white wine vinegar, or in pickles.

Sherry vinegar is produced in Jerez, Spain, and has a nutty mellow flavour and a rich dark brown colour. Try it in a full-flavoured salad dressing, perhaps with walnut oil, to dress a mixed bean salad (see page 143), or add to marinades for red meats and game.

It has a natural affinity with olives, so use it in any dish containing them.

Malt vinegars are made from malted barley and matured to develop a distinctive flavour which is far too strong to use in most recipes or salad dressings but perfect for pickles – their traditional use. Malt vinegar should be combined with sugar for a sweet sharp taste. Recipe books usually suggest using dark malt vinegar with a brown sugar for a rich colour in something like apple chutney, or clear distilled malt vinegar with granulated sugar for a bright clear colour in a cucumber pickle, for instance.

Flavoured vinegars are made with wine, cider or fortified wines such as sherry vinegar. Flavours can be herbs, for example tarragon, which has a delicate delicious taste, and sometimes the vinegars have a sprig of the herb in the bottle. Garlic or shallots can flavour vinegar and so can fruits such as raspberry, which has a quite distinctive full flavour compared with the more delicate blueberry wine vinegar.

Flavoured vinegars are best when matched with sympathetic ingredients, when they will surprise you with their subtlety – a dash of raspberry wine vinegar in a fresh raspberry sauce really concentrates the fruit flavour beautifully (page 208). Or combine a little with sugar and chopped mint and sprinkle over sliced ripe peaches or pears for a very fresh-tasting starter.

Orange and Raisin Salad with Smoked Hams

SERVES 4 AS A MAIN DISH

- 6 oranges
- 90 ml/6 tablespoons olive oil
- 45 ml/3 tablespoons dry sherry
- 15 ml/1 tablespoon chopped fresh thyme
- salt and freshly milled pepper
- 75 g/3 oz pitted black olives
- 25 g/1 oz seedless raisins
- 225–350 g/8–12 oz smoked ham (see method)

Using a vegetable peeler, thinly pare the zest from the rind of one orange. Squeeze the juice and set aside. With a sharp knife, cut the peel into fine shreds. Put the orange shreds in a small saucepan and cover with cold water. Bring to a simmer for 3 minutes to blanch and tenderize, then drain well.

In a mixing bowl combine the olive oil, sherry, thyme, reserved orange juice, orange shreds and a good seasoning of salt and pepper. Using a sharp knife, remove the rind and pith from the remaining oranges and cut across into thin slices, discarding any pips. Layer the slices in a shallow bowl and scatter over the olives and raisins. Spoon over the dressing and marinate until serving time.

Choose individual flat plates large enough to arrange the salad attractively.

Choose a selection of smoked hams from a delicatessen or supermarket. Look for French Bayonne, German Westphalia or Belgian Ardennes ham. Home-produced smoked hams include York, Bradenham and Smithfield hams. They should be sliced very thinly.

Loosely fold each slice of ham and arrange portions on individual plates. Transfer some orange slices, olives and raisins to each plate and spoon over the dressing left in the bowl.

SALT, PEPPERS AND MUSTARDS

Like so many ingredients we use today, these three traditional seasonings have changed with fashion. It is no longer just fine white salt, white pepper and tubs of dry mustard powder that crowd the supermarket shelves but an intriguing variety. As with oils and vinegars, knowing which to use when is important for a good result.

Salt Salt has had a bad press recently and, although it is perfectly possible to cook without it, it really is better to season foods properly in the kitchen. Food tastes dismal without salt, as anyone who has to follow a salt-free diet will tell you. Salt enhances flavours both savoury and sweet – a pinch here and there makes all the difference.

We favour sea salt, made by the natural evaporation of sea waters which has a clean fresh taste. You have a choice of fine or coarse sea salt for cooking and the crunchy white flakes for serving at table. Rock salt is mined underground. It is sold as general-purpose table salt with a free-flowing agent added to ensure a smooth sprinkle from the salt cellar. You can grind coarse sea salt flakes or nibs of rock salt in a salt mill. Similar in appearance to a pepper mill, today's salt mills are made of acrylic because of the corrosive effects of salt. If you choose to use a salt mill in the kitchen, avoid using it over a pan of steaming liquid. Salt attracts moisture and must always be kept dry.

Pepper You can buy tubs of ground black pepper as well as white, but freshly ground peppercorns are much more flavourful. Buy a pepper mill and improve your cooking straight away. A white peppercorn is a black one stripped of its aromatic outer shell, leaving just the more pungent core. Green peppercorns are picked unripe and are artificially dried to retain their delicate green colour. They are not as spicy as the other two. Pink pepper berries are not from the same family and are not peppercorns. They are the berries of a tropical bush called the pepper tree. Flaky in texture and with little flavour, they are used mostly for their visual effect. Green peppercorns and pink pepper berries are used in peppercorn mixtures designed for pepper mills.

Use freshly milled black pepper in recipes, using ground white pepper in light sauces, pale soups and some fish or egg dishes only if you find the dark speckles unappetizing. Seasoned pepper mixes are the latest thing. They are coarsely ground peppercorns with added dried natural flavours such as herbs, onion or citrus. They are most useful as a last-minute seasoning sprinkled over simply cooked vegetables, fish, poultry or salads.

Mustard Mustard is made from mustard seeds which are finely powdered, coarsely ground or left whole. Traditional powdered British mustard uses a mixture of yellow and brown mustard seeds, while the French favour only the black and brown seeds, which give their mustards a characteristic deep beige colour. The heat in mustard comes from the essential oils released when the seeds are crushed. Smooth mustard tends to hit your taste buds straight away, while the flavour of coarse grain mustard spreads more evenly over the palate and you taste it more slowly.

Mustard seeds can be crushed with additional flavours such as peppercorns, allspice or red chillies, tarragon, horseradish or garlic. They are also mixed with honey, wine, beer or cider – the variations are endless. Look for genuine French mustard made in France. A pinch of dry or a teaspoon of traditional hot English mustard adds punch to cheese recipes. Use smooth or wholegrain mustards to add flavour and, with wholegrain, an interesting texture to salad dressings, sauces and marinades.

Mixed Leaves with Bacon and Cheshire Cheese

SERVES 4 AS A MAIN DISH

- 5 slices white bread
- 350 g/12 oz rashers smoked back bacon
- 225 g/8 oz Cheshire cheese
- 30 ml/2 tablespoons tarragon vinegar
- 5 ml/1 level teaspoon wholegrain mustard
- 5 ml/1 level teaspoon caster sugar
- salt and freshly milled pepper
- 60 ml/4 tablespoons extra virgin olive oil
- 1 Iceberg lettuce
- 225 g/8 oz bag mixed salad leaves

Heat the oven to 160°C/325°F/gas mark 3.

Trim the crusts from the bread, then cut the slices into small dice. Spread on a baking tray and dry off in the oven for 30–40 minutes until golden brown and crisp. Leave to cool.

Grill the bacon rashers until crisp and brown, cool slightly, then cut into small pieces. Crumble the cheese into chunky pieces.

In a bowl, whisk the vinegar, mustard, sugar and a seasoning of salt and pepper. Add the olive oil and whisk to a creamy consistency.

Remove the centre core of the Iceberg lettuce and cut or break into bite-sized pieces. Place in a large salad bowl with the mixed leaves. Spoon over the dressing and toss to coat the salad greens. Sprinkle over the bacon pieces, crumbled cheese and *croûtons* and serve.

PERFECT SALADS

The salad should be the last thing you make before a meal so that the ingredients retain their crispness.

- ❦ Soft leaves should be torn rather than cut, but firm hearts of more crunchy salad greens can be shredded, sliced or cut into bite-sized chunks with a sharp knife.
- ❦ The best green salads provide contrasts of colour (from deep green to red, bronze and white), texture and shape. Some of the packs of ready-mixed salad and herb leaves are excellent.
- ❦ For a mild garlic flavour rub the mixing bowl with a crushed clove of garlic. Discard the garlic, then add the salad leaves.
- ❦ Drop the leaves into a big bowl so that you have plenty of room to toss the mixture. Immediately before serving, drizzle in the dressing – but not too much, you should never drown a salad. Then toss with two salad spoons by lifting and rolling the leaves over until they are glazed with the dressing.
- ❦ Ring the changes with different dressings (see pages 50–1).

- It's a nice idea to cut an Iceberg into wedges, then spoon the dressing over on the serving plate; Little Gem or chicory heads cut lengthways look good given the same treatment.
- Put the side plates for serving salad in the refrigerator to chill – this keeps the salad leaves crisp longer.

Tossed green salads look casual, so the simpler you keep them the better, but if you want to add a few extras consider these.

- Sliced or slivered courgette, cucumber or radishes.
- Cooked green vegetables such as blanched mangetout, asparagus tips or broad beans.
- Thinly sliced red onion rings or finely chopped spring onions for a mild onion flavour.
- Slices of peeled orange, sliced or halved strawberries or diced avocado.
- Nuggets of white Stilton, Roquefort or Gorgonzola, grated Cheddar or a sprinkling of grated Parmesan.
- Crunchy bread *croûtons* or salted peanuts add a delicious texture; so do crisply cooked and crumbled bacon rashers.
- Pumpkin or sunflower seeds look interesting and are especially nice if toasted first.
- Fresh flower petals look cool and pretty; gently separate nasturtium heads or the petals of marigolds or crumble in mauve chive flowers.

Lettuce Wedges, Red Onion and Smoked Mackerel Salad

SERVES 4 AS A MAIN DISH V

175 g/6 oz green beans
1 red onion
2 Little Gem lettuces
4 peppered smoked mackerel
225 g/8 oz cherry tomatoes
8 black olives
Vinaigrette Dressing (page 50) or Fresh Chive Mayonnaise (page 52)

Trim the green beans and add to a pan of boiling salted water. Simmer for 6 minutes or until just tender, then drain. Cover with cold water (to fix the green colour) until cool, then drain well. Peel and thinly slice the onion and separate into rings. Trim the lettuces and cut in half lengthways. Halve the mackerel lengthways.

Select a roomy flat platter and arrange everything in a simple 'help yourself' fashion. Pass a bowl of the chosen dressing separately.

HERBS

Fresh herbs give a wonderful flavour and add to the appearance of so many dishes. Now that they are flown in all year round from all over the world, we can enjoy them even in the depths of winter. They will last for several days provided they are kept cool, enclosed in a polythene bag or stored in their vacuum packs. Use them quickly, when they are at the peak of their freshness. When possible, buy punnets or pots of growing herbs. Keep them well watered on the windowsill and snip off what you need – they will last at least a week.

Soft-leaved fresh herbs can be snipped with scissors over the top of foods or chopped with a sharp knife, removing the leaves from any thick stalks first. Basil is an exception – tear the large leaves with your fingers and use small leaves whole.

Robust bay leaves are used whole to infuse the flavour in recipes. Rosemary is another herb with a pungent fragrance. Both these herbs should be removed from dishes before serving.

Dried herbs have a more concentrated flavour, so you need to be more economical in their use. We find the new freeze-dried herbs are the best; they have a reasonable flavour and a good green colour. In marinades, vinaigrette dressings, seasoning mixtures and sauced dishes they can be a perfectly acceptable alternative to fresh herbs. If you use dried herbs in place of fresh use less, about 5 ml/1 level teaspoon of dried for every 30–45 ml/2–3 tablespoons of the fresh chopped herb.

Pink Grapefruit with Prawns in Avocado Cream

SERVES 4 AS A MAIN DISH

- 2 pink grapefruit
- 350 g/12 oz cooked and peeled prawns
- 1 ripe avocado
- 1 thin slice cut across a peeled small onion
- 150 ml/¼ pint soured cream
- salt and freshly milled pepper
- 1 25 ml/½ level teaspoon Dijon mustard
- crisp lettuce leaves
- 15 ml/1 tablespoon chopped fresh chives

Using a small sharp knife, remove the peel and pith from the grapefruit. Slice into each fruit and lift out the grapefruit segments. Discard any pips and drain off the juice. Place the segments in a large bowl and gently stir in the prawns. Chill until serving time.

Halve the avocado, discard the stone and scoop the flesh into a food processor or blender. Add the onion, soured cream, salt, pepper and mustard. Buzz to a smooth purée. Turn the avocado cream into a bowl, cover tightly and chill.

Arrange the lettuce leaves on individual plates and pile the grapefruit and prawns in the centre. Top with spoonfuls of the avocado cream and sprinkle with chopped chives.

NUTS AND SEEDS

Crunchiness is the element here – both nuts of all kinds and seeds are terrific for adding texture and taste to all sorts of dishes.

Nuts in their shells keep best, for up to 6 months, enclosed in nature's protective coating, ready to be served with a good cheese to round off a special meal. For recipes though, shelled nuts are the ones to buy. Along the supermarket shelves you will find nuts on offer in a variety of forms – whole, blanched, slivered, toasted, salted, dry roasted, chopped or ground. Shelled nuts stay fresh for a limited time, especially once the sealed pack has been opened. Buy them in small quantities, keep them tightly sealed in a screw-topped jar in a cool dry cupboard, and use quickly. Chopped and ground nuts deteriorate faster still – like ground coffee, the best flavour is obtained when you chop, toast or grind nuts as you need them.

In cooking, most nuts are interchangeable. If a recipe sounds appealing to you but you don't like the nuts suggested, switch to one you do. The one exception is chestnuts. Chestnuts are quite different from other nuts because you can't eat them raw – they have to be simmered or roasted to make them edible. Their tough outer jackets are hard work to remove and it hardly seems worth the trouble when you can buy whole cooked chestnuts and smooth chestnut purée in tins.

To blanch nuts Almonds in their brown skins and pistachios are the only nuts that require this treatment. Put the nuts in a bowl and pour over boiling water to cover. Let them stand for several minutes then scoop out a nut and test by squeezing – the almond should pop out of the skin effortlessly. Pistachios should be drained and turned on to a dry teatowel. Rub gently, and the skins will flake away to reveal the pretty green nut inside.

To sliver and slice nuts Ready-blanched almonds are often dry and splinter instead of cutting neatly. A quick soak in boiling water makes nuts softer and easier to cut into fine slices or slivers. Cut newly blanched almonds immediately after removing the skins. Brazil nuts also respond to this treatment – after soaking in boiling water for 2–3 minutes they can be cut into neat slices or 'chips'. In a hurry? Dispense with the soaking and remove slivers from brazils with a vegetable peeler. Slivered, sliced or 'chipped' nuts look very pretty toasted.

To chop nuts Sometimes it's easier to use a pair of scissors – on walnuts, for example. Otherwise use a large kitchen knife and a board. Nuts can be chopped in a processor but take care – anything longer than a quick on/off buzz will reduce them to a powder. When using nuts to decorate a cake or pudding follow this tip for a pretty finish – put the chopped nuts into a sieve and shake gently to remove all the very fine bits before sprinkling the chopped nuts on the cake.

To toast (or roast) nuts Browning nuts, whole or cut, enhances their flavour and is well worthwhile if they are to be used in salads or sprinkled on top of dishes such as risottos. The easiest method is roasing in the oven, when the colour will be more even. Spread the nuts on a baking tray (with sides) and place in a preheated oven 190°C/375°F/gas mark 5 for about 6 minutes. Check frequently, giving the tray a gentle shake to encourage even browning on all sides. Nuts can be toasted under the grill or in a dry frying pan (without any oil) but the browning is very uneven – watch them constantly as they will scorch very quickly.

To grind nuts Ground almonds are best left to the experts – buy them ready ground. Walnuts will not grind, as they are too oily and quickly go to a paste. Hazelnuts can be ground very successfully and should be treated to several bursts on the food processor until they are the fineness you require. Toasted hazelnuts coarsely ground look very pretty sprinkled on desserts.

Spiced and seasoned nuts Use 350 g/12 oz of either one kind of shelled and skinned nut or a mixed selection.

Salted Toss the nuts with 30 ml/2 tablespoons olive oil and spread in a single layer in a shallow tin. Bake at 180°C/350°F/gas mark 4 for 8 minutes or until golden brown. Sprinkle generously with coarse sea salt while still hot.

Curried After tossing the nuts in the oil, sprinkle with 10 ml/2 level teaspoons curry powder and a pinch of sugar. Toss to coat the nuts then bake as above. Sprinkle generously with coarse sea salt while still hot.

Oriental Omit the oil and bake the nuts as above until golden. Sprinkle the hot nuts generously with soy sauce (use a bottle with a shaker top) and return to the hot oven for 1 minute for the soy sauce to dry.

Sesame, pumpkin and sunflower seeds are used extensively in cooking, simply sprinkled over salads or eaten as a nibble. Like nuts, their flavour is enhanced by toasting. This can be done either in the oven or in a dry frying pan in the same way as nuts – see above. Once toasted and cooled, they will keep well in a screw-topped jar. The larger seeds, pumpkin and sunflower, are delicious toasted and then sprinkled with sea salt or soy sauce, to serve with drinks.

Tahini is a thick paste made of crushed sesame seeds. Stirred into puréed chick peas it provides the distinctive flavour in hummus. It will also add a rich flavour to salad dressings (see page 50).

Walnut Cheese with Fruits

SERVES 4 AS A MAIN DISH V

2 (227 g) cartons curd cheese
salt and freshly milled pepper
2 large oranges
25 g/1 oz walnuts
2 pink grapefruit
1/2 small melon
a selection of salad greens
Fresh Herb Dressing (see page 50)

Turn the cheese into a bowl and, with a fork, work in a good seasoning of salt and pepper. Finely grate the zest from one orange, add to the cheese and evenly blend in. Divide the mixture into 4 portions and shape each into a 'log'. Finely chop the walnuts on a sheet of greaseproof paper. One at a time, roll the cheese logs in the nuts to lightly coat. Chill the cheeses until serving time.

Choose individual flat plates large enough to arrange the salad attractively. On a hot day, it's rather nice to pop them in the refrigerator to chill at the same time as the cheeses.

Using a small sharp knife, remove the peel and pith from the oranges and grapefruit. Thinly slice the oranges. Cut between the segments of the grapefruit. Remove the melon rind and seeds and cut the flesh into thin wedges.

Arrange a portion of cheese and the fruits with salad greens on each plate. Drizzle over a little of the Fresh Herb Dressing and serve immediately.

WARM SALADS

By mixing something lightly cooked and hot with cool, crisp greens and maybe tossing with a hot dressing, you are creating a *salade tiède* or warm salad – a surprise for the taste buds!

Warm salads must be eaten immediately they are prepared, before the hot ingredients wilt the delicate salad greens. So gather all the ingredients together, cook quickly, and serve either as a main course, together with warm crusty bread, or as a first course. These recipes will serve 2 as a main dish, 4 as a starter.

Spinach Salad with Hot Bacon Dressing
Arrange 225 g/8 oz small spinach leaves, thoroughly washed and dried, and 1 large avocado, peeled and sliced, on serving plates. Trim the rinds from 6 streaky bacon rashers and dice the bacon. Fry slowly to extract as much bacon fat as possible and allow the bacon to get really crisp. Lift the bacon from the pan and keep hot. Add 30 ml/2 tablespoons olive oil, 30 ml/2 tablespoons red wine vinegar, 2.5 ml/½ level teaspoon toasted sesame seeds and stir until hot. Season with freshly milled pepper and drizzle over the spinach and avocado. Scatter the bacon bits over the top and serve with lemon wedges.

Corn Salad with Sautéd Chicken Livers
Arrange 100 g/4 oz corn salad, rinsed and dried, on serving plates and sprinkle with 50 g/2 oz pine-nuts. Separate 6 chicken livers and trim with scissors. Gently sauté in 15 ml/1 tablespoon grapeseed oil for about 5 minutes, or until the livers are firm but still pink in the middle. Lift from the pan, cut in slices and arrange on the salad. Add 30 ml/2 tablespoons walnut oil and 30 ml/2 tablespoons sherry vinegar to the pan and stir until hot. Season to taste with salt and freshly milled pepper and drizzle over the salad.

Grilled Goat's Cheese and Walnut Salad V
Rinse and dry a selection of salad greens including radicchio and curly endive. Tear into bite-sized pieces and place in a bowl. Whisk together 45 ml/3 tablespoons walnut oil, 15 ml/1 tablespoon white wine vinegar and a seasoning of salt and pepper. Spoon over the greens, add 30 ml/2 tablespoons broken toasted walnuts and toss to mix. Arrange on serving plates. Toast 4 slices of French bread, cut diagonally, under the grill on one side only. Slice 2 crottins in half or 1 small log chèvre (about 100 g/4 oz) into thick slices. Arrange on top of the untoasted sides of the bread. Grill until the cheese is just beginning to melt. Serve on top of the salad.

Avocado, Bacon and Watercress Salad

SERVES 4 AS A MAIN DISH

Rinse the watercress, discarding any coarse stems. Roll in a teatowel to dry. Trim the bacon rashers, grill until crisp, then let them cool and coarsely crumble them. Make the chive dressing by measuring the mustard, sugar, lemon juice, oil and a seasoning of salt and pepper into a medium bowl. Whisk untl well blended, then stir in the chives.

Halve the avocados, remove the stones and carefully pull away the skin (see page 13). Dice or slice the flesh into the chive dressing and gently turn to coat with the dressing.

Cut or tear the lettuce into bite-sized pieces and place in a large salad bowl together with the watercress. Add the avocados and dressing and gently toss together. Sprinkle over the bacon bits and serve.

- 1 bunch watercress
- 225 g/8 oz streaky bacon rashers
- 5 ml/1 level teaspoon Dijon mustard
- 5 ml/1 level teaspoon soft brown sugar
- 30 ml/2 tablespoons fresh lemon juice
- 60 ml/4 tablespoons extra virgin olive oil
- salt and freshly milled pepper
- 45 ml/3 tablespoons chopped fresh chives
- 3 ripe avocados
- 1/2 Iceberg lettuce

Autumn Fruits with Stilton Dressing

SERVES 2 AS A MAIN DISH V

Trim the rind off the Stilton, crumble the cheese with a fork, and add to the fromage frais. Lightly blend together and season to taste. Quarter the pears and peel if wished. Remove the cores and cut into thin wedges. Quarter the apples, remove the cores and cut into thin wedges. Sprinkle the fruit with a little lemon juice.

Arrange the fruit wedges on individual plates and tuck in the salad greens and walnuts. Top with the Stilton dressing and serve immediately.

- 100 g/4 oz Stilton
- 150 ml/1/4 pint fromage frais
- salt and freshly milled pepper
- 2 large ripe dessert pears
- 2 red-skinned apples
- a little lemon juice
- salad greens
- 25 g/1 oz walnut halves

SALAD LEAVES – CHOOSING AND STORING THEM

With the choice on offer today, green salads can be really interesting and pretty. Select salad greens that are bright and perky with no brown patches or wilted leaves. Here are just some of the variety of green leaves to be found in the shops today.

- Cabbage or round lettuce are the familiar round varieties with soft green leaves that separate easily.
- Feuille de Chêne (oak leaf) has a floppy head of deeply notched leaves that are green through to bronze and is good for adding colour to an all-green salad; the same goes for Lollo Rosso, with frilly-edged leaves that look interesting and are crisp-textured.
- Cos lettuce is supercrisp and can be torn into pieces. Little Gem (from the same family) is a miniature version, with neat, tightly curled heads. Use the leaves whole or cut the head lengthwise into halves or wedges.
- Webbs Wonderful is round, with crinkly outer leaves protecting the firm heart. Iceberg is a paler version, crunchy but bland-tasting. Both may be shredded or cut into chunky pieces.
- Chicory, those slender spear heads of yellow and white, add a refreshing touch of bitterness to a green salad. They look attractive when sliced lengthwise into wedges or across in chunks.
- Radicchio (from the chicory family) is also slightly bitter, and the deep red leaves with white ribs are closely packed into a round head. Tear the leaves into pieces and use in small amounts – a small head goes a long way.
- Frisée (curly endive) is a mass of coarse frizzy leaves, the dark outer ones having a stronger flavour than the pale centre. Escarole is a broad-leaved variety and not so strongly flavoured.
- Small leaves to use whole in salads include very young leaf spinach, dark and pretty – pull away the stalks. Or corn salad (mâche), clusters of green spoon-shaped leaves – nip off the base of the stalks to separate the leaves.
- Cress makes a pretty sprinkle – snip off the tender green tops with scissors. Or use the flat peppery leaves and tender tips of watercress.
- Rocket has indented dark leaves with a peppery flavour – it is occasionally available in good greengrocers, but try to grow this one yourself. The same goes for dandelion or nasturtium leaves – pick only tender young spring shoots.
- Add a good sprinkling of fresh herbs to salad leaves (instead of mixing them in the dressing) – try chives, coriander, chervil, lovage (a broad-leaved herb with a celery flavour). Hold the bunch of herbs over the salad bowl and scissor-snip them coarsely over the dressed salad greens so that they retain their character and flavour – for maximum impact use just one herb rather than a mixture.

Salads will be good to look at and even better to eat if the ingredients are cool and crisped up in the refrigerator.

- Separate loose-leaved salad greens with the fingers and shake the leaves in a colander under running cold water (don't let them soak). Then spin dry in a salad spinner. Or pile the leaves on a clean teatowel, draw it closed, then give the 'bag' a swing (preferably outside) to remove all the water droplets. Wet salad leaves will make a soggy salad and will also not keep so well in the refrigerator.

- Put the salad leaves in a large freezer bag, secure the opening and refrigerate. The leaves will crisp up beautifully, and stay fresh and ready to serve for at least a couple of days. Even limp lettuce will revive given this treatment.
- Small salad leaves of spinach, watercress and herbs keep fresh this way too. Spinach may need several rinses to remove all the sand it is grown in. Refrigerate ready-mixed green leaves in the unopened supermarket pack.
- Tightly packed salad heads such as Iceberg and Little Gem should be kept whole. Remove any bruised outer leaves and tuck them in the refrigerator salad drawer or in a freezer bag.

POTATO SALADS

With freshly cooked new potatoes as the base and a choice of four different dressings, potato salad is lifted from the everyday standby to something very special. Apart from the Warm Potato Salad, they should be made a few hours before serving so that the ingredients can marinate. Keep covered in a cool place – not in the refrigerator.

Basic Salad Rinse 900 g/2 lb small new potatoes, then add them to boiling salted water and cook until just tender – about 10 minutes. Drain, then shake in the pan over the heat for a moment to dry them. Tip into a large serving bowl.

Warm Potato Salad [V] Whisk together 30 ml/2 level tablespoons wholegrain mustard, 45 ml/3 tablespoons white wine vinegar, 30 ml/2 tablespoons clear honey, 100 ml/4 fl oz olive oil and a good seasoning of salt and freshly-milled pepper. Pour over the hot potatoes and turn gently to coat them all over. Add 1 bunch spring onions, trimmed and finely sliced. Serve while still warm, gently stirring before serving.

Herbed Potato Salad [V] Whisk together 5 ml/1 level teaspoon Dijon mustard, 100 ml/4 fl oz grapeseed oil, 45 ml/3 tablespoons white wine vinegar, 15 ml/ 1 level tablespoon caster sugar and a good seasoning of salt and freshly milled pepper. Pour over the hot potatoes and gently turn to coat with the dressing. Add 1 bunch spring onions, trimmed and finely chopped. Leave to cool at least 1 hour or longer. Before serving gently stir in 30 ml/2 tablespoons finely chopped parsley and 30 ml/2 tablespoons chopped chives.

Creamy Potato Salad Whisk together 75 ml/3 fl oz grapeseed oil, 30 ml/2 tablespoons white wine vinegar, 15 ml/1 tablespoon wholegrain mustard, 30 ml/2 level tablespoons caster sugar and salt and pepper. Pour over the hot potatoes and gently turn. Add 1 bunch spring onions, finely chopped. Leave to cool at least 1 hour or longer. Before serving, mix together 30 ml/2 tablespoons mayonnaise and 30 ml/2 tablespoons natural yogurt. Stir into the potatoes. Serve with chopped chives and crisply cooked and crumbled streaky bacon.

Curried Potato Salad [V] Add 45 ml/3 tablespoons white wine vinegar, salt and freshly milled pepper and, if wished, 1 crushed clove of garlic to the hot potatoes. De-seed and finely chop 1 green pepper and stir in. Mix everything very gently and leave for at least 1 hour. Before serving, whisk 150 ml/$^1/_4$ pint double cream to soft peaks. Fold in 30 ml/2 level tablespoons mayonnaise, the juice of $^1/_2$ a lemon and 15 ml/1 level tablespoon mild curry paste. Add to the potatoes and mix through. Add a sprinkling of paprika on top.

DRESSINGS

Explore the wealth of flavours produced by combining oil with different vinegars, juices and a variety of other ingredients. Even the consistency can be varied – a combination of ingredients shaken in a screw-topped jar will retain their individuality. Buzz the same ingredients in a processor or blender and you will get a thick creamy consistency that will not separate. Unless otherwise stated, the quantities given are for salads serving 4–6. Store any unused dressings in a screw-topped jar. Dressings made in a jar will need to be well shaken again before use.

Vinaigrette Put a good seasoning of salt and freshly milled pepper, 15 ml/1 tablespoon caster sugar or clear honey, 10 ml/2 teaspoons wholegrain or Dijon mustard and 75 ml/3 fl oz wine vinegar into a screw-topped jar or blender with 225 ml/8 fl oz grapeseed oil and 50 ml/2 fl oz olive oil. Shake well or buzz until blended. Makes about 300 ml/½pint.

Using a herbed vinegar such as tarragon will add the appropriate herb flavour. Red wine vinegar will make a richer-coloured dressing than white or cider vinegar. Chopped fresh herbs or crushed garlic may also be added to vary the flavour.

Vinaigrette is a useful all-purpose dressing to use with mixed or green salads and to marinate lightly cooked vegetables.

Creamy Poppy Seed Measure 45 ml/3 tablespoons red wine vinegar, 30 ml/2 level tablespoons caster sugar, a seasoning of salt and freshly milled pepper, 5 ml/1 level teaspoon mustard powder, 15 ml/1 tablespoon finely chopped onion and 150 ml/¼ pint grapeseed oil into a processor or blender. Cover and buzz until emulsified. Add 60 ml/4 tablespoons cold water and 30 ml/2 tablespoons poppyseeds. Buzz briefly to combine.

Spoon over wedges of Iceberg lettuce or sliced tomatoes.

Oriental Measure 15 ml/1 tablespoon tahini, 30 ml/2 tablespoons sherry vinegar, a seasoning of salt and freshly milled pepper and 15 ml/1 tablespoon clear honey into a jar or blender. Add 30 ml/2 tablespoons dark soy sauce, grapeseed oil and 15 ml/1 tablespoon sesame seed oil. Shake well or buzz until blended.

Dark, rich and intensely flavoured, this dressing is delicious stirred into cooked rice or added to bean salads.

Fresh Herb Spoon 45 ml/3 tablespoons white wine vinegar or fresh lemon juice, 1 crushed clove of garlic, a seasoning of salt and freshly milled pepper, 5 ml/1 teaspoon Dijon mustard and 10 ml/2 level teaspoons caster sugar into a jar or blender. Add 75 ml/3 fl oz extra virgin olive oil and 75 ml/3 fl oz olive or grapeseed oil. Shake well or buzz until blended. Add 45 ml/3 tablespoons snipped fresh summer herbs – basil, chives, oregano or coriander. Shake or buzz until just combined.

For a milder flavour, cut the garlic clove in half and add to the completed dressing. Allow to stand for 1 hour then remove. Spoon this pretty green-flecked dressing over seafood or chicken salads.

Honey Mustard Measure 45 ml/3 tablespoons white wine vinegar, 30 ml/2 tablespoons wholegrain mustard, a seasoning of salt and freshly milled pepper and 30 ml/2 tablespoons clear honey into a jar or blender. Add 175 ml/6 fl/oz olive oil. Shake or buzz until combined.

Spoon this slightly sweet and creamy dressing over cold roast beef, chicken or ham salads.

Spicy Chilli Spoon 45 ml/3 tablespoons cider vinegar, 30 ml/2 tablespoons sweet chilli sauce, 15 ml/1 tablespoon soft brown sugar, a seasoning of salt and freshly milled pepper and 1 crushed clove of garlic into a jar or blender.

Add 175 ml/6 fl oz olive oil and 5 ml/1 teaspoon crushed dried pepper flakes. Shake or buzz until blended.

A tomato-coloured tangy dressing – for a more pungent flavour use hot chilli sauce. Spoon over pasta or seafood salads.

Blue Cheese Measure 45 ml/3 tablespoons white wine vinegar, 5 ml/1 teaspoon Dijon mustard, a seasoning of salt and freshly milled pepper, 25 g/1 oz Roquefort, Stilton or Danish Blue, 30 ml/2 tablespoons single cream and 175 ml/6 fl oz grapeseed oil into a jar or blender. Shake or buzz until smooth (if making in a jar, mash the cheese with a fork first).

A creamy dressing with a 'bite'. Spoon over greens such as chicory or curly endive and add diced celery, apples or pears and walnuts.

COLESLAW SALADS

With a basis of very finely shredded cabbage, coleslaw can also contain a wide variety of other vegetables and fresh or dried fruits. The dressing can vary too, with either a creamy mayonnaise base or a well seasoned oil and vinegar mixture.

Basic Salad Remove outer leaves from ½ a small white cabbage and cut into two. Cut away the hard core and then very finely cut across the wedges to make fine slivers of cabbage. The secret of a good coleslaw is to take the time to cut it very finely. (The cabbage can be put through a food processor on the slicer plate but the finished result will not be so nice.)

Put the cabbage into a large bowl. Peel and finely chop one small sweet red onion or trim and finely slice 1 bunch spring onions. Add to the cabbage. Add the remaining ingredients (see below) and the dressing and toss well. Cover and leave in a cool place for at least 2 hours.

Pepper and Apple Slaw [V] Quarter 1 green pepper, remove the stem, core and seeds and very finely slice. Quarter 2 red-skinned apples, remove the core and thinly slice. Add the pepper and apples to the cabbage. Whisk together 150 ml/¼ pint mayonnaise, 150 ml/¼ pint soured cream, the juice of ½ a lemon and 15 ml/1 tablespoon wholegrain mustard. Season well with salt and freshly milled pepper. Add to the cabbage as above.

Coleslaw Vinaigrette [V] Peel and grate 1 large carrot, trim and very finely slice 3 celery stalks and cut 50 g/2 oz ready-to-eat dried apricots into slivers. Add the carrot, celery and apricots to the cabbage. Dissolve 30 ml/2 tablespoons caster sugar in 30 ml/2 tablespoons boiling water. Add 30 ml/2 tablespoons white wine vinegar, 30 ml /2 tablespoons olive oil, and a good seasoning of salt and freshly milled pepper. Add to the cabbage as above. *Illustrated on Plate Nine.*

FLAVOURED MAYONNAISE

Don't just stop at salads when serving these delicious versions of that traditional favourite – mayonnaise. They make flavoursome dressings for cold meat, poultry, seafood and fruits.

Start with 175 ml/6 fl oz of your favourite prepared mayonnaise recipe or a good shop-bought variety and add the flavourings of your choice. Cover and chill for at least 1 hour to allow the flavours to develop. Each recipe makes 4–6 servings. Unused dressings may be kept tightly covered in the refrigerator for up to 5 days, ready for dipping into when making a sandwich or quick salad.

Yogurt Mayonnaise Combining natural yogurt and mayonnaise in equal amounts makes a lighter less rich-tasting dressing that's lower in calories too.

Use instead of the whole amount of mayonnaise in our recipes or serve plain, seasoned to taste with salt and freshly milled pepper.

Fresh Chive Add 30 ml/2 tablespoons soured cream, 45 ml/3 tablespoons finely chopped chives, 15 ml/1 tablespoon fresh lemon juice and seasoning to taste.

Use for making new potato salad, spoon on to hot baked potatoes, or gently combine with freshly cooked tiny green beans and crisp crumbled bacon.

Double Mustard Add 30 ml/2 tablespoons soured cream, 15 ml/1 tablespoon each of Dijon and wholegrain mustard and seasoning to taste.

Add to blanched 'matchsticks' of celeriac or spoon on to individual servings of mixed citrus fruits. Delicious with cold roast beef or duck.

Mild Garlic Crush 1 clove of garlic and rub it round the inside of the mixing bowl. Remove and discard it (for a stronger flavour leave in the bowl). Spoon in the mayonnaise and add 30 ml/2 tablespoons soured cream. Stir and season to taste.

Use to dress cold chicken salad or spoon over raw thinly sliced button mushrooms.

Coleslaw Add 30 ml/2 tablespoons soured cream, 5 ml/1 teaspoon Dijon mustard and 15 ml/1 tablespoon white wine vinegar. Season to taste.

Use as the dressing for shredded cabbage leaves or white cabbage salads.

Blue Cheese Mash 50 g/2 oz Stilton, Danish blue or Roquefort with a fork. Add to the mayonnaise with 30 ml/2 tablespoons soured cream and 5 ml/1 teaspoon chopped shallot or chives. Season to taste.

Spoon over wedges of crisp Iceberg or Webbs lettuce, on to wedges of fresh ripe pear or as a dip for crudités.

Tangy Tomato Add 45 ml/3 tablespoons single cream, 30 ml/2 tablespoons tomato relish and a few drops of hot pepper sauce. Season to taste.

Spoon over servings of cold prawns or poached salmon, or into the hollows of buttery avocado halves.

Lemon and Green Add 5 ml/1 teaspoon finely grated lemon rind, 30 ml/2 tablespoons lemon juice, 15 ml/1 tablespoon finely chopped parsley and 15 ml/1 tablespoon finely chopped gherkin. Season to taste.

Combine with chunks of tuna or other cooled and diced firm-fleshed fish such as monkfish or salmon. Gently stir into freshly cooked and cooled baby vegetables such as broad beans. Spoon over hot asparagus.

Apple Horseradish Add 30 ml/2 tablespoons soured cream, 15 ml/1 tablespoon horseradish relish, 45 ml/3 tablespoons unsweetened apple sauce and seasoning to taste.

Serve with cold beef, chicken or pork, or spoon over sliced tomato and red onion salad.

Honey and Orange Add 30 ml/2 tablespoons natural yogurt, 30 ml/2 tablespoons clear honey and 5 ml/1 teaspoon finely grated orange rind. Season to taste.

Serve with fresh fruit and vegetable salad platters, with scoops of cottage cheese on

PLATE ONE
Orange and Sweet Onion Salad (page 15) and Vegetable Chowder (page 8)

PLATE TWO

Winter Vegetables: Paprika Wedges (page 20), Red Cabbage with Apple and Orange (page 33), and Carrots with Orange and Ginger (page 32)

pineapple slices, or with cold smoked duck or chicken.

Fruited Curry Add 5 ml/1 teaspoon tomato purée, 10 ml/2 teaspoons curry paste, 15 ml/1 tablespoon mango chutney (chop pieces of fruit small) and 15 ml/1 tablespoon lemon juice. Season to taste.

Use as a dressing for cold cooked chicken, for spooning over hard-boiled eggs or for mixing a simple crunchy cauliflower salad.

CHAPTER FOUR

Fish

The simple easy ways to cook fresh fish are all here, plus good sauces and relishes to serve with them. For something different choose from dishes that are lightly spiced, baked in the oven or cooked in a sauce – good enough to serve as party food. Try fish served cold too.

CHOOSING AND STORING FISH

When shopping for fish, look for a good refrigerated display, with the fish on lots of ice and absolutely no smell. Always ask the fishmonger for help if you are not sure how to cook unusual fish or which fish to choose for a certain recipe. He will also clean, gut and fillet fish for you.

Fresh fish is always firm textured and springy, not limp. The scales should have a good sheen and the eyes should be bright, not cloudy. Mussels should be still alive and their shells tightly closed. If they have opened, they should close up when you touch them.

Transfer fish from the shop to your refrigerator as soon as possible, preferably using a cool bag and frozen ice packs. Store fish at the bottom of the refrigerator so that it cannot drip on other foods. Make sure it is well wrapped.

Cook fresh fish within 1 day of purchase. Live mussels should keep for 2 days if stored damp (not wet). Smoked fish has a longer shelf life of 4–5 days. If the fish is prepacked or vacuum packed, observe the 'use by' date.

Salmon Salad Platter

Illustrated on Plate Three

SERVES 6–8

8 skinned salmon fillets
olive oil
salt and freshly milled pepper
450 g/1 lb French beans
1 red onion
700 g/1½ lb small new potatoes
1 bunch (6–8) spring onions
100 g/4 oz black olives
30 ml/2 tablespoons red wine vinegar
1 (50 g) can anchovy fillets

Heat the grill to hot and set the grill pan 7.5 cm/3 inches below the heat source. Arrange the salmon fillets on an oiled baking tray, brush with olive oil and season with salt and pepper. Grill for 4 minutes – there is no need to turn them. Leave to cool.

Trim the French beans and cut any long ones in half. Add to a pan of boiling salted water and simmer for 6 minutes, until tender. Drain and rinse with cold water. Peel the red onion and cut into thin slices. Cover with boiling water, leave for 1 minute, then drain. Cook the potatoes in boiling salted water for 10–15 minutes until tender, then drain. Trim the spring onions. Break the cooled salmon into chunky pieces.

For the dressing whisk together 100 ml/4 fl oz olive oil, the vinegar and a good seasoning of salt and freshly milled pepper. Drain and chop the anchovy fillets. Toss the cooked potatoes with 45 ml/3 tablespoons of the dressing and the chopped anchovies.

On a large flat platter arrange the salmon pieces, French beans, potatoes, and red onion rings. Tuck in the spring onions and scatter over the olives. Drizzle the remaining dressing all over the salad.

Grilled Salmon Fillets with Tomato Cream

SERVES 6

- 6 salmon fillets
- 100 g/4 oz Garlic and Herb Butter (page 31)
- salt and freshly milled pepper
- 8 sun-dried tomatoes in oil
- 150 ml/1/4 pint double cream

If necessary skin the salmon and remove any tiny bones. Melt the seasoned butter and use a little to brush a baking tray with a rim or a shallow baking dish. Arrange the fillets on the tray (or dish) and brush them generously with the remaining butter. Season with freshly milled pepper. Lift the tomatoes out of their jar with a fork on to a plate. Scissor-snip into chunky pieces.

Heat the grill to moderately hot and set the grill rack 7.5 cm/3 inches from the heat source. Grill the salmon for about 4 minutes until it is just turning golden brown. There is no need to turn it.

Meanwhile make the sauce. Heat the double cream in a small saucepan with the tomato pieces and any oil from them left on the plate. When just beginning to bubble around the edges, remove from the heat and season with salt and pepper. Serve with the salmon.

SALMON FOR SERVING COLD

Baking salmon in foil is by far the easiest method of cooking a whole fish which is to be served cold, but you do have to watch the size of the fish you choose. Before you buy the fish, check the inside measurement of your oven. A 1.5–1.75 g/3–3½ lb fish is the largest that will fit in an average oven without bending it. Fish of this size are sea trout or small farmed salmon. If you want to cook a larger salmon, you can perhaps lay it diagonally across the baking sheet or, as a last resort, cut off the head before cooking.

Rinse the fish inside and out under cold water, and pat dry with absorbent kitchen paper. Season inside the fish with salt and freshly milled pepper. Rub the outside of the fish with oil.

Heat the oven to 180°C/350°F/gas mark 4.

Set the fish on a large square of oiled kitchen foil and add 2–3 slices of lemon. Draw the foil up and over the fish and seal the edge by folding along the top to make a baggy parcel loose enough to allow air to circulate inside it. Turn up the ends of the foil to seal. Lift the wrapped fish on to a baking tray. Bake for 30–40 minutes, or calculate the cooking time allowing 10 minutes per 450 g/1 lb.

At the end of the cooking time remove the salmon from the oven but do not open the foil – cool then refrigerate undisturbed for 24 hours.

Open the foil carefully (the fish will be firm enough to handle) and discard the lemon slices. Gently peel away the skin, turning the fish carefully to get at the second side. Lift the fish on to a flat serving platter.

At this stage the fish can be served with the bone in. Alternatively, it is easier and neater to serve if the bone is removed. To remove the bone, use a palette knife to lift off the top fillets carefully, remembering which part of the fish they came from. Then snip the backbone with scissors, just below the head and above the tail. Lift the bone away. If you prefer, remove the head too. Carefully replace the salmon fillets.

Loosely cover with clingfilm and chill until serving time. Sprinkle the fish with a little dill If you like, but resist over-decorating it. Serve with a good mayonnaise or choose from the Flavoured Mayonnaises on pages 52–3.

Fresh Salmon Kedgeree

SERVES 4

350 g/12 oz long-grain rice
750 ml/1¼ pints hot vegetable stock
450 g/1 lb salmon tail fillet
150 ml/¼ pint double cream

Add the rice to the hot stock and bring to the boil, stirring. Cover and cook gently for about 20 minutes or until the rice is tender and the stock absorbed. Skin the salmon fillet and cut the flesh into chunks. Combine the double cream, curry paste and a seasoning of salt and pepper. Peel and finely chop the onion.

Melt the butter in a large frying pan. Add the salmon pieces and fry for a few minutes, turning them gently, until tinged with brown and cooked through. Using a slotted spoon, transfer them to a plate and keep warm. Add the onion to the hot butter and fry gently for about 5 minutes until very soft. Stir in the cream and curry paste mixture and bring to a simmer. Add the cooked rice and turn to heat through. Add the salmon pieces and heat gently for a moment or two. Serve piping hot, garnished with lemon wedges.

10 ml/2 level teaspoons curry paste
salt and freshly milled pepper
1 medium onion
50 g/2 oz butter
lemon wedges

Salmon and Wild Rice in Filo Pastry

SERVES 6–8

1.1–1.5 kg/2½–3 lb middle cut of salmon
100 g/4 oz long-grain and wild rice mix
1 clove of garlic
100 g/4 oz soft butter
30 ml/2 tablespoons chopped fresh chives
15 ml/1 tablespoon olive oil
5 sheets filo pastry
poppy seeds
175 g/6 oz fine-cut marmalade
50 ml/2 fl oz white vermouth
30 ml/2 tablespoons white wine vinegar
10 ml/2 level teaspoons cornflour

Ask the fishmonger to slice the salmon piece into 2 fillets, removing the bone and skin. Cook the rice according to the packet directions. Peel and crush the garlic and add to half the butter. Add the chives and blend together. Fork the seasoned butter into the rice.

Melt the remaining butter with the oil. Take 4 of the filo pastry sheets and lightly brush each with the butter and oil mixture. Lay the sheets out on a baking tray, overlapping each other to form a 35 cm/14 inch square.

Place one salmon piece in the centre of the pastry. Spoon the buttered rice on top and cover with the second piece of salmon. Draw the pastry up and over the salmon, overlapping it along the join. Fold the pastry ends under the fish to form a neat parcel. Chill until baking time.

Heat the oven to 180°C/350°F/gas mark 4.

Brush the remaining pastry sheet with the melted butter and oil and cut into long 1 cm/½ inch strips. Brush the pastry-wrapped salmon with the remaining butter and oil, then arrange the filo strips decoratively on top. Sprinkle generously with poppy seeds. Bake for 40 minutes.

Meanwhile, make the orange sauce. Spoon the marmalade into a medium saucepan with the vermouth and vinegar. Set over medium heat, stirring, until the marmalade has melted. Blend the cornflour with 15 ml/1 teaspoon cold water and add to the pan. Cook, stirring constantly, until the sauce comes to the boil and is slightly thickened. Pour into a serving jug.

For easier cutting, let the baked salmon stand for 10–15 minutes in a warm place.

Monkfish Gumbo

SERVES 4

175 g/6 oz long-grain rice
1 small onion
1 green pepper
3 stalks celery
2 cloves of garlic
175 g/6 oz okra
350 g/12 oz monkfish fillets
15 ml/1 tablespoon plain flour
5 ml/1 level teaspoon paprika
30 ml/2 tablespoons olive oil
600 ml/1 pint vegetable stock
1 (397 g) can chopped tomatoes
1 bouquet garni
100 g/4 oz cooked and peeled prawns
juice of 1 lemon
10 ml/2 teaspoons Worcestershire sauce
dash of Tabasco sauce

Cook the rice according to package directions and keep hot. Peel and finely chop the onion. Halve the pepper, removing the seeds and chopping the flesh finely. Pull away any tough strings from the celery then chop finely. Peel and crush the garlic. Trim the okra and cut across into slices. Cut the monkfish into bite-sized pieces. Combine the flour and paprika on a plate and roll the pieces of fish in the mixture to coat all over.

Heat the oil in a large saucepan, add the pieces of fish and fry to brown them all over. Lift from the pan with a slotted spoon. Add the onion, pepper, celery, garlic and okra to the hot oil, turn and fry gently for about 5 minutes to soften. Add the vegetable stock, the tomatoes and bouquet garni. Bring just to the boil, lower the heat, cover, and simmer gently for 15 minutes.

Return the pieces of monkfish to the pan. Add the prawns, lemon juice, Worcestershire sauce and a good dash of Tabasco to taste. Simmer 3–5 minutes longer. Remove the bouquet garni.

To serve, place a good spoonful of cooked rice in each warmed soup bowl, then ladle in the Gumbo.

Monkfish in Green Chilli and Coconut Cream

SERVES 6

Cut the monkfish into chunky pieces. Peel and finely chop the onion, peel, core and dice the apple, de-seed and chop the chilli, peel and grate the root ginger. Heat the oil in a large frying pan (use one that has a lid), add the monkfish and gently fry for 2–3 minutes just to firm up the flesh. Remove from the pan using a slotted spoon.

To the hot oil add the onion, apple, chilli and ginger. Stir the mixture over a low heat until soft – about 8 minutes. Add the coriander, cumin and turmeric and stir over the heat for a minute. Stir in the vermouth, 225 ml/ 8 fl oz water and the single cream.

Return the fish pieces to the pan and bring to a simmer. Cover and cook gently for 10 minutes. Crumble the coconut into the sauce and continue to cook, stirring, until the coconut has melted and the sauce is slightly thickened. Serve garnished with the lemon wedges.

- 700 g/1½ lb monkfish tail fillets
- 1 medium onion
- 1 small cooking apple
- 1 green chilli
- 2.5 cm/1 inch fresh ginger
- 30 ml/2 tablespoons olive oil
- 2.5 ml/½ level teaspoon ground coriander
- 2.5 ml/½ level teaspoon ground cumin
- 2.5 ml/½ level teaspoon ground turmeric
- 50 ml/2 fl oz white vermouth
- 300 ml/½ pint single cream
- 50 g/2 oz creamed coconut

SEASONED FLOUR

Seasoned flour is nothing more than plain flour with salt and freshly milled pepper added. It is used to coat pieces of fish, meat or chicken prior to frying or adding to a casserole. Seasoned flour forms a protective coating and browns or thickens according to the way it is used. To make it up as you go along, simply spoon a couple of tablespoons of plain flour (or as much as you think you will need) on to a plate and add a good seasoning of salt and several turns of the pepper mill. Mix together before dipping in the fish, meat or chicken pieces. A simple way for meat or chicken pieces is to spoon the flour and seasonings into a freezer bag, add 2–3 pieces of meat or chicken at a time, close securely and shake – it's less messy this way.

Seasoned flour can be stored ready mixed by sifting together 250 g/8 oz plain flour, 15 ml/1 level tablespoon salt, 5 ml/1 level teaspoon pepper (24 grinds of the mill) and 1.25 ml/¼ teaspoon mace or nutmeg – the latter gives the mixture a faintly aromatic flavour. Store in a clearly labelled jar and spoon out as required. Use seasoned flour to thicken gravies too.

FRESH RELISHES

The idea of serving a fresh vegetable or fruit relish or salsa with simply cooked fish or meats comes from California. There, the abundance of locally grown fruit and vegetables all the year round influences the style of cooking. Unlike pickles, these relishes are served freshly made while the ingredients are still crunchy. Allow time to hand chop the vegetables and fruit into tiny dice, as using a processor will turn them to a purée.

Perhaps on a cold wet day the thought of a cold relish with hot food may not seem very appealing but, when the weather warms up, do try them. Serve any one with hot or cold grilled, barbecued or poached fish. They are also delicious with steaks, hamburgers, chops or with cold sliced meat and poultry.

Corn and Sweet Peppers Drain a 326 g can of whole kernel sweetcorn and turn into a mixing bowl. De-seed 1/2 a yellow and 1/2 a red pepper and cut into tiny dice. Very finely chop 1/2 a red onion. Add the peppers and onion to the corn along with 15 ml/1 tablespoon caster sugar, salt and freshly milled pepper to taste, 15 ml/1 tablespoon white wine vinegar and 15 ml/1 tablespoon olive oil. Toss to mix.

Tomato and Avocado Cut out the stalk end of 4 large tomatoes and cover with boiling water for 1 minute to remove the skins. Halve, de-seed and finely dice the flesh. Place in a bowl and generously season with salt and freshly milled pepper. Peel and finely chop 1/2 a red onion. Halve, de-seed and finely chop 1 green chilli. Add the onion and chilli to the tomato along with 30 ml/2 tablespoons chopped parsley, 15 ml/1 tablespoon red wine vinegar and 30 ml/2 tablespoons olive oil. Peel and finely dice 1 ripe avocado, add to the bowl and gently mix together.

Courgette with Red and Green Onions Trim and finely dice 3 medium courgettes and turn into a bowl. Very finely chop 1/2 a red onion and 6–8 trimmed spring onions. De-seed 1/2 a green pepper and cut into tiny dice. Add both onions and the pepper to the bowl. Season well with salt and freshly milled pepper and spoon over 15 ml/1 tablespoon red wine vinegar, 30 ml/2 tablespoons olive oil and 60 ml/4 tablespoons chopped chives. Lightly toss together.

Minted Melon Halve and de-seed 1 small Ogen melon, cut off the rind and cut the flesh into tiny dice. Strip the leaves from 15 g/1/2 oz mint sprigs, pile them on a chopping board and sprinkle with 15 ml/1 tablespoon granulated sugar. Chop finely – the sugar draws out the flavouring oils. Place the diced melon, the mint and the sugar in a bowl. Add 30 ml/2 tablespoons raspberry vinegar and a good seasoning of salt and pepper. Toss lightly together.

Smoked Mussels in Tomatoes

SERVES 4

- 4 beefsteak tomatoes
- salt
- 5 ml/1 level teaspoon tomato purée
- vegetable stock (see method)
- 1 medium onion
- 1 clove of garlic
- 30 ml/2 tablespoons olive oil
- 5 ml/1 level teaspoon dried thyme
- 100 g/4 oz bulgar wheat
- 25 g/1 oz grated Parmesan
- 1 (105 g) can smoked mussels
- olive oil for brushing

Slice the stalk end off the tomatoes and reserve. Carefully scoop out the tomato pulp and seeds. Sprinkle the inside of each tomato shell with salt and turn upside down to drain. Place the tomato pulp and seeds in a processor with the tomato purée, buzz until smooth and strain into a measuring jug. Or press the pulp through a sieve and mix in the purée. Make the tomato liquid up to 300 ml/$^1/_2$ pint with vegetable stock.

Peel and finely chop the onion, peel and crush the garlic. Heat the oil in a medium saucepan, add the onion and cook gently until softened. Stir in the garlic and thyme and fry for a few moments longer. Stir in the bulgar and then the tomato stock. Bring to a simmer, cover, and cook gently for 15 minutes. Draw off the heat and allow to stand for 10 minutes without removing the lid.

Heat the oven to 180°C/350°F/gas mark 4.

Fork the Parmesan and mussels into the bulgar. Spoon into the tomato shells, filling them to the brim and packing the bulgar down gently. Cover each with a tomato lid and arrange in a shallow baking dish. Brush the tomatoes all over with olive oil and add 30 ml/2 tablespoons water to the dish. Bake for 20 minutes. Serve hot.

Mussels in Curried Cream

SERVES 4

1 kg/2 lb fresh mussels
45 ml/3 fl oz dry white wine
1 medium onion
25 g/1 oz butter
5 ml/1 level teaspoon mild curry paste
300 ml/½ pint double cream
salt and freshly milled pepper
juice of ½ a lemon

Turn the mussels into a bowl of cold water. Rinse them well, scrub and pull away the beards. Discard any that have not closed.

Lift the mussels straight from the water into a large saucepan. Add the wine. Cover and set over high heat to steam the mussels open. Give the pan an occasional shake and after 2–3 minutes draw off the heat. Pick the mussels from the open shells, discarding any that have not opened. Strain the cooking liquor and reserve. Spoon the mussels into a lightly buttered heatproof serving dish.

Heat the oven to 180°C/350°F/gas mark 4.

Peel and finely chop the onion. Melt the butter in a medium saucepan, add the onion, cover and soften over low heat. Stir the curry paste into the onions, add the cooking liquor and the cream. Bring to a simmer, stirring and cook gently for 3–5 minutes to reduce and thicken the sauce. Season with freshly milled pepper and salt if needed. Stir in the lemon juice.

Spoon the sauce over the mussels. Bake for 15 minutes until bubbling hot. Very nice served with freshly cooked rice.

Pan-fried Trout in Oatmeal

SERVES 2

Trim the trout fillets and pull out any tiny bones. Remove the skin. Measure the oatmeal (or cornmeal or flour) on to a sheet of greaseproof paper and season with salt and pepper. Coat the fillets by pressing each side into the oatmeal. Shake away any loose oatmeal. Trim the bacon rashers.

Melt the butter in a large frying pan, add the bacon rashers and fry gently until the bacon fat begins to run. Push the bacon to the side of the pan and add the trout fillets, best side down. Cook over medium heat for 4–5 minutes, turning the fish once. Lift the bacon and trout on to hot serving plates, add the lemon wedges and serve piping hot with buttered toast.

- 4 pink trout fillets
- 50 g/2 oz medium oatmeal, cornmeal or flour
- salt and freshly milled pepper
- 2 rashers smoked back bacon
- 25 g/1 oz butter
- 2 lemon wedges
- hot buttered toast

Grilled Trout in Mustard Butter

SERVES 4

Rinse each fish and pat dry. With a sharp knife, slash through the thickest part of the fish two or three times on each side. Beat the English and wholegrain mustard with the soft butter. Add a good seasoning of salt and freshly milled pepper.

Heat the grill to moderately hot and arrange the grill pan about 7.5 cm/3 inches from the heat source. Place the trout on the grill rack and spread generously with the flavoured butter, pushing it into the knife slashes. Grill for 5 minutes – the skin will brown and crisp up. Carefully turn the fish over and spread with the remaining butter. Grill the second side for about 5 minutes.

- 4 whole cleaned trout
- 5 ml/1 level teaspoon hot English mustard
- 45 ml/3 level tablespoons wholegrain mustard
- 100 g/4 oz soft butter
- salt and freshly milled pepper

SIMPLE FISH SAUCES

Lemon wedges are so simple and so good but occasionally it's nice to try something more exciting.

Each recipe serves 4.

Butter Sauce Melt 75 g/3 oz unsalted butter and slowly pour into a jug, leaving the white sediment behind. Stir in one of the following: 15 ml/1 tablespoon capers, or 15 ml/1 tablespoon wholegrain mustard, or 15 ml/1 tablespoon chopped chives, tarragon or parsley. Season with freshly milled pepper.

Mayonnaise Sauces Spoon 150 ml/$^1/_4$ pint mayonnaise into a bowl and add one of the following: 5 ml/1 teaspoon finely grated lemon rind, 15 ml/1 tablespoon lemon juice and 15 ml/1 tablespoon parsley, or 2 dill pickles, very finely chopped, or 10 ml/2 level teaspoons sweet chilli sauce. Season with freshly milled pepper.

Cream Sauces Heat 150 ml/$^1/_4$ pint double cream until bubbling and stir in one of the following: 3 sun-dried tomatoes (packed in oil), finely chopped, or 10 ml/2 level teaspoons curry paste, or 6 anchovies, drained on kitchen paper and coarsely chopped. Add 15 ml/1 tablespoon finely chopped chives, tarragon or parsley. Season with freshly milled black pepper.

Wine Sauce Use 150 ml/$^1/_4$ pint of the liquid used for poaching fish. If this already has wine in it, use as it is. If not, add 30 ml/2 tablespoons white vermouth. Blend together 15 g/$^1/_2$ oz soft butter and 10 ml/2 level teaspoons plain flour until smooth. Over medium heat, gradually blend the butter/flour mixture into the liquid until the sauce is smooth and just comes to the boil. Season with salt and freshly milled pepper.

Plaice with Anchovy Crumb Stuffing

SERVES 6

6 filleted plaice, about 225 g/8 oz each
salt and freshly milled pepper
1 small onion
3 celery stalks
50 g/2 oz butter
2 (50 g) cans anchovy fillets
1 bunch fresh parsley, about 50 g/2 oz
225 g/8 oz soft white breadcrumbs
Caper Butter Sauce (see above) or lemon wedges

With a sharp knife, skin the plaice, then separate each into two narrow fillets to make 12 pieces of fish altogether. Sprinkle lightly with salt.

Peel and finely chop the onion. Trim and cut the celery stalks lengthwise and chop finely. Heat the butter in a large frying pan. Add the oil from the cans of anchovies and stir in the onion and celery. Cover and cook gently until very soft but not brown – about 20 minutes.

Meanwhile, nip the tops from the parsley and chop them finely. In a bowl, combine the parsley and breadcrumbs. (If you are making the crumbs in a processor, add the parsley tops and buzz at the same time.) Chop the anchovies and add to the bowl with the softened vegetables, the juices from the frying pan and a seasoning of pepper. Mix together with a fork. Take golf-ball-sized portions of the stuffing, press them gently into a round shape and roll up inside a plaice fillet.

Heat the oven to 180°C/350°F/gas mark 4.

Lightly butter a shallow baking dish and add the fillets, standing them close together and on edge to show the stuffing. Cover with buttered foil. Bake for 20–25 minutes or until the plaice is white and flakes to the touch. Drizzle a little of the Caper Butter Sauce over each fillet and serve the rest separately.

Haddock and Pasta Bake

SERVES 6

- 450 g/1 lb smoked haddock
- 450 g/1 lb fresh haddock
- 450 ml/3/4 pint milk
- 150 ml/1/4 pint white vermouth
- 50 g/2 oz plain flour
- freshly milled pepper
- grating of nutmeg
- 50 g/2 oz butter
- 225 g/8 oz green tagliatelle
- 3 thick slices white bread
- 25 g/1 oz fresh parsley
- finely grated rind of 1 lemon
- 30 ml/2 tablespoons grated Parmesan

Place the fish in a large frying pan and pour over the milk. Gently poach over medium heat for 6–8 minutes. With a slotted spoon carefully lift the fish from the pan and, when cool enough to handle, remove all the skin and any bones. Break the fish into chunky pieces.

Strain the hot milk from the frying pan into a saucepan and add the vermouth. Add the flour, a seasoning of pepper and the nutmeg. Flake in half the butter. Stir over a medium heat until the butter has melted, then whisk until the sauce comes to a boil and is thickened. Cook the pasta according to the packet directions, and drain.

Heat the oven to 200°C/400°F/gas mark 6.

Turn the drained pasta into a lightly buttered 1.1 litre/2 pint baking dish. Add the flaked fish to the sauce, stir well and spoon evenly over the pasta. Trim away the bread crusts and buzz the bread in a processor with the parsley tops. Melt the remaining butter and stir in the lemon rind, crumbs and parsley. Spoon around the edge of the dish and sprinkle the Parmesan over the centre. Bake for 15–20 minutes until golden brown.

PERFECT POACHED FISH

Poaching is a gentle cooking method for fish fillets (usually rolled or folded) and for fish steaks.

- Use a frying pan with a lid and butter it lightly. Arrange the fish pieces in the pan. Add sufficient warm liquid to just cover the fish. This could be half milk and water or all skimmed milk. Or use half dry white wine or dry cider and water, fish or vegetable stock. Season with salt and freshly milled pepper.
- Cover and cook over a low heat. The liquid should just simmer – do not allow it to boil or evaporate.
- Use the rule of thumb for the cooking time – 10 minutes for each 2.5 cm/ 1 inch thickness – fillets take about 5 minutes, steaks a little longer. Fish is cooked when it looks opaque and quite white. If you press gently on the thickest part, the flesh will separate into flakes. Don't overcook fish, it becomes dry and chewy.
- Use the cooking liquor to make a sauce (see page 66), or serve with lemon wedges. Poached fish, especially salmon, is delicious served cold with mayonnaise (page 52).

PERFECT MICROWAVED FISH

The microwave is the ideal appliance for cooking fish – quick, no smells and a perfect result. It is suitable for cooking steaks and fillets as well as whole fish. The fish can be cooked just with a little butter, with stock, milk or wine, or in a sauce. The microwave can't cook fish with a crumb coating – it would simply go soggy.

- Place the fish on a shallow plate (this could be the serving plate if you are cooking one portion), brush or dot with butter and lightly season. The thin end of fillets should be folded underneath to give an even thickness of fish. Loosely cover with greaseproof paper and cook on HIGH/100%. One portion would need 2–4 minutes – be guided by the manufacturer's handbook.
- Alternatively place the fish (fillets could be rolled around a stuffing or folded) in a shallow dish and add milk, wine or stock (see the suggestions for Perfect Poached Fish, above). Loosely cover with greaseproof paper and cook on HIGH/100% (check the handbook for times – 450 g/1 lb fish takes about 4–6 minutes).

PERFECT SHALLOW FRIED FISH

Small whole fish, fish fillets or steaks are suitable for shallow frying. Fish fillets look very attractive cut across into thick strips before frying. These are called *goujons*.

- Fish cooked this way is usually dipped in a coating which helps to keep the fish moist and gives an appetizing golden crunchy crust. Whichever coating you choose, first dip the fish on all sides in seasoned flour. Then choose one of the following: dip the floured fish in milk and then coat with fine oatmeal or dip the floured fish in lightly beaten egg and then crisp breadcrumbs or cornmeal.
- Fish can be shallow fried dipped in seasoned flour only, without any additional coating.
- Using a large frying pan, heat sufficient grapeseed oil or half oil, half butter to cover the base of the pan to a depth of 5 mm/¼ inch.
- Slide in the fish and fry quickly to seal in the juices. Turn once during a cooking time of 3–5 minutes.
- Drain the fish on absorbent kitchen paper before serving. Serve with wedges of lemon to sharpen the taste and add a sauce if wished (page 66).

PERFECT GRILLED FISH

Grilling is a quick way of cooking small whole fish, fish steaks or fillets. Whole fish such as trout, mackerel and herrings grilled on the bone taste sweet, and the skin protects the flesh, keeping it moist.

- Preheat the grill to moderately hot and set the grill rack 7.5 cm/3 inches below the heat source. Oil the grill rack to prevent the fish sticking.
- Slash the flesh of whole fish two or three times along the thick part of the body (both sides) to help the heat penetrate.
- Brush the fish with oil or melted butter. If wished use a Flavoured Butter (see pages 30–1).
- Turn whole fish once during grilling, brushing again with oil or butter. Cooking time 8–10 minutes. Fish fillets or smaller pieces of fish can be cooked without turning. Cooking time 4–5 minutes.
- To keep leaner fish steaks moist, set a fireproof dish with a knob of butter in the grill pan (remove the rack) and set under the heat until the butter has melted. Add the fish steaks and turn them, so both sides are coated with the butter. Grill for 8–10 minutes, turning the fish once.

PERFECT BAKED FISH

Baking is suitable for whole fish, fish fillets and steaks.

- Heat the oven to 180°C/350°F/gas mark 4 for large whole fish or to 200°C/400°F/gas mark 6 for joints, fillets and steaks.
- Whole fish can be wrapped in buttered or oiled foil, especially when the fish is to be served cold. Wrap the foil loosely so that the air can circulate inside the parcel and place on a baking tray. Fish steaks can be wrapped in individual parcels. Add herbs, a Flavoured Butter (page 31) or slices of lemon, and season with salt and freshly milled pepper.
- There is a rule of thumb for determining cooking time for baked fish, often recommended by fishmongers. You should allow 10 minutes for each 2.5 cm/1 inch fish thickness. This makes foil-wrapped fish steaks easy to calculate. Bake whole fish for 10 minutes per 450 g/1 lb – usually about 30–40 minutes.
- Fish fillets (possibly rolled with a stuffing – see Plaice with Anchovy Crumb Stuffing page 66) or fish steaks can be cooked in a buttered or oiled baking dish, and wine or fish stock used as a baste. Cover with buttered or oiled foil and bake for 10–20 minutes, depending on the thickness of the fish.

Bombay Crêpes

SERVES 4

12 crêpes (see page 184)
225 g/8 oz curd cheese
30 ml/2 tablespoons mango chutney
5 ml/1 level teaspoon curry paste
225 g/8 oz peeled prawns
salt and freshly milled pepper
50 g/1 oz butter
pinch of curry powder
lemon wedges

Heat the oven to 180°C/350°F/gas mark 4.

Tip the curd cheese into a bowl. Add the chutney, first cutting up any large pieces of fruit, and the curry paste. Beat with a wooden spoon until well combined. Coarsely chop the prawns. Add to the cheese with salt and freshly milled pepper and mix.

Spoon an equal amount on to the centre of each crêpe. First fold over each side of the crêpes and then the top and bottom to form neat rectangular parcels. Arrange on a buttered baking tray, folded side down. Melt the butter and stir in the curry powder. Brush generously over the top and sides of each crêpe. Bake for 12–15 minutes until heated through.

Serve piping hot, with the lemon wedges.

Seafood Gratin

SERVES 6

---

6 slices white bread
30 ml/2 tablespoons olive oil
450 g/1 lb smoked haddock fillet
450 g/1 lb fresh halibut fillet
300 ml/½ pint dry white wine
150 ml/¼ pint water
225 g/8 oz smoked mussels or shelled cooked mussels
40 g/1½ oz butter
40 g/1½ oz plain flour
salt and freshly milled pepper
1 egg yolk
150 ml/¼ pint double cream
75 g/3 oz grated Gruyère

Heat the oven to 160°C/325°F/gas mark 3.

Trim the crusts from the bread and cut into triangles. Quickly fry in the olive oil until golden brown on both sides. Keep hot in the oven.

Trim the fish, removing any skin, and cut each into 6 pieces. Arrange the fish in a large frying pan, add the wine and water and bring to a simmer. Cover and poach gently for 6–8 minutes or until the fish is cooked. With a slotted spoon, lift the fish on to a hot shallow gratin dish. Sprinkle over the mussels. Cover with a piece of buttered kitchen foil and keep warm in the oven.

Strain the fish poaching liquid into a measuring jug and make up to 375 ml/¾ pint with water if necessary. Pour into a saucepan and add the butter and flour. Cook, stirring constantly, over medium heat until the sauce comes to a boil and is smooth and thickened. Season with pepper and remove from the heat. Beat the egg yolk with the cream and stir into the hot sauce.

Heat the grill to hot. Spoon the sauce over the hot fish and sprinkle with the cheese. Grill until golden brown and bubbling. Arrange the bread triangles around the edge of the dish and serve immediately.

CHAPTER FIVE

Poultry

Chicken is everybody's first choice and fresh new ideas are here for serving it, but new-look turkey and duck portions are now widely available too and adapt to any cooking method with impressive results. Baked, sauced, stir-fried or casseroled, chicken, turkey, duck and pheasant provide inspired dishes for every occasion. Even the classic roast is brought up to date with new seasonings, bastes and stuffings.

Crunchy Chicken Pieces with Tomato Dip

SERVES 6

- 6 boned and skinned chicken breasts
- 2 eggs
- 15 ml/1 tablespoon olive oil
- 6 large slices white bread
- 15 ml/1 level tablespoon paprika
- 30 ml/2 level tablespoons dried chilli flakes
- 60 ml/4 level tablespoon cornmeal
- freshly milled pepper
- 5 ml/1 level teaspoon salt
- 150 ml/¼ pint mayonnaise
- 150 ml/¼ pint soured cream
- 30 ml/2 tablespoons tomato relish or chutney

Cut each chicken breast into 3 chunky pieces. Crack the eggs into a shallow bowl, add the olive oil and whisk with a fork to break up the eggs.

Remove the crusts from the bread and break into pieces. Buzz in a food processor or blender to fine crumbs. Add the paprika, chilli flakes, cornmeal, pepper and salt and buzz to blend well. Turn out on to a sheet of greaseproof paper.

Using 2 forks, dip each chicken piece first in the egg and drain well, then coat with the spiced crumbs. Arrange the coated pieces on a clean sheet of greaseproof paper.

Heat the oven to 190°C/375°F/gas mark 5.

Set 2 large baking trays in the oven as it heats up. Transfer the chicken pieces to the hot baking trays, crowding them on but not allowing the pieces to touch. Bake for 15–20 minutes or until they are crunchy and golden brown and cooked right through.

While the chicken is cooking, whisk together the mayonnaise, soured cream and tomato relish. Serve the chicken in a paper-lined basket with the dip in a small bowl.

FOR EXTRA FLAVOUR

Simply grilled chicken portions or roasted chicken gain a boost of flavour when treated to extra seasonings. It can just be a sprinkling of spices or herbs, a brush with a quick basting mixture as the chicken cooks, or tucking a herb or two inside the body cavity.

Brush the skin of chicken portions or a whole bird with olive oil and rub in the dry spice mixtures before grilling or roasting. Store any unused spice mixture in a screw-topped jar for future use. Brush the glazes on both before and during the cooking.

Dry Spice Mixes

Cajun Spice Combine 30 ml/2 level tablespoons paprika, 15 ml/1 level tablespoon coarse-ground black pepper, 30 ml/2 level tablespoons dried oregano, 15 ml/1 level tablespoon dried thyme, 15 ml/1 level tablespoon dried onion flakes,2.5 ml/½ level teaspoon salt and 2.5 ml/½ level teaspoon cayenne.

Hot Indian Spice Combine 30 ml/2 level tablespoons paprika, 15 ml/1 level tablespoon ground cumin, 15 ml/1 level tablespoon ground coriander, 5 ml/1 level teaspoon chilli powder, 30 ml/2 level tablespoons soft brown sugar, 15 ml/1 level tablespoon hot pepper flakes and 2.5 ml/½ level teaspoon five-spice powder.

Allspice and Ginger Combine 30 ml/2 level tablespoons whole allspice with 15 ml/1 level tablespoon ground ginger.

Glazes

Wholegrain Mustard with Honey Stir together 30 ml/2 level tablespoons wholegrain mustard and 30 ml/2 level tablespoons clear honey. Season with salt and freshly milled pepper.

Orange and Soy Sauce Stir together 30 ml/2 tablespoons orange juice, 30 ml/2 tablespoons clear honey, 30 ml/2 tablespoons lemon juice and 15 ml/1 tablespoon soy sauce. Season with salt and freshly milled pepper.

Honey and Lemon Glaze Stir together 45 ml/3 tablespoons clear honey, finely grated rind and juice of 1 lemon, 45 ml/3 tablespoons olive oil, salt and freshly milled pepper.

'Tuck-ins' for Whole Roasting Chickens

Choose from a bouquet garni, a few lemon or orange slices, a small onion stuck with cloves, a quartered apple, some sprigs of rosemary or thyme or just a knob of garlic butter. Tuck into the body cavity before cooking. The flavour from the 'tuck-ins' will enrich the pan juices to make a gravy or sauce.

Chicken with Honey-mustard Glaze

Serves 6

- 6 chicken quarters
- 50 g/2 oz butter
- 100 g/4 oz clear honey
- 60 ml/4 level tablespoons Dijon mustard
- 15 ml/1 level tablespoon curry paste

Heat the oven to 180°C/350°F/gas mark 4.

Trim the chicken quarters and arrange them in a single layer, skin side up, in a large roasting tin or baking dish. Melt the butter in a small saucepan and draw off the heat. Add the honey, mustard and curry paste and stir to mix them well.

Spoon the honey-mustard glaze over the chicken. Cover with a large piece of foil, loosely tenting it so that it doesn't touch the chicken. Set the pan in the heated oven. After 20 minutes, remove and discard the foil and baste the chicken with the glaze in the pan. Return to the oven for a further 20–30 minutes, basting frequently with the hot glaze to encourage a golden brown, shiny skin.

THE SAFE HANDLING OF FRESH AND FROZEN POULTRY

- The term 'oven-ready' means a plucked and fully-prepared bird, ready to be cooked. You may or may not get the giblets; sometimes the butcher will offer them to you separately.
- Transfer fresh poultry from the supermarket or butcher to the home refrigerator as quickly as possible – preferably using a cool-bag with frozen icepacks.
- Open the end of any packaging to allow a fresh bird to 'breathe'; remove any giblets from the body cavity and store the bird at the bottom of the refrigerator. Cook a fresh bird within 2 days of purchase.
- Thaw a frozen smaller bird – chicken, duck or pheasant – in the refrigerator. Place on a plate on a layer of absorbent kitchen paper and set on the lowest shelf – 24 hours or overnight is usually sufficient time.
- Small birds may be thawed in the microwave. Stand the bird on a microwave trivet, remove any metal ties, and open the end of the packaging to allow the thawed liquid to drain out. Follow the manufacturer's handbook for the method and time. Always stop the microwave if the bird begins to feel warm, and finish thawing in the refrigerator. Remove any giblets as soon as they are loose.
- Larger birds such as turkey and goose are best thawed at cool room temperature (not in the refrigerator). It is very important that a turkey (indeed, all poultry) is properly thawed before cooking. Check the instructions on the packaging well ahead of time, as a very large bird can take 1–2 days to thaw totally. Slit the plastic wrapping and set the bird on a trivet or upturned plate on a tray to contain the thawed juices. Remove the giblets as soon as they are loose, and use to make stock immediately or store in the fridge.
- To check that poultry is completely thawed, make sure there are no ice crystals in the body cavity and that the legs are quite flexible.
- Once thawed, poultry should be covered and stored in the fridge. Cook as soon as possible.
- Always wash your hands with hot soapy water both before and after handling raw poultry.
- Never use the same knives or chopping boards for raw and cooked poultry without washing them, your hands and the work surface between each use.
- Always place raw poultry on the bottom shelf in the refrigerator so that no drips fall on cooked foods.

Chicken in Tomato and Pesto Sauce

SERVES 6

30 ml/2 tablespoons olive oil
6 boned chicken breasts
1 (200 ml) carton crème fraîche
1 (230 g) can chopped tomatoes
45 ml/3 level tablespoons prepared pesto (or see page 118)
salt and freshly milled pepper
fresh basil leaves and black olives

Heat the oil in a 25 cm/10 inch frying pan (use one that has a lid). Add the chicken breasts and fry to brown on both sides. In a bowl combine the crème fraîche, the tomatoes and the pesto. Stir and season with salt and freshly milled pepper.

Pour the pesto sauce over the chicken and bring to a simmer. Lower the heat, cover with the pan lid and cook gently for 20 minutes. When the chicken is tender, strew with fresh basil leaves and black olives and serve.

COOKING CHICKEN TO SERVE COLD

There could be a number of occasions when you wish to serve chicken cold – sliced on its own or with other cold meats as part of a platter. Add a salad or two and perhaps some home pickled fruits (page 109) or a Fresh Relish (page 62) and you have a very easy meal. Or the cold chicken could be destined for a grander presentation, dressed with a Flavoured Mayonnaise (page 52) or Vinaigrette (page 50). Either way you want chicken that is moist and tender.

We think we've found the simplest and most successful method, and the bonus is that the chicken is all tender lean breast meat. This way there is no picking meat off the carcass of a roast or simmered bird and no need to hide the dark leg meat underneath the best pieces of breast meat at serving time. Cook the chicken breast portions with the skins on – it helps to keep them moist. Once they have cooled, simply lift the skin away, then slice, dice or do what you will with the tender meat.

Heat the oven to 180°C/350°F/gas mark 4. Arrange as many chicken breasts as you require, skin side up, in a deep baking dish (or roasting tin), selecting one the right size to hold them closely packed, then brush with melted butter. Pour in sufficient vegetable stock to come part-way over the chicken breasts but not completely submerge them. Leave uncovered and bake for 30–35 minutes, by which time the chicken will be tender and the skin golden. Let the chicken cool in the stock, then refrigerate (in the stock) until you are ready to use it.

If you prefer to have a whole cooked chicken to serve cold, we suggest that the best method is to cook the chicken in a roasting bag. Follow the manufacturer's instructions and leave the chicken in the bag to cool and for storing in the refrigerator.

PERFECT ROAST CHICKEN

Choose a plump oven-ready bird, allowing 225–350 g/8–12 oz weight per serving; for example, a 1.5–2 kg/3–4½ lb chicken will give 6 servings. If the occasion is a special one, look out for various distinctively labelled speciality fresh chickens such as Poulet Noir, Landais Forest, Duc de Bourgogne or Conservation Grade. These will be more expensive but have a better flavour. The creamy colour and moist texture of a cornfed chicken is particularly good when serving cold.

- Loosely stuff the neck end of the chicken only. Place a quartered onion or apple, or a lump of butter and some herbs, in the body cavity to keep the flesh moist and to add flavour to the pan juices for a gravy or sauce.
- Sage and onion stuffing is traditional with roast chicken – for other suggestions see page 79. Stuffing may also be rolled into balls and cooked alongside the chicken.
- Alternatively, it is very easy to loosen the skin over the chicken breast and thighs and a soft mixture such as sautéd chopped mushrooms or a herbed butter can then be carefully spread between the skin and flesh.
- Truss the chicken into a compact shape, making sure the legs are tied close to the body.
- Preheat the oven to 200°C/400°F/gas mark 6. Calculate the roasting time allowing 20 minutes per 450 g/1 lb, plus 20 minutes. Remember that a frozen chicken will lose approximately 225 g/ 8 oz of its original weight when thawed.
- Place the chicken on one side of its breast on a rack standing in a roasting tin. Brush the chicken skin with olive oil or melted butter and season with salt and freshly milled pepper. After 20 minutes of cooking time, turn the bird to the second breast side, brush again with oil or melted butter and roast for a further 20 minutes. Finally turn the bird breastbone uppermost and baste with the pan juices for the remainder of the roasting time.
- To test if the chicken is cooked through, push a knife tip or skewer into a thigh. The juices should run clear. If there is any hint of pink, return the chicken to the oven for a further 15 minutes, then test again.
- Transfer the roasted chicken on to a warmed platter and cover loosely with foil. Leave to stand for 10 minutes. This allows the meat to 'settle', making it much easier to carve in neat slices.
- While the chicken is standing, use the pan juices to make a gravy – see page 103.
- To roast chicken portions, choose chicken quarters or portions still with the bones in and skin on. Boneless chicken breasts, especially those with the skin removed, need a more moist form of cooking (see page 77). Trim off excess skin and fat. Place skin side uppermost on a roasting rack standing in a roasting tin. Brush with oil or melted butter and season with salt and freshly milled pepper. Roast at 200°C/400°F/gas mark 6 for 45–50 minutes. Baste occasionally, but do not turn the pieces over.

Chicken with Tarragon Sauce

SERVES 4

- 4 boned and skinned chicken breasts
- 225 ml/8 fl oz hot vegetable stock
- 50 ml/2 fl oz dry white vermouth
- 2–3 slices of onion
- 15 ml/1 tablespoon soft butter
- 10 ml/2 teaspoons level plain flour
- 150 ml/¼ pint single cream
- salt and freshly milled pepper
- 30 ml/2 tablespoons chopped fresh tarragon

Place the chicken breasts in a single layer in a large frying pan (use one with a lid). Combine the stock, vermouth and onion slices and add to the pan. Bring to a gentle simmer, reduce the heat to low and add the pan lid. Cook for 20–30 minutes until the chicken is tender. Transfer the chicken to a warm plate, cover with foil and keep warm.

Bring the cooking liquid to the boil and cook rapidly for about 10 minutes to reduce by half and concentrate the flavour. Remove the onion slices with a slotted spoon and discard. On a plate blend the butter and flour to make a soft paste. Draw the frying pan off the heat, add the butter paste in small pieces and stir until it has melted into the liquid. Add the cream and return the pan to the heat. Bring to a simmer, stirring all the time to make a smooth sauce. Season with salt and freshly milled pepper and stir in the chopped tarragon.

Cut the chicken into thick slices and arrange on a warm serving platter. Stir any chicken juices on the plate into the sauce then spoon a little over the chicken. Pass the remainder in a jug.

STUFFINGS

Old-fashioned bread stuffing and lighter vegetable mixtures are just as delicious with chicken as they are with turkey. We don't recommend stuffing goose, duck or small birds such as pheasant – the natural fat from goose and duck can make stuffing greasy and unpalatable, and pheasant is cooked so briefly that the stuffing won't be cooked by the time the meat is done.

You can prepare stuffing up to a day in advance, then cover and refrigerate until required. Do not stuff a bird until just before cooking. These days the recommendation is that poultry is stuffed only at the neck end, not in the body cavity. This ensures that the oven heat penetrates the whole bird efficiently. Cook the remaining stuffing separately. A well-flavoured stuffing, served hot, would also extend portions of cold leftover poultry.

The following recipes are made using an American method where the bread is in cubes rather than crumbs. Quicker to make, cubes look particularly good when the stuffing is baked separately. Do be sure to use day-old bread or the stuffing will mix to a mush. If the bread is fresh, spread the cubes in a shallow layer in a roasting tin and bake for 15 minutes at 150°C/300°F/gas mark 2 to dry them out.

We have made suggestions as to which stuffing to serve with which bird, but do mix and match your own choice.

To cook stuffing separately Turn the prepared stuffing into a buttered 1.1 litre/2 pint baking dish and spread evenly. Drizzle over a little melted butter and cover with foil. Bake alongside the poultry (or at 180°C/350°F/gas mark 4) for 45–50 minutes, uncovering after 30 minutes to brown and crisp the top.

Or spoon into well-buttered deep muffin pans, drizzle with butter and bake for 25–30 minutes.

Or shape into large balls with wet fingers and arrange on a buttered baking sheet. Brush with melted butter and bake for 25–30 minutes.

Basic Recipe Remove the crusts from 6 slices of white or wholemeal bread, cut into 1.25 cm/½ inch cubes, and place in a large mixing bowl. Break 1 egg into a small bowl, add 30 ml/2 tablespoons cold water and lightly mix with a fork.

Sage and Onion Melt 50 g/2 oz butter in a frying pan and add 2 large onions, peeled and finely chopped. Cover and cook over a medium heat for 10 minutes until very soft. Add a further 50 g/2 oz butter, 15 ml/1 tablespoon finely chopped fresh or 10 ml/2 teaspoons dried sage, 5 ml/1 teaspoon dried mixed herbs, salt and freshly milled pepper. Draw off the heat and stir until the butter is melted.

Stir into the breadcubes, add the beaten egg, and lightly but thoroughly mix with a fork.

Serve with chicken or turkey.

Green Onion, Lemon and Parsley Trim and finely slice 1 bunch (6–8) spring onions, including all the green stems. Finely grate the rind of 1 lemon and squeeze the juice. Wash, dry and finely chop 25 g/1 oz fresh parsley. Melt 75 g/3 oz butter and stir in the spring onions, lemon rind and juice and the parsley. Season well with salt and freshly milled pepper.

Stir into the breadcubes, add the beaten egg and mix lightly but thoroughly with a fork.

Serve with chicken or pheasant.

Courgette and Lemon Melt 50 g/2 oz butter in a frying pan. Add 1 large onion, peeled and finely chopped, and 4 courgettes, sliced lengthways and across into small dice. Cover and cook over a medium heat for 10 minutes until very soft. Add a further 50 g/2 oz butter, 1.25 ml/½ teaspoon dried thyme, the finely grated rind of 1 lemon, 60 ml/4 tablespoons chopped parsley and a seasoning of salt and freshly milled pepper. Draw off the heat and stir until the butter is melted.

Stir into the breadcubes, add the beaten egg, and mix lightly but thoroughly with a fork.

Serve with chicken or duck.

Cranberry and Raisin Pick over and rinse 225 g/8 oz fresh or frozen cranberries. Put in a saucepan with 50 g/2 oz caster sugar and 15 ml/1 tablespoon cold water. Cook until the berries soften and burst – about 10 minutes. Draw off the heat, add 50 g/2 oz butter, and stir until the butter is melted. Add 50 g/2 oz seedless raisins, the finely grated rind of 1 orange, 1.25 ml/½ teaspoon ground cinnamon, salt and freshly milled pepper.

Stir into the breadcubes, add the beaten egg, and mix lightly but thoroughly with a fork.

Serve with goose, turkey or duck.

Apple and Bacon Melt 25 g/1 oz butter in a frying pan. Add 1 large onion, peeled and finely chopped, and 6 rashers streaky bacon, trimmed and finely chopped. Cover and cook over a medium heat for 10 minutes until the onion is very soft. Stir in 1 dessert apple, peeled and grated, and season with salt and freshly milled pepper.

Stir into the breadcubes, add the beaten egg and mix lightly but thoroughly with a fork.

Serve with chicken or turkey.

Chestnut and Celery Melt 25 g/1 oz butter in a frying pan. Add 1 large onion, peeled and finely chopped, and 3 medium celery stalks, cut lengthways and across into small dice. Cover and cook over a medium heat for 10 minutes until very soft. Add a further 50 g/2 oz butter, draw off the heat, and stir until the butter is melted. Coarsely chop 1 (350 g) can vacuum-packed whole chestnuts. Add to the softened vegetables with 30 ml/2 tablespoons chopped parsley, salt and freshly milled pepper.

Stir into the breadcubes, add the beaten egg, and mix lightly but thoroughly with a fork.

Serve with turkey, goose or pheasant.

Chicken in Gingered Mango Cream

SERVES 4

- 150 ml/¼ pint double cream
- 2.5 cm/1 inch fresh ginger
- 4 boned and skinned chicken breasts
- 12 ready-to-eat dried apricots
- 4 slices *prosciutto* (Parma ham)
- 60 ml/4 tablespoons dry white vermouth
- 1 ripe mango
- salt and freshly milled pepper

Pour the cream into a small saucepan. Pare off the outer brown skin of the ginger and grate the flesh into the cream. Over a low heat bring just to the boil. Remove from the heat, cover, and leave to infuse while cooking the chicken.

Heat the oven to 190°C/375°F/gas mark 5.

Arrange 3 apricots on top of each chicken breast and wrap each chicken breast in a slice of *prosciutto*. Place in a single layer in a small baking dish and add the vermouth. Cover with kitchen foil and bake for 20–25 minutes until tender.

Meanwhile, halve the mango by cutting each side of the stone. Score one half into slices (for the garnish) and criss-cross the other into small pieces (for the sauce). Then turn the mango skin inside out and detach the flesh from the skin.

Lift the cooked chicken pieces on to a warm serving plate, cover and keep hot. Tip the pan juices into a small saucepan. Strain the cream into the juices, pressing the ginger gently to get the maximum flavour from it. Bring the mixture to a simmer, taste for seasoning and add the chopped mango pieces. Spoon the sauce over the chicken and garnish with the mango slices.

Chicken and Artichokes in Parmesan Sauce

SERVES 6

- 6 boned chicken breasts
- 300 ml/½ pint vegetable stock
- 1 (400 g) can artichoke hearts
- 50 g/2 oz butter
- 50 g/2 oz plain flour
- 300 ml/½ pint single cream
- salt and freshly milled pepper
- grated nutmeg
- 75 g/3 oz grated Parmesan
- 2 large slices fresh bread
- finely grated rind of 1 lemon
- 15 ml/1 tablespoon chopped parsley

Place the chicken breasts in a single layer in a 25 cm/10 inch frying pan (use one that has a lid). Add the stock and bring to a simmer. Cover and cook gently for 20 minutes. Lift the chicken pieces from the pan and let them cool slightly. Reserve the cooking liquor. Drain the artichoke hearts and slice each one in half through the centre.

Melt the butter in a saucepan, stir in the flour and cook for 1 minute. Gradually stir in the reserved cooking liquor, beating all the time to make a smooth sauce. Stir in the cream and bring just to the boil. Draw off the heat and season with salt, pepper and a pinch of nutmeg. Stir in half the Parmesan. Cut the cooled chicken breasts in half at an angle to make nice serving portions.

Heat the oven to 180°C/350°F/gas mark 4.

Pour a little of the sauce into a 1.1 litre/2 pint baking dish. Add the chicken pieces and the artichoke hearts, then pour over the remaining sauce. Trim the crusts from the bread, cut each slice into small cubes and place in a bowl. Add the lemon rind, parsley and remaining Parmesan. Mix lightly with a fork and sprinkle over the chicken. Bake for 20–25 minutes or until the top is golden and the chicken bubbling hot.

CHICKEN SALADS

Chicken salad is always popular for a summer lunch or a buffet party. These recipes, made with poached chicken breast meat (see page 77), are equally good made with cold turkey breast meat or with roast chicken. For each recipe you need about 900 g/2 lb of cold poultry, cut into bite-sized chunks. Each recipe serves 4–6.

Curried Chicken with Mango Finely chop 1 small onion and fry in 15 ml/1 tablespoon grapeseed oil until very soft but not brown. Stir in 15 ml/1 level tablespoon curry paste, 15 ml/1 level tablespoon tomato purée, 100 ml/4 fl oz red wine and 15 ml/1 tablespoon red wine vinegar. Bring to a simmer and cook gently for about 10 minutes to make a thick, spicy sauce. Draw off the heat, stir in 30 ml/2 tablespoons mango chutney and leave to cool. Buzz the dressing in a processor, or for a smoother texture, press through a sieve.

Turn 1 (500 g) tub fromage frais into a bowl and stir in the curried sauce. Stir in the chicken pieces and chill until serving time. Peel and slice a large mango. Spoon the chicken salad on to a large serving platter and add the mango slices. Sprinkle with 50 g/2 oz toasted flaked almonds and serve.

Chicken with Apples and Pecans Whisk together 150 ml/¼ pint mayonnaise, 1 (150 g) tub natural yogurt, 5 ml/1 teaspoon Dijon mustard, 10 ml/2 teaspoons tarragon wine vinegar and a seasoning of salt and freshly milled pepper. Finely chop 4 stalks celery and a bunch (6–8) spring onions. Add to the dressing with the chicken pieces and chill until serving time.

Just before serving stir in 2 red-skinned apples, cored and diced, and 50 g/2 oz chopped pecan nuts.

Chicken and Fruit in Ginger Dressing In a large mixing bowl whisk together 150 ml/¼ pint good quality mayonnaise, 1 (150 g) tub natural yogurt and a seasoning of salt and freshly milled pepper. Very finely chop 2 pieces of stem ginger and add to the dressing along with 30 ml/2 tablespoons stem ginger syrup.

Stir in the chicken pieces, 225 g/8 oz small seedless green grapes, 1 bunch (6–8) spring onions and 4 finely chopped stalks of celery. Drain 1 (227 g) can pineapple slices, cut into quarters and stir in. Chill until serving time. Serve sprinkled with salted peanuts.

PERFECT ROAST PHEASANT

For most of us pheasant will come plucked and oven-ready from the butcher or supermarket. They are not big birds and it is usual to cook them in pairs – a brace, traditionally a cock and hen. Pheasant are served either carved or cut in half – allow $^1/_2$ a bird per serving.

- Put a generous knob of butter and some fresh thyme or marjoram in the body cavity. Then truss the pheasant to a neat compact shape – like a chicken.
- A pheasant purchased 'oven-ready' should already have a slice of larding fat or streaky bacon wrapped over the breast. If not, add 1 or 2 slices of streaky bacon to keep the breast meat moist.
- Heat the oven to 200°C/400°F/gas mark 6.
- Generously butter a roasting tin just large enough to hold the birds without touching one another. (A thick slice of onion or carrot in the roasting pan will add flavour to the gravy.) Arrange the birds breast side down and roast for 30 minutes.
- Turn the pheasants breast side up and lift off the bacon rashers. Baste with the pan drippings. Lightly sprinkle with flour and baste again. Roast for a further 20 minutes for rare, 30 minutes for well done.
- Transfer the roasted pheasant to a warmed platter and tent loosely with foil. Leave to stand for 5 minutes.
- While the pheasant is standing use the pan juices to make a gravy – see pages 103–4.

Pheasant with Rich Fruit Gravy

SERVES 4

1 brace (2) pheasants
4 streaky bacon rashers
butter
few sprigs fresh thyme
2 thick slices fresh white bread
1 large onion
flour for dusting
200 ml/6 fl oz red wine
45 ml/3 tablespoons quince or rowan jelly

Heat the oven to 200°C/400°F/gas mark 6.

Your pheasant may come with a slice of larding bacon over the breasts. If not, tie 2 streaky bacon rashers over each bird to baste the flesh. Put a generous knob of butter and a sprig of thyme in each body cavity and truss the pheasant into a compact shape. Trim the crusts from the bread and pull the bread into small pieces.

Generously butter a roasting pan just big enough to hold both birds without touching each other. Peel and thinly slice the onion and arrange in an even layer in the tin. Place the birds on top breast-side down, and roast for 30 minutes.

Meanwhile, heat a generous knob of butter in a large frying pan and stir in the bread pieces. Cook over a high

PLATE THREE
Salmon Salad Platter (page 56)

PLATE FOUR
Duck with Spiced Apples (page 86)

heat, stirring constantly, until crisp and brown. Spoon on to kitchen paper and keep hot.

Turn the birds right side up and lift off the bacon. Sprinkle the breasts lightly with flour, baste with the pan drippings and roast for a final 20–30 minutes. Transfer the pheasant to a warmed platter and keep hot.

Skim any excess fat from the pan juices and place the pan over a medium heat. Add the wine and bring to the boil, stirring to lift off the crusty bits on the bottom of the pan. Stir in the jelly and continue to bubble until the jelly has melted and the gravy has reduced slightly. Strain into a warm jug and keep hot.

Using sharp scissors or poultry shears, cut the birds in half along the breast bone. Serve with the gravy, and sprinkled with the crisp breadcrumbs.

Pheasant with Winter Vegetables

SERVES 4

- 50 g/2 oz butter
- 50 g/2 oz fresh breadcrumbs
- 2 oven-ready pheasants
- 8 button onions or shallots
- 5 ml/1 level teaspoon caster sugar
- 150 ml/¼ pint red wine
- 150 ml/¼ pint chicken stock
- 30 ml/2 tablespoons redcurrant jelly
- 2 pieces pared orange rind
- juice of 1 orange
- 15 ml/1 tablespoon red wine vinegar
- 5 ml/1 level teaspoon tomato purée
- salt and freshly milled pepper
- 450 g/1 lb parsnips

Heat the oven to 160°C/325°F/gas mark 3.

Melt 25 g/1 oz butter in a large frying pan and stir in the breadcrumbs. Cook, stirring, over a high heat until crunchy and golden brown. Tip out on to a plate.

Wipe out the pan with kitchen paper. Melt the remaining butter, add the pheasants, breast side down, and brown on all sides. Transfer to a casserole.

Peel the onions or shallots, leaving them whole. Add to the pan drippings and sprinkle with the sugar. Fry, shaking the pan to brown them on all sides. Add to the casserole.

Pour the wine into the hot pan drippings and stir to pick up the dark flavouring bits. Add the stock, redcurrant jelly, orange rind, orange juice, vinegar and tomato purée. Bring to a simmer, stirring to melt the jelly. Season with salt and pepper and pour over the pheasant and onions. Cover and cook in the preheated oven for $1^1/_2$ hours.

Meanwhile, pare the parsnips and cut into chunky pieces. Cover with cold water, bring to the boil for 1 minute to blanch, then drain. Add to the casserole halfway through the cooking time.

When the pheasants are fully cooked, lift them from the casserole, and cut each in half with sharp scissors or poultry shears to make 4 portions. Return them to the casserole, sprinkle with the crisp breadcrumbs and serve.

Duck with Spiced Apples

Illustrated on Plate Four

SERVES 6

- 6 duck leg portions
- 175 ml/6 fl oz dry white vermouth
- 150 ml/$^1/_4$ pint vegetable stock
- 1 large cooking apple
- finely grated rind and juice of 1 lemon
- salt and freshly milled pepper
- 2 red-skinned dessert apples
- 25 g/1 oz butter
- 15 ml/1 level tablespoon granulated sugar
- pinch of ground cinnamon

The day before serving, heat the oven to 180°C/350°F/gas mark 4. Arrange the duck portions in a large casserole dish, placing them skin side down. Add the vermouth and stock. Cover and cook for 1 hour. Remove from the oven, cool, and chill overnight.

Next day, remove and discard the layer of duck fat from the surface. Lift out the duck portions and pour the cooking liquor into a saucepan.

Peel, core and cut up the cooking apple. Add to the cooking liquor along with the rind and juice of the lemon. Cover and simmer until the apple is quite soft, about 10–15 minutes. Pass the apple mixture through a sieve to make a smooth apple sauce. Season with salt and freshly milled pepper and leave to cool.

Heat the oven to 200°C/400°F/gas mark 6.

Arrange the duck portions in a shallow baking dish, placing them skin side up. Roast for 15–20 minutes, until they are a rich golden brown. Reheat the apple sauce and pour over the duck portions. Turn the oven down to 160°C/325°F/gas mark 3, just to keep the duck hot.

Meanwhile, core and slice the dessert apples. Melt the butter in a frying pan, stir in the sugar and cinnamon, then add the apple slices and fry for 2–3 minutes until soft and golden brown, turning them over once. Arrange the apple slices over the duck portions and serve.

Five-spice Duck with Clementines

SERVES 4

- 4 duck breasts
- 10 ml/2 level teaspoons five-spice powder
- 10 ml/2 level teaspoons caster sugar
- 30 ml/2 tablespoons red wine vinegar
- 300 ml/½ pint orange juice
- 45 ml/3 tablespoons diced stem ginger
- 30 ml/2 tablespoons ginger syrup from the jar
- 3 clementines or small oranges
- salt and freshly milled pepper

With a sharp knife, score the skin on each duck breast with about 4–6 neat lines. Combine the five-spice powder and the sugar to make a seasoning mixture and rub well into the scored duck skin. Let the seasoned breasts stand for 30–60 minutes to take the flavour.

Heat a good-sized dry frying pan (with no added fat). Add the duck breasts, skin side down, and fry over a moderate heat until well browned. Then turn to seal the other side – sufficient fat will come from the duck as heat is applied. Lift the duck pieces from the pan.

Pour off the excess pan drippings, leaving behind any dark flavouring bits. Add the red wine vinegar and stir well. Add the orange juice, diced stem ginger and ginger syrup. Bring to a simmer. Return the duck pieces to the pan, placing them skin side upwards – the skin should stay out of the liquid in order to stay crisp. Simmer gently, uncovered, for 35–40 minutes.

Quarter the clementines and add to the pan 10 minutes before the cooking time is up, to tenderize them. Transfer the duck breasts and clementines to a warmed serving dish and keep hot. Bring the sauce just to the boil and simmer for 5 minutes to reduce. Season, spoon over the duck and fruit, and serve.

PERFECT ROAST DUCK

Always err on the generous side when choosing a duck, as they have a larger carcass than most other poultry. As a guide, select a 2.5 kg/5 lb oven-ready duck to serve 4 and allow 2 1.8 kg/4 lb oven-ready birds for 6 servings.

- Since a duck has a high proportion of bone to flesh, it is usually served cut into quarters rather than carved. Any stuffing mixture should be cooked separately – see page 80.
- Rinse then completely dry the inside and outside of the duck with absorbent kitchen paper – a damp duck will not crisp up well.
- Place a quartered onion or 1 or 2 cut-up oranges or apples in the body cavity to enhance the pan juices.
- Prick the skin all over with a fork so that the fat can drain off during roasting. Rub the skin all over with salt.
- Truss the duck to a neat shape.
- Heat the oven to 200°C/400°F/gas mark 6 and calculate the roasting time – 20 minutes per 450 g/1 lb for 'slightly underdone' or 25 minutes per 450 g/1 lb for 'just cooked'.
- Place the duck on a rack in a roasting tin – raising the duck ensures that the drippings can drain freely into the roasting pan – there is no need to baste a duck. Remove excess fat from the roasting tin part-way through the cooking – the easiest way to do this is with a bulb baster.
- About 30 minutes before the end of the cooking time, the duck skin can be brushed with soy sauce or honey or sprinkled with caster sugar to encourage it to turn a rich golden colour.
- Insert the tip of a sharp knife between the thigh and breast – if cooking the duck to 'slightly underdone' the juices may be just slightly pink. If cooking to 'just cooked' they should run clear.
- Lift the duck on to a carving board or warm serving platter and tent loosely with foil. Allow to stand for 5 minutes before cutting into portions. With kitchen scissors cut along the breastbone and then cut each half in half again.
- While the duck is standing, use the pan juices to make a gravy – see pages 103–4.
- To roast duck portions: prick the skin all over with a fork and rub with salt. Place, skin side up, on a roasting rack in a roasting tin. Roast at 200°C/400°F/gas mark 6 for about 45 minutes.

Chinese-style Duck with Oranges

SERVES 6

4 duck breast fillets
45 ml/3 tablespoons clear honey
30 ml/2 tablespoons dark soy sauce
4 oranges

Prick the skin of each duck fillet with a fork. Blend 15 ml/1 tablespoon honey with 15 ml/1 tablespoon soy sauce and brush all over them. Arrange skin side up in a single layer in a baking dish or roasting tin. Refrigerate while preparing the sauce.

2.5 cm/1 inch fresh ginger
300 ml/½ pint orange juice
50 g/2 oz granulated sugar
juice of 1 lemon
15 ml/1 level tablespoon cornflour
30 ml/2 tablespoons cold water

Slice away the outer peel and white pith from the oranges. With a sharp knife, cut into the fruits, lift out the segments and reserve them. Remove the brown skin of the ginger and finely grate the flesh. Heat the orange juice just to boiling.

Measure the sugar into a dry frying pan. Set over a medium heat and stir continuously until the sugar has melted and turned to a caramel. Gradually stir in the hot orange juice to make a smooth sauce.

Add 30 ml/2 tablespoons honey, 15 ml/1 tablespoon soy sauce, the lemon juice and the grated ginger to the sauce. Blend the cornflour with the cold water until smooth and add to the pan. Cook, stirring, until the sauce thickens and comes to the boil. Remove from the heat.

Heat the oven to 200°C/400°F/gas mark 6.

Roast the duck breasts for 30 minutes until the skins are crisp. Reheat the sauce and add the orange segments. Slice the duck breasts diagonally and arrange on a warm serving dish. Spoon over a little of the sauce and serve the rest separately.

Turkey in Coconut Curry Sauce

SERVES 4

8 ready-to-eat dried apricots
450 ml/¾ pint water
2 medium onions
30 ml/2 tablespoons oil
5 ml/1 level teaspoon caster sugar
4 turkey escalopes
½ (192 g) jar Thai hot curry paste
75 g/3 oz creamed coconut

Soak the apricots in 300 ml/½ pint of the water for at least 15 minutes. Drain, reserving the liquid.

Peel the onions and slice thinly. Heat the oil in a large frying pan (use one that has a lid). Add the onions, sprinkle with the sugar and, over a low heat, fry until soft and a deep golden brown – about 20 minutes.

Meanwhile, place the turkey escalopes between sheets of clingfilm and beat out thinly with a rolling pin. Divide the apricots between the escalopes, then roll up the escalopes to enclose the fruit. Tie with thin string or secure with wooden cocktail sticks.

Stir the Thai curry paste into the cooked onions. Add

the reserved liquid from the apricots and the remaining water. Stir until the mixture is simmering. Add the turkey rolls. Cover and cook gently for 30 minutes.

Crumble the creamed coconut and add to the pan. Stir until melted – the coconut will thicken the sauce. Cover and cook for a further 5 minutes before serving.

Turkey Parcels with Glazed Chestnuts

SERVES 6

- 6 skinless boned turkey breast fillets
- 6 bay leaves
- 1 bunch (6–8) spring onions
- 75 g/3 oz butter
- 5 ml/1 level teaspoon ground mace
- 225 g/8 oz lean sliced ham
- 1 (350 g) can vacuum-packed chestnuts
- 1 egg
- salt and freshly milled pepper
- 300 ml/$^1/_2$ pint chicken stock
- 50 ml/2 fl oz dry sherry

Take each turkey fillet and beat it between sheets of greaseproof paper sprinkled with cold water. Use a rolling pin to flatten each fillet enough to wrap around a piece of the stuffing. Set aside, along with the bay leaves.

To make the filling, first trim the spring onions then finely chop all the white and some of the green stems. Melt 50 g/2 oz of the butter in a frying pan, add the spring onions and soften gently. Stir in the ground mace and draw off the heat.

Coarsely chop the ham and place in a bowl. Drain the chestnuts and set 12 aside for the garnish. Mash the remainder and add to the ham. Add the softened spring onions, the egg, and salt and pepper. Mix well.

Divide the filling between the turkey breasts. Draw the meat over to enclose the filling – shape each one to a neat round shape and turn over. Place a bay leaf on top and tie each stuffed fillet with string.

Melt the remaining butter in a flameproof casserole. Add the turkey parcels and turn to brown on all sides. Add the chicken stock, cover, and simmer for 30 minutes.

Lift the turkey fillets from the pan and keep hot. Add the sherry to the pan liquid and simmer rapidly for a few minutes until reduced by half and and concentrated. Add the reserved chestnuts and heat through, turning to glaze them. Return the turkey fillets to the casserole, spoon over the glaze and serve.

PERFECT ROAST TURKEY

A medium to large bird is the best buy for roasting. Small turkeys have a larger proportion of bone to meat and don't offer such good value. Choose a fresh bird with a breast broad in proportion to its length – this means there will be plenty of tender white meat. A flare of white fat up either side of the breast indicates a thin layer of fat under the skin which will baste the flesh, keeping it moist. Allow 350 g/12 oz weight per serving portion – for example a 3.7 kg/8 lb turkey will serve 9–10 people.

❦ Make a note of the weight of the bird when purchased. If the turkey is frozen, allow adequate time for it to thaw – large birds can take 24–48 hours (read the package instructions). Remove the neck and giblets from the body cavity of a fresh turkey – they may be in a separate pack.

❦ Rinse the inside of the turkey and dry with absorbent kitchen paper. Loosely stuff the neck end of the turkey only. For a choice of stuffings see pages 79–81. Fold the neck skin over to cover the stuffing and secure under the bird with a skewer. If you prefer, the stuffing can be cooked alongside the turkey.

❦ Place a quartered onion, lemon or apple in the body cavity. This will add flavour to the pan juices when making the gravy or sauce.

❦ Truss the turkey to a neat shape – twist the wing tips under the breast and tie the legs close to the body. Carving neat slices is easier if the wishbone is removed before cooking. Open up the neck skin, cut around the bone with a small sharp knife and pull out the bone.

❦ Calculate the roasting time. Remember that a frozen turkey will lose about 450 g/1 lb of its weight when thawed. Cooking times are: 3.7–4.6 kg/8–10 lb, 3–3½ hours; 4.6–6.4 kg/10–14 lb, 3½–4 hours; 6.4–8.2 kg/14–18 lb, 4–4½ hours; 8.2–9.2 kg/18–20 lb, 4½–5 hours.

❦ Roast turkeys up to 5.5 kg/12 lb in an oven heated to 220°C/425°F/gas mark 7 for the first 30 minutes, then lower the temperature to 180°C/350°F/gas mark 4 for the remaining cooking time. Roast turkeys over 5.5 kg/12 lb at 220°C/425°F/gas mark 7 for the first 30 minutes, then lower to 160°C/325°F/gas mark 3 for the remaining cooking time.

❦ Stand the turkey on a rack in a large roasting tin (make sure it fits the oven). To keep the bird moist brush generously with olive oil or melted butter, and season with salt and freshly milled pepper.

❦ Arrange a layer of rindless streaky bacon rashers over the breast meat. Alternatively, soak a square of double thickness butter muslin in melted butter or oil and drape over the breast meat. You can baste the turkey through the muslin.

❦ Place the turkey in the heated oven. Baste 2–3 times with the pan drippings during the roasting time. This is easiest to do using a baster, or you can use a large spoon. Remove the bacon slices or butter muslin 30 minutes before the end of the cooking time. Baste well and finish cooking.

❦ To check whether the turkey is fully cooked, pierce with the tip of a knife between the thigh and the breast. The juices should run clear. If there is even a hint of pink, return the turkey to the oven for about another 15 minutes, then check again.

❦ When fully cooked, lift the turkey on to a carving board or platter. Lightly tent with foil and leave to stand for at least 15 minutes to allow the juices to settle, making carving easier.

❦ While the turkey is standing, use the pan juices to make a gravy – see pages 103–4.

Turkey and New Potatoes in Blue Cheese Sauce

SERVES 4

- 4 turkey breast fillets
- 450 g/1 lb small new potatoes
- 25 g/1 oz butter
- 2 cloves of garlic
- 75 ml/3 fl oz dry white wine
- 150 ml/¼ pint chicken stock
- 5 ml/1 level teaspoon dried *herbes de Provence*
- 100 g/4 oz blue cheese (Stilton, Danish Blue, Roquefort)
- 30 ml/2 tablespoons double cream

Trim the turkey fillets and scrub the potatoes. Melt the butter in a large frying pan (use one that has a lid), add the turkey fillets and fry until golden brown on both sides. Lift from the pan on to a large plate.

Stir the potatoes into the hot butter in the pan and cook for a few minutes, stirring once or twice, until they are just beginning to brown. With a slotted spoon, lift out the potatoes and add to the turkey fillets. Peel and crush the garlic.

Add the white wine to the hot pan drippings and stir to pick up the flavouring bits. Add the chicken stock, the garlic and the *herbes de Provence*. Bring to the boil. Return the potatoes to the pan and arrange the turkey fillets on top. Cover and simmer gently for 20–25 minutes, or until the turkey is tender and the potatoes cooked.

With a slotted spoon, lift the potatoes and turkey fillets on to a warm serving dish. Crumble the cheese and add to the pan juices with the cream. Heat gently, stirring, until the cheese has melted. Season with freshly milled pepper and spoon over the turkey and potatoes.

PERFECT ROAST GOOSE

Fresh goose is still a seasonal bird, available from the end of September until Christmas, naturally reared and fattened, but frozen goose is available all the year round. Goose costs a little more than other poultry, but the flavour is delicious and the flesh very moist as it is a relatively fatty bird. Goose is usually marketed in three basic sizes. The smallest birds weigh around 3.7 kg/8 lb and will serve 6, medium-sized ones weigh 4.6 kg/10 lb and will serve 9–10, while the larger birds average 5.5 kg/12 lb and will serve 12.

- Make a note of the weight of the bird when purchased. If frozen allow adequate time for thawing (refer to packing instructions).
- Remove the neck and giblets from the body cavity and pull away any surplus fat from inside the tail end.
- Lightly stuff the neck end of the goose only, to form a smooth rounded shape. For a choice of stuffing see pages 79–81. Fold the neck skin over to cover the stuffing and secure with a skewer. If you prefer, the stuffing can be cooked alongside the goose.
- Truss the goose to a neat shape, then prick the skin all over so that the fat can drain off during roasting. Rub the skin with salt.
- Heat the oven to 220°C/425°F/gas mark 7 and calculate the cooking time allowing 15 minutes per 450 g/1 lb plus 15 minutes.
- Place the goose breast side uppermost on a roasting rack standing in a deep roasting tin – there will be a lot of fat. Roast for 20 minutes, then lower the temperature to 180°C/350°F/gas mark 4 for the remaining cooking time.
- Do not baste the goose but remove excess fat from the pan as it accumulates – this is most easily done with a bulb baster. Goose fat makes particularly good roast potatoes.
- About 30 minutes before the end of the cooking time, increase the oven temperature to 220°C/425°F/gas mark 7. At this stage the goose skin may be brushed with soy sauce or honey or sprinkled with caster sugar, to encourage it to turn a rich golden brown.
- To check whether the goose is fully cooked, pierce with the tip of a knife between the thigh and breast. The juices should run clear. If there is even a hint of pink, return the goose to the oven for about 15 minutes, then check again.
- Lift the goose off the roasting rack on to a carving board or platter. Lightly tent with foil and leave to stand for 15–20 minutes before carving.
- While the goose is standing, use the pan juices to make a gravy (see pages 103–4).

CHAPTER SIX

Meat

Recipes are getting simpler and quicker thanks to the variety of new cuts of meat available today. Whether you are looking for a fast grill or pan-fry, or an interesting casserole, none of these recipes will keep you in the kitchen long. We've taken into account that the Sunday roast is as popular as ever – look for the tips on gravy and unusual accompaniments.

MARINADES

Traditionally marinades are used to tenderize meats, but we like to put the emphasis on flavour. The marinades that follow are interesting because they use spices, soy sauce, chilli, garlic and fresh ginger among the ingredients; oil blends them together and a little sugar mellows the flavours. Season with freshly milled pepper if you wish but leave out salt, which tends to draw the meat juices.

Marinate cubes of beef rump steak, fillet end of leg or shoulder of lamb, or pork fillet for kebabs. Chicken or turkey fillets look good cut into thick strips for threading on skewers. Chicken breast portions, drumsticks and thighs should be slashed with a sharp knife so that the marinade can penetrate. A well-flavoured marinade adds that little extra to beef steaks, lamb chops or leg steaks, and pork spareribs or loin chops before grilling, barbecuing or baking. Joints of meat such as beef fillet or pork loin can be soaked in an oil-based marinade before roasting, especially when the meat is to be served cold.

Basic method Combine the marinade ingredients, then pour into a non-metallic shallow dish that will take the meat or poultry pieces in one layer. Add the meat and turn it several times to coat with the marinade. Or, better still, put the marinade in a suitably sized freezer bag, add the meat pieces (or joint), close securely and give the bag several turns to coat the meat with the marinade. Allow a minimum of 4 hours for the flavours to penetrate, or leave overnight (especially with joints), always in the refrigerator, turning the meat portions or the freezer bag several times. When ready to cook, lift the meat or poultry from the marinade with a fork. Any marinade remaining in the dish or bag may be used as a baste during cooking or to flavour the gravy.

The following marinades are sufficient for 450–700 g/1–1½ lb meat pieces, 4–6 steaks, chops or chicken breasts or a single joint of up to 1.5 kg/3 lb.

Spicy Peanut Marinade Combine 45 ml/3 tablespoons dark soy sauce, 45 ml/3 level tablespoons smooth peanut butter, 15 ml/1 level tablespoon soft brown sugar, 5 ml/1 teaspoon hot chilli sauce and 75 ml/3 fl oz grapeseed oil. Add 2 crushed cloves of garlic and stir to mix.

Teriyaki Marinade Mix together 30 ml/2 tablespoons dark soy sauce, 30 ml/2 level tablespoons soft brown sugar and 15 ml/1 tablespoon grapeseed oil. Add 5 ml/1 teaspoon unsweetened ginger purée, 1 crushed clove of garlic and the juice of 1 lemon. Stir to mix.

Sesame Mustard Marinade Toast 30 ml/2 tablespoons sesame seeds in a dry frying pan. Add to 30 ml/2 tablespoons red wine vinegar, 30 ml/2 level tablespoons Dijon mustard and 100 ml/4 fl oz grapeseed oil. Add 1 crushed clove of garlic and 30 ml/2 tablespoons sesame oil and stir to mix.

Chilli Barbecue Marinade Combine 30 ml/2 tablespoons clear honey, 15 ml/1 tablespoon Dijon mustard, 15 ml/1 tablespoon red wine vinegar, 30 ml/2 level tablespoons tomato purée, 15 ml/1 level tablespoon hot chilli sauce and 100 ml/4 fl oz grapeseed oil. Add 2 crushed cloves of garlic and mix well.

Spiced Lamb with Pears and Dates

SERVES 4

3 medium onions
30 ml/2 tablespoons olive oil
5 ml/1 teaspoon clear honey
1 thin-skinned lemon
1 clove of garlic
5 ml/1 level teaspoon ground allspice
2.5 ml/½ level teaspoon ground cinnamon
700 g/1½ lb lean lamb (leg or shoulder)
seasoned flour for coating
600 ml/1 pint hot vegetable stock
15 ml/1 tablespoon tomato purée
salt and freshly milled pepper
3 firm pears
8 stoned dates
25 g/1 oz butter

Peel and finely chop 2 of the onions. Heat the oil in a frying pan (use one with a lid) and add the chopped onions and the honey. Cover and cook gently until softened and pale golden brown, stirring occasionally.

In a pan, cover the whole lemon with cold water, bring to the boil, then lower the heat and simmer for 10 minutes.

Peel and crush the garlic. Stir the garlic, allspice and cinnamon into the softened onions, then draw the pan off the heat. Drain the lemon.

Heat the oven to 160°C/325°F/gas mark 3.

Cube the lamb and toss in seasoned flour. Turn the onion mixture into a large casserole dish and add the floured meat pieces. Combine the stock and tomato pureé and pour over the meat. Season with salt and freshly milled pepper.

On a plate to catch the juices, cut the lemon into 6 wedges lengthwise. Discard the pips. Quarter the pears, removing the core, and peel.

Add the lemon wedges, juice and pear quarters to the casserole. Cover and cook for about 45 minutes. Stir in the dates, re-cover the casserole, and continue to cook for about 30 minutes or until the meat is tender.

Peel the remaining onion and cut into thin slices. Separate into rings and coat with seasoned flour. Melt the butter in a large frying pan, add the onion rings, and fry quickly until crisp and golden.

Transfer the lamb to a serving dish and sprinkle the onion rings on top. Serve with rice or couscous (see page 133).

Minted Lamb Kebabs

Illustrated on Plate Five

SERVES 6

700 g/1½ lb lamb neck fillets
300 ml/½ pint Greek-style yogurt
3–4 strands saffron
15 ml/1 tablespoon dried mint
30 ml/2 tablespoons olive oil
30 ml/2 tablespoons clear honey
freshly milled pepper
12 small onions

Trim the lamb, cut into chunky pieces, and arrange in a single layer in a shallow dish. Whisk together the yogurt, saffron, dried mint, olive oil, honey and a good seasoning of pepper. Spoon over the lamb and turn the meat to coat it on all sides. Cover and refrigerate for at least 4 hours or overnight, stirring once or twice. Remove from the refrigerator 30 minutes before cooking.

Top and tail the onions, then peel, leaving them whole. Put them in a pan, cover with cold water, bring to the boil, then simmer for 5 minutes. Drain.

Thread the lamb pieces and onions on to 6 skewers. Heat the grill. Set the skewers on the grill rack about 7.5 cm/3 inches below the heat source (or cook on a barbecue). Cook for 15–20 minutes, turning once or twice, until the meat is tender and golden brown.

Serve with hot rice, or remove the lamb and onions from the skewers and slip inside warm pitta breads with some shredded lettuce.

Grilled Lamb in a Lemon Marinade

SERVES 6–8

1 fillet end of leg of lamb, about 1.5 kg/3 lb
45 ml/3 tablespoons clear honey
finely grated rind and juice of 2 lemons
45 ml/3 tablespoons grapeseed oil

With a sharp knife cut across the skin of the lamb through to the bone. Follow the bone, cutting round and under until you can lift it out, then open the meat out flat. Score the meat, criss-cross fashion in diamonds, on both the flesh and skin side.

Spoon the honey, finely grated rind and lemon juice and the oil into a large freezer bag. Slide in the boned meat. Tie the bag securely and turn to coat the meat with the marinade on all sides. Refrigerate for 24 hours, turning the bag as often as you can, so that the meat takes the flavour of the marinade on all sides.

Heat the grill to hot, line the grill pan with foil and set the rack in it. Preheat the grill rack 7.5 cm/3 inches below the heat source for about 5 minutes. Lift the lamb from the marinade and place on the grill rack. Grill for about 20 minutes on each side, turning the meat just once. Alternatively, heat the oven to 220°C/425°F/gas mark 7 and roast the meat on a rack for about 50 minutes. It could also be barbecued. Whichever way you choose, the meat should be blackened and crusty on the outside and pink in the middle.

Serve hot or cooled to room temperature, cut in thin slices at an angle across the grain.

PERFECT ROAST LAMB

Lamb is available all the year round with meat from home or abroad. Lamb comes from animals under one year old, and has pale pink flesh and light creamy white fat.

A butcher will tell you a shoulder has more flavour – if the carving puts you off, ask him to either part-bone it by removing the blade bone or completely bone it. The pocket left by the removal of the blade bone makes a good spot for filling with a well-flavoured stuffing. When the opening is stitched the joint is still shoulder 'shaped'. A fully boned shoulder can be opened out, spread inside with a thin layer of stuffing, rolled up and tied at intervals to make a neat roll. A 'melon' of lamb is a stuffed and boned shoulder shaped and tied into a cushion-shape. Leg of lamb is sold whole or halved into the shank end and the fillet end. Rack of lamb may be sold whole for a crown roast or guard of honour.

- Allow 225–350 g/8–12 oz uncooked meat on the bone and 125–175 g/4–6 oz uncooked meat off the bone per person.
- Follow the tips listed in For the Very Best Roasts (see page 101).
- Calculate the cooking time: for joints on the bone allow 25 minutes per 450 g/1 lb plus 25 minutes for medium (pink); 30 minutes per 450 g/1 lb plus 30 minutes for well done. For a boned and rolled joint allow 35 minutes per 450 g/1 lb plus 35 minutes for medium (pink); 40 minutes per 450 g/1 lb plus 40 minutes for well done.
- For added flavour, pierce the skin with a pointed knife and insert slivers of garlic or sprigs of rosemary.
- Preheat the oven to 180°C/350°F/gas mark 4.
- About 20 minutes before the end of the cooking time spread the fat with a little redcurrant, rowan, quince or mint jelly. The jelly caramelizes to a beautiful golden glaze.

Lamb Steaks with Herbs and Lemon

SERVES 4

- 1 medium onion
- 100 g/4 oz carrots
- 4 cloves of garlic
- 15 ml/1 tablespoon olive oil
- 25 g/1 oz butter
- 4 lamb steaks
- 5 ml/1 teaspoon dried oregano
- 45 ml/3 tablespoons tomato purée
- 10 ml/2 level teaspoons caster sugar
- 1 lemon
- 175 ml/6 fl oz vegetable stock
- freshly milled pepper
- 45 ml/3 tablespoons chopped fresh parsley

Peel and chop the onion. Pare the carrots, then slice lengthwise and across to chop finely. Peel and crush the garlic.

Heat the oil and butter in a large frying pan (use one with a lid), add the lamb steaks and brown them on both sides. Transfer the steaks to a plate.

Add the chopped onion and carrot to the hot butter. Stir in the garlic. Lower the heat, cover the pan and cook until the vegetables are softened – about 10 minutes. Stir in the oregano.

In a small bowl stir together the tomato purée and the sugar. Remove the lemon rind with a vegetable peeler and squeeze out the juice. Add the juice to the bowl along with the stock. Return the lamb steaks to the pan and pour over the tomato mixture. Bring to a simmer, season with pepper, cover and cook gently for 40 minutes.

Meanwhile, finely chop the lemon rind and mix with the chopped parsley. Sprinkle over the lamb just before serving.

USING A MEAT THERMOMETER

Using a meat thermometer takes all the guesswork out of calculating roasting times, especially if you prefer a rare result.

Push the thermometer into the thickest part of the joint, making sure it is not touching any bone. (Bone gets hotter than the surrounding flesh so you would get a false reading.)

While the meat is roasting keep an eye on the dial and remove the roast when the desired result is reached.

BEEF		
rare	–	60°C/140°F
medium	–	70°C/160°F
well done	–	80°C/175°F
LAMB		
medium (pink)	–	70°C/160°F
well done	–	80°C/175°F
PORK		80–85°C/175–185°F
HAM		80°C/175°F

THE SAFE HANDLING OF FRESH AND FROZEN MEAT

- Transfer frozen and fresh meat from the shop to the home refrigerator as quickly as possible – preferably using a cool-bag with frozen icepacks.
- Store raw meat at the bottom of the refrigerator. Raw meat must never be placed above cooked foods.
- Small joints or portions of frozen meat may be thawed in the microwave. Stand them on a microwave trivet, remove any metal ties and open the end of the packaging to allow thawed liquid to drain out. Follow the manufacturer's handbook for the method and time. Always stop the microwave if the meat begins to feel warm, and finish thawing in the refrigerator.
- Once thawed, meat should be covered and stored in the fridge. Cook as soon as possible.
- Always wash your hands with hot soapy water both before and after handling raw meat.
- Never use the same knives or chopping boards for raw and cooked meat without washing them, your hands and the work surface between each use.

FOR THE VERY BEST ROASTS

- Meat should be allowed to come to room temperature before cooking – this will take about 2 hours for an average-sized joint.
- Frozen meat must be completely thawed.
- The surface of the meat must be quite dry. Pat thawed or marinated cuts of meat with kitchen paper on all sides before cooking.
- Prick the outer skin or layer of fat with a fork and lightly brush joints with oil or melted butter and season with salt and freshly milled pepper about 2 hours before cooking. Salt will ensure a crisp brown crust on the fat of beef and lamb, and crisp crackling on pork.
- Place a few thick slices of onion or carrot under the roast as the basis of a good gravy (see page 103). Place the roast fat side uppermost. Insert a meat thermometer if wished, making sure it is inserted into the thickest part of the flesh. If the thermometer is touching bone it will give a false reading.
- Always place a roast in a preheated oven.
- Baste lamb and beef once or twice during cooking, using the hot fat in the roasting tin.
- When roasting is completed, lift the meat on to a heated platter or board and keep warm. Leave to stand for 15–20 minutes to allow the juices to settle and the meat to relax, making carving easier. Add to the gravy any juices which accumulate on the platter during this time.
- If you intend to serve the meat cold, allow it to cool at room temperature.

PERFECT ROAST PORK

Available all the year round, virtually every bit of the pig is edible and is used in a wider variety of food products than any other meat. Over the years breeding has produced a leaner pig and, more recently, traditionally reared animals with extra succulence and tenderness. Look for labels identifying these in the shops.

All cuts of pork are tender and suitable for roasting. Choose leg or loin joints with a good area of rind to make the prized crisp crackling. Make sure it is well scored (use a sharp Stanley knife) or carving will be difficult.

- Allow 350 g/12 oz uncooked meat on the bone and 175 g/6 oz uncooked meat off the bone per person.
- Follow the tips listed in For the Very Best Roasts (see page 101), especially rubbing salt well into the scored rind for a crisp finish.
- Calculate the cooking time: for joints on the bone allow 25 minutes per 450 g/1 lb plus 25 minutes. For boned and rolled joints allow 30 minutes per 450 g/1 lb plus 30 minutes.
- Preheat the oven to 220°C/425°F/gas mark 7.
- Increase the oven heat for the last 10 minutes of the calculated time to crisp the crackling. Alternatively, lift off the rind with a knife, crisp it under a hot grill and serve it separately.
- Serve roast pork with apple sauce (try stirring in a little creamed horseradish for an extra kick).

Pork Steaks with Caramelized Onions

SERVES 6

2 large onions
6 pork loin steaks
seasoned flour
30 ml/2 tablespoons olive oil
30 ml/2 level tablespoons granulated sugar
2.5 ml/½ level teaspoon ground allspice
2.5 ml/½ level teaspoon ground cinnamon
30 ml/2 tablespoons red wine vinegar
100 g/4 oz ready-to-eat dried apricots
300 ml/½ pint vegetable stock
salt and freshly milled pepper

Peel and thinly slice the onions. Coat the meat with seasoned flour. Heat the oil in a large frying pan, add the pork steaks and brown each one on both sides. Transfer to a large casserole.

Add the onions to the hot oil in the frying pan and stir to soften over a medium heat. Sprinkle with the sugar and cook, stirring, until the onions are a rich golden brown. Stir in the spices, vinegar and 30 ml/2 tablespoons water. Simmer until the onions are syrupy – 2–3 minutes.

Heat the oven to 160°C/325°F/gas mark 3. Pour the caramelized onions over the pork. Add the apricots and stock. Cover and cook in the oven for 1½ hours. Season with salt and pepper to taste before serving.

Pork in Gingered Tomato Sauce

SERVES 4

- 2 pork fillets, weighing about 700 g/1½ lb in total
- 30 ml/2 tablespoons olive oil
- freshly milled pepper
- 2 medium onions
- 5 ml/1 teaspoon caster sugar
- 10 ml/2 level teaspoons ground cumin
- 10 ml/2 level teaspoons ground coriander
- 2.5 cm/1 inch fresh ginger
- 1 (397 g) can chopped tomatoes
- 15 ml/1 tablespoon tomato purée
- 15 ml/1 level tablespoon cornflour
- 50 ml/2 fl oz water
- 15 ml/1 tablespoon clear honey
- 1 vegetable stock cube
- 5 ml/1 teaspoon red wine vinegar

Trim the pork fillets and score them lengthways with 2–3 long cuts. Rub them all over with a little of the oil and season with freshly milled pepper. Cut each pork fillet across in half. Peel the onions and slice thinly.

Heat the remaining oil in a large frying pan (use one with a lid). Add the pork pieces and brown in the hot oil, turning once. Remove from the pan. Add the onion to the pan and sprinkle with the sugar. Fry gently until soft and golden brown – about 15 minutes. Stir in the ground cumin and coriander. Grate the ginger and add to the pan.

Press the contents of the can of tomatoes through a sieve to remove the seeds. To the tomato liquid add the tomato purée, cornflour, water, honey, crumbled stock cube and vinegar. Stir to blend and pour into the pan. Stir until simmering. Replace the pork pieces, cover and cook gently for 30–35 minutes.

THE GOOD GRAVY GUIDE

For many, a traditional thick gravy is the essential accompaniment to a roast joint of meat or poultry, but a well-seasoned thin gravy is also delicious. For something different try a cream gravy – especially good with roast chicken or turkey. Make a thin gravy, then stir in a little double cream and cook until bubbling hot.

- ❦ A well-flavoured stock is important; simmer the giblets from poultry or game with onion slices, a bay leaf and water to cover, then strain and season. Or use vegetable cooking water boosted with a suitably flavoured stock cube. You will need 600 ml/1 pint stock to make gravy for 8 servings.
- ❦ For gravy with a rich flavour and colour, arrange thick slices of onion or carrot under the poultry or joint before roasting. During cooking the natural sugar in the vegetables caramelizes in the pan juices.
- ❦ To enrich a gravy, use red or white wine as part of the stock; stir in a tablespoon or so

of redcurrant or quince jelly; add a good dash of vinegar – try red or white wine, sherry or balsamic; season well with freshly milled pepper or add a teaspoon of sugar.

To make a thin gravy Pour off the fat from the roasting tin, leaving behind the dark drippings and coagulated pan juices. Remove the onion or carrot pieces with a fork. Add 600 ml/1 pint of hot stock and bring to the boil, stirring to pick up and blend in the crusty drippings. Simmer to concentrate the gravy, strain into a serving jug, and season to taste.

To make a thick gravy Leaving the crusty bits behind, pour off the fat in the roasting tin into a bowl. Measure and return 45 ml/3 tablespoons of the fat to the roasting tin, and add 45 ml/3 level tablespoons plain flour. Over a medium heat, stir with a wire whisk until frothy and coloured to a light tan. Add 600 ml/1 pint hot stock. Stir to blend and loosen the crusty bits and bring to a simmer. Cook for 5 minutes then strain into a serving jug and season to taste.

Many of today's ovens come with particularly large roasting tins which are impractical to make gravy in. If you have one of these, first pour off the fat after removing the roast. To make thin gravy add part of the stock to the roasting tin and return it to the hot oven for a few minutes to allow the pan drippings to soften. Pour the stock and pan drippings from the roasting tin into a saucepan, add the remainder of the stock and continue as above. To make thick gravy pour off the fat into a bowl and again return the roasting tin to the oven with part of the stock. Measure the fat and flour into a saucepan, add the stock and pan drippings from the roasting tin, the remainder of the stock and continue as above.

Pork and Pepper Stir-fry

SERVES 4

175 g/6 oz pork fillet (tenderloin)
1 bunch (6–8) spring onions
2.5 cm/1 inch fresh ginger
1 yellow pepper
1 orange pepper
175 g/6 oz fresh beansprouts
30 ml/2 tablespoons soy sauce
100 ml/4 fl oz vegetable stock
15 ml/1 level tablespoon cornflour
15 ml/1 tablespoon stem ginger syrup or clear honey

Cut the pork fillet in very fine slivers across the grain of the meat. Trim the spring onions, then slice into 2.5 cm/1 inch pieces. Peel and grate the ginger. Halve and de-seed both the peppers, then cut lengthwise into thin slivers. Rinse and dry the beansprouts.

To make the glaze, measure the soy sauce, stock, cornflour and ginger syrup into a small bowl. Stir until smooth.

Heat the oil in a wok or large frying pan and add the nuts. Cook, stirring constantly, until golden brown. Remove from the pan with a slotted spoon. Add the spring onion and ginger and stir-fry for 30 seconds. Add the pork slivers and stir-fry for 2–3 minutes. Stir in the peppers and beansprouts and stir-fry for 2 minutes.

Stir the glaze, add to the pan, and stir until the sauce is bubbling and the meat and vegetables are glazed. Add the nuts, stir, and serve straight from the pan.

30 ml/2 tablespoons grapeseed oil
50 g/2 oz cashew nuts

Bacon and Apple Cassoulet

SERVES 4

2 red-skinned apples
100 g/4 oz baby onions
50 g/2 oz butter
4 bacon chops
25 g/1 oz soft brown sugar
1 (432 g) can cannellini beans
15 ml/1 level tablespoon cornflour
1 vegetable stock cube
2.5 cm/1 inch fresh ginger
300 ml/½ pint English apple juice

Using an apple corer, remove the core of both apples and cut each across into four slices. Trim and peel the onions, leaving them whole. Melt half the butter in a large frying pan (use one with a lid). Add the apple slices and cook until golden brown on both sides. Remove from the pan.

Add the bacon chops to the pan and quickly brown on both sides. Remove the chops and wipe out the pan with kitchen paper.

Melt the remaining butter in the pan, add the onions and sprinkle over the sugar. Cook gently, stirring frequently, until golden brown – about 10 minutes. Drain the beans and rinse under cold water. Drain well and add to the onions.

In a mixing bowl combine the cornflour, the crumbled vegetable stock cube, the grated ginger and the apple juice. Blend well and add to the pan. Stir until the mixture comes to a simmer and the sauce has thickened. Add the bacon chops, cover, and simmer for 15 minutes. Remove the pan lid, add the apple slices and simmer for a further 5 minutes before serving.

PERFECT ROAST GAMMON

Gammon is the hind leg of a bacon pig which has been brine cured. It can be bought smoked or unsmoked. Oven roasting is the easiest way to cook gammon – the meat is lean and tender and has a delicious flavour served hot or cold. Choose a whole gammon for a large party or a half gammon for a family celebration. If in doubt go for a larger joint, as the meat is so good served cold. Whole and half gammon are usually sold on the bone, middle cuts are usually boned. Look for a cut with a good area of rind – the cooked joint will look most attractive whether served with the crackling or glazed (see below). For roast gammon with crackling always choose an unsmoked gammon joint.

- Allow 225–350 g/8–12 oz uncooked meat on the bone and 125–175 g/4–6 oz uncooked meat off the bone per person.
- Make a note of the weight of the gammon and remove any wrappings.
- Even though today's methods of curing are milder than they used to be, we still think it is a good idea to soak all gammon joints before roasting. Overnight for a whole or half gammon, 3–4 hours for a smaller joint, in cold water to cover. Drain and pat dry with absorbent kitchen paper before roasting.
- Calculate the cooking time: 20 minutes per 450 g/1 lb for a whole gammon; 30 minutes per 450 g/1 lb for other joints, reducing the time to 25 minutes per 450 g/1 lb for joints over 3 kg/6 lb.
- Heat the oven to 180°C/350°F/gas mark 4 for a whole gammon; 190°C/375°F/gas mark 5 for half a gammon or joints.

ROAST GAMMON WITH CRACKLING

- Score the rind in straight close lines (like pork) with a sharp kitchen or Stanley knife. Rub the rind first with oil, then with coarse salt, and sprinkle with plenty of cracked pepper for a pretty finish.
- Line a roasting tin with foil. Add the gammon skin side up.
- At the end of the cooking time, leave the gammon to stand for 20 minutes before carving.

GLAZED ROAST GAMMON

- Cut a large enough piece of foil to completely enclose the gammon in a loose parcel. Place the gammon, skin side up, in the centre of the foil, and add a bay leaf or sprig of fresh rosemary. Draw the foil up and over the joint and fold closed in a baggy parcel so that the air can circulate. Turn the ends up to seal.
- Stand the foil parcel in a roasting tin.
- Remove the gammon from the oven 15–20 minutes before the end of the calculated cooking time.
- Increase the oven temperature to 200°C/400°F/gas mark 6.
- Open the foil (take care – there will be meat juices and steam inside).
- With a sharp knife, strip off the rind and score the fat in close straight lines or in a criss-cross pattern. Spread the fat with Dijon mustard and press on a generous layer of demerara sugar. Alternatively, spread with fine-cut orange marmalade or with redcurrant jelly.
- Return the gammon to the hot oven for the remaining cooking time to brown and glaze the joint.
- At the end of the cooking time, leave the gammon to stand for 20 minutes before carving.

GOOD GRILLS

Grilling is a fast and fierce method of cooking that calls for tender, quick-cooking cuts of meat or poultry. It's also an easier and healthier (low fat) method which relies on little more than thoughtful presentation and the addition of an attractively cooked vegetable or a crisp salad.

Nowadays there is a wide choice of well trimmed meat cuts to choose from. Modern Continental cutting methods have produced leaner, boneless new cuts ideal for the fast cook, so don't just stick with the old familiar ones. For good results let chilled meat come to room temperature before cooking and make sure frozen meat is thawed – especially chicken. To be sure of tender moist results select, or ask for, meat cuts that are thickly sliced; between 1.25–2.5 cm/½–1 inch is ideal. Meat cuts that are thin will dry out very fast, making them tough to eat.

Basic grilling Line the grill pan with foil, tucking it firmly around the edges of the pan. Preheat the grill for 3–5 minutes and set the grill rack at least 7.5 cm/3 inches from the heat source. Rub or brush the meat surfaces with olive or grapeseed oil (it is best to season with salt and freshly milled pepper on serving). If foods have been marinated, lift from the marinade and drain. Use the marinade to baste the food during cooking if you wish. Turn the food over to the second side just once, halfway through the cooking time. If the foods spit furiously they are too close to the heat source – check the rack level and lower it. Timing is determined by the thickness of the food, not the size or weight. The recommended times (see below) can only be approximate but they are a good guide. Timing is important – too long under the grill and your precious food is past its best.

Serve grilled meat with a squeeze of lemon juice, top with Flavoured Butters (see pages 30–1) or with melted butter with chopped spring onion, crushed garlic or fresh herbs added. Pass some of the interesting new varieties of flavoured mustards.

Beef Only the best cuts of steak are suitable – sirloin (also called entrecôte), fillet or rump. For a subtle flavour, rub a crushed clove of garlic over the raw steak. An extra aid to the cooking time required can be determined by the 'feel' of the meat. Press gently on the centre of the cooked steak with a finger (or back of a spoon). If the meat gives easily the steak is rare, if meat resists but is still soft it's medium done, and if the meat feels firm, then it is cooked right through. Begin to test 2–3 minutes before the recommended cooking time is up.

Time for thick-cut steaks: rare 6 minutes, medium 8–10 minutes, well-done 12–15 minutes.

Lamb Choose from leg or shoulder chops and steaks, butterfly (also called valentine) chops, loin chops or cutlets. Lamb tastes delicious with a mixture of 30 ml/2 level tablespoons Dijon mustard and 30 ml/2 level tablespoons soft brown sugar spread on the second side when turned – it goes appetizingly golden brown.

Time 10–12 minutes.

Pork Choose loin or sparerib chops, loin steaks or escalopes. Trim off excess fat and snip at 1.25 cm/½ inch intervals to prevent buckling while grilling. A sprinkling of ground allspice from a pepper mill is a nice seasoning. Or, for a delicious sweet-sharp flavour and rich golden colour, rub the raw meat with equal parts of caster sugar and dry mustard – about 15 ml/1 level tablespoon of each is sufficient for 4 chops.

Time 15–20 minutes.

Chicken Choose from chicken quarters or part-boned breasts, drumsticks, thighs, halves or spatchcock poussin. Leave the skin on, as it protects the flesh from becoming dry. Start grilling with the bone side towards the heat – bone acts as a heat conductor and speeds up the cooking. Test the chicken pieces by pushing a knife tip into a thick part; the juices that run should be clear with no tinges of pink.

Time 20–25 minutes.

Gammon Steaks, bacon chops and thick-cut bacon rashers can all be grilled successfully. Nick the fat on gammon steaks or bacon chops at intervals to prevent buckling while grilling. Lightly brushing gammon steaks on both sides with oil prevents the meat becoming dry and tough. Arrange bacon rashers with the fat part of each rasher covering the lean part of the next one.

Time for steaks and chops 10–12 minutes. Rashers 3–4 minutes.

Sausages There are dozens of special recipe sausages to choose from at the butcher's and supermarkets. Place the sausages close together on the grill rack and brush with a little oil to encourage even browning. There is no need for seasoning, nor is it necessary to prick them.

Time 10–15 minutes.

Kebabs Can be made with beef, pork, lamb or chicken. It's better to cut your own neat pieces from tender cuts you recognize (see page 107) than to take a chance on pre-cut meat. Cut into good-sized chunky pieces – small pieces shrink during cooking, becoming dry and chewy. Choose flat skewers, so the meat pieces don't twirl around when the kebabs are turned over, and remember that all the items on one skewer should require the same cooking time so it's better to keep vegetables for separate skewers.

Time on average 15–20 minutes.

Frikadeller with Red Berry Sauce

SERVES 4

- 450 g/1 lb ground (minced) pork
- 1 medium onion
- 50 g/2 oz plain flour
- salt and freshly milled pepper
- pinch grated nutmeg
- 1 egg
- 30 ml/2 tablespoons milk
- 50–75 g/2–3 oz butter for frying
- 1 orange
- 30 ml/2 tablespoons cranberry sauce (with whole berries)
- 30 ml/2 tablespoons redcurrant sauce

Turn the pork into a mixing bowl. Peel and finely chop the onion. Add the onion, flour, a good seasoning of salt and pepper, nutmeg, egg and milk to the pork. Mix very thoroughly with a wooden spoon until the mixture is quite smooth and soft. Chill until cooking time.

Heat the butter in a large frying pan. Drop the pork mixture by tablespoonfuls into the hot butter – you should get about 8. Fry over a moderate heat, turning them to brown on both sides, for about 15 minutes.

Transfer the *frikadeller* to a plate. Finely grate the orange rind and squeeze the juice. Add both to the pan with the cranberry sauce and redcurrant jelly. Return to the heat, stirring to melt the jelly. Return the *frikadeller* to the pan and heat for a few minutes.

RELISHES AND PICKLES

A platter of cold meats, whether home-cooked or from the delicatessen, comes to life when served with one or two homemade pickles. Keep the ingredients chunky and bold, in bite-sized pieces. Cool the pickles after cooking, pack in clean glass jars with airtight lids, and store in the refrigerator for at least 48 hours before serving to allow the flavours to merge and mellow. They may be kept in the refrigerator for 4–6 weeks. Serve in shallow dishes with a little of the marinade or syrup, or lift out of the jar with a fork and pile in the centre of the platter of meats. All of these recipes make 6–8 servings.

Cranberry Relish Heat the oven to 160°C/325°F/gas mark 3. Place 450 g/1 lb fresh or frozen cranberries with 450 g/1 lb caster sugar in a casserole. Stir in the grated rind and juice of 1 orange. Cover and bake 30–40 minutes or until the cranberries are tender and bubbling in a bright red syrup. Cool and stir in 50 g/2 oz chopped pecans or walnuts.

Pickled Pineapple Cut away the rind from 1/2 a fresh pineapple and cut the flesh into bite-sized pieces. Measure 100 ml/4 fl oz white wine vinegar, 100 ml/4 fl oz water and 275 g/10 oz caster sugar into a saucepan. Add 2–3 pieces finely pared lemon rind, 4 whole cloves, 5 cm/2 inches stick cinnamon and 2.5 cm/1 inch fresh ginger, finely chopped. Stir over a low heat until the sugar has dissolved, then bring to the boil. Add the pineapple pieces, lower the heat and simmer for 6–8 minutes or until the fruit is glazed.

Spiced Prunes Put 225 g/8 oz stoned, tenderized prunes into a mixing bowl. Add 300 ml/1/2 pint white wine vinegar, 150 ml/1/4 pint cold water, 225 g/8 oz soft brown sugar and 5 cm/2 inches stick cinnamon. Cover and leave overnight. Turn the contents of the bowl into a saucepan and bring to the boil. Reduce the heat to a simmer and cook for 10 minutes.

Chilli Onions Peel 450 g/1 lb small pickling onions, leaving them whole. Cover with cold water in a saucepan and bring to a simmer. Cook for 5 minutes then drain. Return the onions to the pan and add 150 ml/1/4 pint cold water, 60 ml/4 tablespoons white wine vinegar, 25 g/1 oz caster sugar, 30 ml/2 tablespoons olive oil, 5 ml/1 teaspoon chilli sauce and a seasoning of salt and pepper. Halve and de-seed 1 small red pepper, chop finely and add. Bring to the boil, cover and simmer for 20 minutes or until the onions are tender. Using a slotted spoon, transfer the onions to the jar. Boil the liquid in the saucepan for 2–3 minutes to reduce and concentrate the flavour. Pour over the onions.

Spiced Peaches or Pears Drain the fruit pieces from 1 (822 g) can peach or pear halves in juice. Pour 225 ml/8 fl oz of the juices from the can into a saucepan. Add 75 g/3 oz caster sugar, 6 whole cloves, 100 ml/4 fl oz white wine vinegar and 5 cm/2 inches stick cinnamon. Stir over a low heat until the sugar has dissolved, then bring to the boil. Lower the heat to a gentle simmer, add the pieces of fruit and cook for 4–5 minutes.

Sausages and Cabbage in Soured Cream

SERVES 4

- 450 g/1 lb herb-flavoured pork sausages
- 4 rashers smoked back bacon
- 1 large onion
- 15 ml/1 tablespoon olive oil
- 5 ml/1 teaspoon caster sugar
- 1 small green cabbage
- 150 ml/¼ pint vegetable stock
- freshly milled pepper
- 5 ml/1 teaspoon white wine vinegar
- 5 ml/1 teaspoon coarse-grain mustard
- 1 (142 ml) carton soured cream

Separate the sausages (do not prick the skins) and fry gently without any oil in a large frying pan (use one with a lid) until just browned on all sides. Remove from the pan. Trim and roughly chop the bacon. Peel and thinly slice the onion.

Heat the oil in the frying pan, stir in the onion and sprinkle with the sugar. Cover and cook gently for about 10 minutes, until soft and golden brown. Add the bacon pieces and cook for 2–3 minutes.

Meanwhile, quarter and core the cabbage then cut across the leaves into fine shreds. Pack the cabbage into the pan – it will soften as it cooks. Add the stock, a seasoning of pepper and the vinegar. Cover and cook gently for 20 minutes or until the cabbage has softened and is tender, adding a little extra water if necessary.

Combine the mustard with the soured cream and stir into the cabbage. Replace the sausages, cover, and cook for a further 5 minutes to heat them through.

PERFECT ROAST BEEF

Beef must be well hung to ensure a superb flavour and tenderness. There is no way to recognize this in raw meat. Make good friends with your butcher, ask where he buys his meat, and seek his opinion as to which cut of meat to choose for which method of cooking. Look in the supermarkets for meat labelled as being from traditionally reared animals and from well-known breeds such as Aberdeen Angus. Animals allowed to grow at their natural pace, rather than by intensive rearing, produce meat with a noticeably superior flavour and tenderness. For the best flavour, choose beef which is lightly marbled with thin strands of creamy-coloured fat, This marbling will open up the fibres of the meat and baste it while cooking.

The best cuts for roasting are sirloin, ribs and topside, in that order. A joint under 1.5 kg/3 lb is really too small to roast successfully – it will quickly become dry.

❦ Allow 225–350 g/8–12 oz uncooked meat on the bone and 125–175 g/4–6 oz uncooked meat off the bone per person.

- Follow the tips listed in For the Very Best Roasts (see page 101).
- Calculate the cooking time: for joints on the bone allow 15 minutes per 450 g/1 lb plus 15 minutes for a rare result; 20 minutes per 450 g/1 lb plus 20 minutes for medium; 25 minutes per 450 g/1 lb plus 25 minutes for well done. For boned and rolled joints calculate 20 minutes per 450 g/1 lb plus 20 minutes for rare; 25 minutes per 450 g/1 lb plus 20 minutes for medium; and 30 minutes per 450 g/1 lb plus 20 minutes for well done.
- Preheat the oven to 220°C/425°F/gas mark 7. Place the prepared roast in the hot oven and cook for 15 minutes, then lower the temperature to 190°C/375°F/gas mark 5 for the rest of the cooking time.
- Serve roast beef with hot or mild mustard or horseradish sauce.

Teriyaki Steaks with Fresh Pineapple

SERVES 6

6 beef fillet steaks
30 ml/2 tablespoons soft brown sugar
30 ml/2 tablespoons dark soy sauce
juice of 1 lemon
15 ml/1 tablespoon grapeseed oil
5 ml/1 teaspoon grated fresh ginger
salt and freshly milled pepper
1 clove of garlic
25 g/1 oz butter
6 slices fresh pineapple
150 ml/¼ pint red wine
45 ml/3 tablespoons redcurrant jelly
5 ml/1 teaspoon Dijon mustard

Trim the steaks and place in a single layer in a shallow dish. To make the marinade, combine the sugar, soy sauce, lemon juice, oil and grated ginger in a bowl. Peel and crush the garlic, stir into the marinade, then pour over the steaks. Cover and refrigerate for up to 8 hours or overnight, turning the meat occasionally.

Melt the butter in a large frying pan. Lift the steaks from the marinade and cook in the hot butter, turning them once or twice. Cook for about 5 minutes for rare, 6–8 minutes for medium-done. Lift from the pan and keep warm. Add the pineapple slices to the pan and cook just until golden brown on both sides. Lift out and keep hot with the steaks.

Pour the red wine into the pan, stir to pick up any residue and let it bubble. Add the strained marinade from the meat, the redcurrant jelly and the mustard. Stir to dissolve the jelly and bring to a simmer. Season with salt and pepper. Return the steaks to the pan and heat through briefly.

Arrange the steaks on top of the pineapple slices and spoon over the sauce.

Beef Casserole with Chestnuts and Dumplings

SERVES 8

8 small onions
3 celery stalks
50 g/2 oz plain flour
5 ml/1 teaspoon dried mixed herbs
salt and freshly milled pepper
1.5 kg/3 lb thick cut rump steak
30 ml/2 tablespoons olive oil
600 ml/1 pint beef stock
150 ml/¼ pint red wine
15 ml/1 tablespoon tomato purée
30 ml/2 tablespoons red wine vinegar
700 g/1½ lb parsnips
1 (350 g) can whole chestnuts
175 g/6 oz self-raising flour
5 ml/1 level teaspoon mustard powder
75 g/3 oz shredded suet

Heat the oven to 160°C/325°F/gas mark 3.

Peel the onions, leaving them whole. Trim and finely chop the celery. Combine the plain flour, herbs and a good seasoning of salt and pepper. Cut the meat into 8 portions and coat with the seasoned flour.

Heat the oil in a large frying pan, add the onions and fry over a moderate heat until golden brown. Add the celery and cook a little longer to soften it. With a slotted spoon transfer the vegetables to a large deep casserole.

Add the meat to the hot oil and seal on both sides. Add to the vegetables in the casserole. Pour the stock, wine, tomato purée and vinegar into the frying pan and bring to the boil. Pour over the meat and vegetables, cover, and cook in the oven for 1 hour.

Meanwhile peel the parsnips and cut into chunky pieces. Stir into the casserole with the chestnuts. Re-cover and cook for a further 45 minutes.

Towards the end of the cooking time make the dumplings: sift the flour, salt and pepper and mustard powder into a bowl, add the suet, and stir in enough cold water to make a soft but not sticky dough. Turn on to a floured worktop and divide into 8 portions. Lightly roll each portion into a ball with floured fingers.

Arrange the dumplings on top of the meat and vegetables. Replace the lid and cook for a final 15–20 minutes, then serve.

YORKSHIRE POPOVERS

Yorkshire Pudding is traditionally served with roast beef and we have adapted the recipe to make Yorkshire Popovers. The batter is baked in individual bun/muffin pans and puffs up into light crisp popovers. Try them with other meats, sausages or chops.

Basic Batter Place the ingredients in a processor or blender in the order listed: 150 ml/ 1/4 pint milk, 150 ml/1/4 pint cold water (or 300 ml/1/2 pint skimmed milk), 4 eggs, 100 g/ 4 oz plain flour and a pinch of salt. Buzz until you have a smooth batter. Alternatively, sift the flour and salt into a bowl, make a well in the centre and crack in the eggs. Add the liquid. Stir the eggs and liquid from the centre, drawing in the flour from the sides, and mix to a smooth batter. Whichever method you follow pour the batter into a jug and chill for at least 1 hour.

Heat the oven to 220°C/425°F/gas mark 7.

Heat 5 ml/1 teaspoon beef dripping or oil in each of 12 bun or muffin tins for 8–10 minutes until really hot. Stir the batter and pour into each tin – not more than half full. Return to the oven immediately and bake for 15–20 minutes. Do not open the oven door during the cooking time. Loosen from the tins and turn out to serve. Makes 12 popovers.

Steak and Onion Pan-fry

SERVES 2

- 2 thick-cut sirloin or fillet steaks
- freshly milled pepper
- 2 medium onions
- 50 g/2 oz butter
- 5 ml/1 level teaspoon caster sugar
- 15 ml/1 tablespoon white wine vinegar
- salt and a grating of nutmeg
- 45 ml/3 tablespoons crème fraîche

Take the steaks out of the refrigerator 30 minutes beforehand and season both sides with freshly milled pepper. Peel the onions, leaving them whole, then slice finely and separate the onion rings.

Set a good-sized dry frying pan over the heat for a moment, and add the butter so it sizzles and melts. Add the steaks. Cook over a high heat for a moment or two, then lower to a medium heat. Cook the steaks 6 minutes for rare, 8–10 minutes for medium and 12–15 minutes for well done. Turn the steaks once only, half-way through the cooking time. Lift the steaks from the pan and keep warm.

Add the onion rings to the hot fat in the pan and sprinkle with the sugar. Stir and cook the onions over a medium heat until soft and golden – about 10 minutes. Stir in the vinegar, season with salt and a grating of nutmeg. Add the crème fraîche and stir until the sauce comes to the boil. Serve the steaks with the creamy onion sauce.

Steak and Kidney Pudding

SERVES 4

700 g/1½ lb rump steak
225 g/8 oz beef kidney
1 large onion
300 ml/½ pint beef stock
150 ml/¼ pint red wine
salt and freshly milled pepper
5 ml/1 teaspoon tomato purée
1 bay leaf
225 g/8 oz self-raising flour
100 g/4 oz shredded suet
1.25 ml/¼ teaspoon dried mixed herbs

Ahead of time: heat the oven to 180°C/350°F/gas mark 4.

Trim the meat and cut into bite-sized pieces. Using scissors, snip away the core from inside the beef kidney and cut the kidney into small pieces. Peel and slice the onion. Put the steak, kidney and onion in a casserole dish. Add the stock, wine, salt and pepper, tomato purée and bay leaf. Cover and place in the oven for 1½ hours. Allow the meat filling to cool.

Butter a 1.1 litre/2 pint pudding basin. Sift the flour into a bowl and mix in the suet, salt and pepper and herbs. Add 150 ml/¼ pint cold water and mix with a fork to a soft but not sticky dough. Lightly knead on a floured worktop. Cut off one-third of the dough and set aside.

Roll the larger portion of dough to a circle large enough to line the basin plus about 5 cm/2 inches to spare all round. Dust the circle of pastry with flour, fold in half, carefully lift into the basin and open out again. Gently press the pastry to the sides of the basin, working with the fingertips from the bottom to the top. There should be about 10 cm/4 inches excess pastry all round the top.

Using a slotted spoon, spoon in the meat filling. Add gravy to three-quarters fill the basin. Reserve the remainder.

Heat the oven to 180°C/350°F/gas mark 4.

Turn the excess rim of pastry in over the filling. Roll

out the reserved pastry to make a lid. Damp the pudding pastry rim with water and place the lid on top. Press to seal and trim the edges. Cut a double thick piece of foil large enough to fold a pleat across the centre (to give the pudding crust room to rise). Cover the pudding, tucking the foil snugly around the edge of the basin.

Stand the pudding in a roasting tin and add boiling water to come at least 2.5 cm/1 inch up the sides of the pudding basin. Completely enclose the tin with foil to seal in the steam. Carefully place in the hot oven and leave to steam cook for 2 hours – there is no need to top up the water. Serve the pudding from the basin, wrapped in a clean napkin. Reheat the reserved gravy for serving separately.

PERFECT ROAST VENISON

Modern farming methods have produced venison with a rich gamey flavour and guaranteed succulence and tenderness. At local farm shops you can often buy wild venison, but only in season. Farmed venison is increasingly available in supermarket meat departments and butcher shops, prepacked in a variety of cuts for roasting, grilling and casseroling. Classed as a red meat, venison compares very favourably in calories and fat content with fish and chicken. The flesh is darker than beef but leaner, which means extra attention is needed in the cooking. Usually sold boned and rolled, the saddle joint (loin) and haunch joint (leg) provide the best roasting joints.

- Allow 175 g/6 oz uncooked meat per person.
- Follow the tips listed in For the Very Best Roasts (see page 101), especially rubbing in plenty of oil to overcome venison's natural dryness. The oil could be flavoured with garlic or lemon zest. Leave the meat to soak up the oil for several hours before cooking. Alternatively, wrap the joint in rashers of streaky bacon.
- Calculate the cooking time: allow 20 minutes per 450 g/1 lb.
- Place the venison in the roasting tin and loosely cover with a tent of foil, or use a covered roasting tin.
- Preheat the oven to 190°C/375°F/gas mark 5.
- Baste frequently with the hot fat in the roasting tin.
- Open the foil (or remove the roasting tin lid) for the last 20 minutes of the cooking time to allow the meat to brown.
- At the end of the cooking time, turn the oven heat off and let the venison stand in the warm oven for 20 minutes. This allows the pink juices to disperse within the meat.
- Carve venison in very thin slices and serve on very hot plates.
- Serve roast venison with a sharp fruit jelly such as quince, rowan or redcurrant.

PLATE FIVE
Courgette with Green and Red Onion Relish (page 62) with Minted Lamb Kebabs (page 98), and Corn and Sweet Pepper Relish (page 62)

PLATE SIX

Spaghetti with Seafood Sauce and Anchovy Crumbs (page 125)

CHAPTER SEVEN

Pasta

Pasta must surely be one of the original convenience foods, it's so quick to cook. Just add a simple sauce or dressing for a satisfying lunch or supper – these recipes are easy to make and sure to please.

FRESH PESTO

You only need to touch the leaves of fresh basil and you are aware of their enticing fragrance. Leafy potted basil plants or vacuum packs of basil leaves are readily available in the supermarket or greengrocer. Simply strew the leaves over a sliced tomato salad or over a bowl of hot pasta tossed with a good olive oil. When basil is abundant, make fresh pesto, in which the leaves are pounded with Parmesan, pine-nuts and olive oil. In a food processor or liquidizer, it takes just seconds – the colour is a wonderful green and the flavour deliciously pungent.

Some cooks wouldn't consider making pesto without including garlic, others like to include pine-nuts, walnuts or even hazelnuts. Use nuts simply shelled, or toast them to bring out even more of their flavour. Either stir the nuts in a frying pan (without any oil) over a low heat or place them in a baking tin and heat in the oven when cooking something else. Cook until pale golden brown and cool before use. Another way to vary the sauce is to use other herbs in place of basil. The following recipes are all equally delicious.

Classic Basil Pesto Place about 40 g/1½ oz basil leaves (about 2 basil plants) in a food processor with 2 cloves of garlic, peeled and sliced. Add 25 g/1 oz pine-nuts, a seasoning of salt and freshly milled pepper and 50 g/2 oz grated Parmesan. Cover and buzz to make a thick purée. With the processor running, pour in 100 ml/4 fl oz olive oil to make a thick green dressing. Don't over-process – the pesto shouldn't be completely smooth.

Black Olive and Basil Pesto Place about 40 g/1½ oz basil in the food processor with 75 g/3 oz pitted black olives, a seasoning of salt and freshly milled pepper and 25 g/1 oz grated Parmesan. Cover and buzz to a thick purée. With the processor running, add 100 ml/4 fl oz olive oil to make the dressing.

Parsley and Walnut Pesto Rinse 25 g/1 oz parsley (the nipped-off tops of a 50 g/2 oz supermarket bag) in cold water and thoroughly dry in a teatowel. Place in a food processor with 2 cloves of garlic, peeled and sliced, and 25 g/1 oz chopped chives. Add 50 g/2 oz broken walnuts, 50 g/2 oz grated Parmesan and a seasoning of salt and freshly milled pepper. Cover and buzz to a coarse purée. With the processor running, pour in 225 ml/8 fl oz olive oil to make a thick green dressing.

Chive and Hazelnut Pesto Coarsely cut up 40 g/1½ oz chives. Place in the food processor with 2 cloves of garlic, peeled and sliced. Add 50 g/2 oz toasted hazelnuts, 50 g/2 oz grated Parmesan and a seasoning of salt and freshly milled pepper. Cover and buzz to a coarse purée. With the processor running, pour in 225 ml/8 fl oz olive oil to make the dressing.

To serve fresh pesto To 225 g/8 oz freshly cooked pasta add 30–45 ml/2–3 tablespoons pesto and an extra 15 ml/1 tablespoon olive oil. Lightly toss together. Serve hot or cold. Stir a spoonful or two into vegetable soup for a pungent flavour boost; add to a vinaigrette for dressing vegetable or rice salads or use in place of garlic butter for hot herb breads.

To store fresh pesto Pesto will keep in the refrigerator for up to 4 weeks. Spoon into a screw-topped jar and pour a thin layer of olive oil over the surface to seal it and preserve the beautiful colour. Stir this oil in before using the pesto.

Ricotta and Courgette Lasagne

SERVES 6 [V]

- 3 medium onions
- 2 cloves of garlic
- 450 g/1 lb courgettes
- 30 ml/2 tablespoons olive oil
- 2 (400 g) cans chopped tomatoes
- 30 ml/2 tablespoons tomato purée
- 15 ml/1 tablespoon red wine vinegar
- 5 ml/1 level teaspoon dried oregano
- 5 ml/1 level teaspoon sugar
- salt and freshly milled pepper
- 450 g/1 lb ricotta or curd cheese
- 1 bunch (6–8) spring onions
- 2 eggs
- 600 ml/1 pint milk
- 50 g/2 oz butter
- 50 g/2 oz plain flour
- pinch of nutmeg
- 6–8 lasagne sheets, regular or spinach-flavoured
- 50 g/2 oz grated Parmesan

The day before serving: start with the vegetable sauce. Peel and finely chop 2 of the onions. Peel and crush the garlic. Trim and slice the courgettes. Heat the oil in a large saucepan, add the onions and cook, covered, over a low heat until soft and just beginning to brown. Add the garlic and cook for a moment longer, then add the courgettes. Cover and cook for about 10 minutes, then stir in the tomatoes, tomato purée, vinegar, oregano, sugar and a seasoning of salt and pepper. Cover and cook for 15–20 minutes or until you have a soft vegetable ragoût. Draw off the heat.

While the ragoût is cooking make the cheese filling. Turn the ricotta or curd cheese into a large bowl. Trim the spring onions, then finely chop all the white part and some of the green stems. Add to the cheese with the eggs and a seasoning of salt and pepper. Mix well – the texture should be soft and easy to spread. Set aside while making the béchamel sauce.

Pour the milk into a saucepan and add the remaining onion, peeled and cut in half. Bring to a simmer, then draw off the heat and leave to infuse for about 15 minutes. Remove the onion and add the butter, flour and nutmeg. Cook over a medium heat, whisking continuously until the sauce is smooth and thickened. Season to taste. ([M] Combine the ingredients in a large bowl. Cook for 3–4 minutes, stirring every minute, until the sauce boils and thickens. Season to taste.)

Lightly grease a 1.7 litre/3 pint rectangular baking dish with sides about 5 cm/2 inches deep. Evenly cover the base of the dish with half the vegetable ragoût and cover with a layer of lasagne sheets. Spoon over the cheese mixture and spread evenly. Top with another layer of lasagne and the remaining vegetable ragoût. Cover with a final layer of pasta and pour over the béchamel sauce, making sure the pasta is completely covered. Lightly cover and refrigerate for 12 hours or overnight.

Heat the oven to 190°C/375°F/gas mark 5.

Sprinkle with the Parmesan. Set in the preheated oven for 45 minutes or until the top is golden brown and the pasta tests soft throughout when pierced with a knife. Remove from the oven and leave to stand for 10 minutes before cutting into portions.

HOW TO COOK BETTER PASTA

- Use a large saucepan with plenty of water to allow the pasta to move around – allow 1.1 litres/2 pints for every 225 g/8 oz pasta. Add 5 ml/1 teaspoon salt for every 1.1 litres/2 pints water.
- Let the water come to a rolling boil then feed the pasta in gradually so the water stays at a brisk bubble. Tease out or shake loose coils of fresh pasta before adding them to the water or you may finish up with a sticky clump.
- Filled pasta such as ravioli must be cooked only at a gentle simmer or they may puff and burst. It may be easier to cook these in a single layer in a large frying pan.
- Follow the cooking directions on the packet for dried pasta, as times do vary. Fresh pasta cooks more quickly than dried – when it rises to the surface of the cooking water it's ready. Test the pasta by lifting out a piece and biting into it. Pasta should be *al dente*, meaning it still has some bite to it and is not completely soft.
- Pasta left to stand in the cooking water will continue to soften, so drain it immediately it is cooked – tip it into a colander, then shake gently to remove excess water.
- Turn drained pasta into a hot serving bowl and add any sauce or, if the pasta is to be served plain, gently stir in a little good olive oil, melted butter or a couple of spoonfuls of the cooking water (see Simple Additions to Pasta, page 122).
- In the microwave: use a very large bowl and quantities as above. Cook uncovered on HIGH/100%. 225 g/8 oz needs 7 minutes, 450 g/1 lb 10 minutes, stirring gently half-way through the cooking time. At the end of the cooking time, stir, cover and leave to stand 5 minutes. (Timings given are for 650 watt ovens.)
- Oven-baked pasta: baked pasta dishes such as lasagne do not need pre-cooked pasta so long as a sufficiently moist sauce is used and the prepared dish is allowed to stand, covered, for 12 hours or overnight in the refrigerator before baking. This way the pasta sheets have time to absorb the liquid and soften.

  Cook at 190°C/375°F/gas mark 5 for about 45 minutes or until the top is golden brown and the pasta feels soft throughout when tested with the point of a knife. Layered dishes such as lasagne will cut more neatly if allowed to stand 10 minutes after removing from the oven.

Ravioli with Grilled Peppers and Sweet Onions

SERVES 4 V

2 large yellow peppers
2 medium red onions
350 g/12 oz fresh ravioli (vegetable or cheese filling)
90 ml/6 tablespoons extra virgin olive oil
30 ml/2 tablespoons lemon juice
30 ml/2 tablespoons fresh thyme leaves
salt and freshly milled pepper

Quarter the peppers lengthwise and remove the seeds. Peel the onions and slice into rings. Line the rack of the grill pan with foil and lightly brush with oil. Arrange the peppers and onions in a single layer and lightly brush with oil. Place under a preheated grill about 7.5 cm/3 inches from the heat. Grill until the peppers are blistered and charred, the onions golden brown. Cover with a cloth and leave for 10 minutes, by which time the peppers should be cool enough to handle. Peel off the charred skins of the peppers and cut into chunky pieces. Keep the peppers and onions warm.

Meanwhile, cook the ravioli according to the packet directions in boiling salted water. To avoid breaking them, this is most easily done using a large frying pan instead of a saucepan. When cooked, drain well and turn into a large bowl. Whisk together the olive oil, lemon juice, thyme and a good seasoning of salt and pepper. Turn the ravioli to coat them with the dressing.

Arrange the peppers and onion slices on hot serving plates. Add the ravioli and serve hot.

ITALIAN CHEESES

Parmesan Parmesan is a hard cheese with a distinctive grainy texture. Look for the name 'Parmigiano Reggiano' on the crust for genuine Parmesan. For the fullest flavour buy in a piece and keep well wrapped until required. Use a swivel-type potato peeler to shave off flakes to eat with fruit or shower over salads. Buzz in a processor or blender to coarse crumbs for sprinkling on pasta, or grate for a flaked effect.

In addition to using in Italian-style recipes, combine Parmesan with Cheddar for a very well-flavoured cheese sauce; add to a pastry mix when making a quiche; sprinkle over vegetable soups or green salads.

Gorgonzola Ranked as one of the world's greatest blue cheeses together with Stilton and Roquefort, Gorgonzola combines a sharp flavour with a rich creamy texture. Choose cheese that is soft, not discoloured where it has been cut, and that smells sweet.

Fold nuggets of Gorgonzola into hot pasta; arrange fresh pear wedges on a piece of buttered toast, top with a slice of Gorgonzola and grill until bubbling and brown; combine with a sliced avocado, drizzle with an oil and lemon juice dressing and serve as a starter.

Dolcelatte A semi-soft blue-veined cheese with a milder flavour than Gorgonzola.

Serve with fresh fruit and biscuits for dessert.

Mozzarella A true mozzarella is made with buffalo milk, but it is more easily found made with cow's milk. A soft, spongy, bland cheese, it has a slightly creamy taste. It is sold packed in whey or ready grated.

Drain and slice to top pasta dishes or *crostini*; combine with sliced tomatoes, black olives and a well-seasoned olive oil dressing for a salad; grate and sprinkle over pizzas.

Bel Paese A semi-soft cheese with a mild creamy taste and a dark yellow waxy rind. It is usually served as a dessert cheese but also melts well and could be used in place of mozzarella in cooking.

Mascarpone A rich, fresh cream cheese with the texture of thick whipped cream, mascarpone is usually sold packed in tubs. Make sure you buy it very fresh.

Serve spooned on to fresh fruit; fold in chopped glacé fruits or grated chocolate or flavour with a liqueur, and spoon into small glasses and serve with Italian Amaretti biscuits for a very rich dessert.

Ricotta A plain, bland, milky-tasting whey cheese, ricotta is sold packed in tubs in supermarkets or loose in Italian delicatessens. It should be used very fresh. It is used in both sweet and savoury recipes – curd cheese could be used as a substitute.

Combine with meat, fish or vegetables to fill pasta and pancakes; sweeten and flavour with fruits or liqueurs to serve as a simple dessert or to stuff crêpes.

SIMPLE ADDITIONS TO PASTA

Quickly cooked pasta is ideal as a side dish when time is short. Add extra flavour and interest by tossing the freshly cooked and drained pasta with one of the following:

- Sesame oil and sesame seeds.
- Garlic or herb butter.
- Breadcrumbs cooked until crisp in butter or olive oil.
- Extra virgin olive oil and torn basil leaves.
- Melted butter flavoured with sweet chilli sauce.
- Hazelnut oil and finely chopped toasted hazelnuts.
- Soy sauce.
- Lots of chopped fresh herbs plus a knob of butter.
- Thinly sliced onion fried until golden brown and crisp.
- Finely chopped spring onions or chives.
- Pesto with a little extra olive oil (see page 118).

Penne with Yellow Peppers and Gorgonzola

SERVES 3–4 [V]

2 large yellow sweet peppers
1 medium onion
175 ml/6 fl oz vegetable stock
225 g/8 oz penne (pasta quills)
2–3 fresh sage leaves
100–175 g/4–6 oz Gorgonzola

Halve the peppers and remove the stem, core and seeds. Cut the flesh into fine shreds. Peel the onion and slice into thin rings. Put the vegetables into a saucepan and add the stock. Simmer gently until tender – about 10 minutes. ([M] Cook 7 minutes or until tender, stirring once or twice.)

Meanwhile, add the pasta to a large pan of boiling water and stir until the water comes back to the boil. Cook the pasta for 8–10 minutes. (Or [M].) Drain well.

Tip the pasta into a warm serving bowl and add the vegetables, with any remaining stock, and the sage. Break the cheese into small pieces and stir in. Serve quickly before the cheese has completely melted.

REHEATING PASTA

If you have over-estimated quantities, pasta without a sauce reheats well from chilled or frozen. Pack the cooled pasta in freezer bags and chill (for up to 3 days) or freeze.

- To reheat: place the bag (no need to thaw first) in a pan of simmering water, with the sealed end held above the water. Simmer until the pasta feels soft and hot.
- To reheat in the microwave: remove any metal ties and fold the open end under the frozen pasta. Heat 225 g/8 oz for 1–2 minutes on HIGH/100% until piping hot.
- To reheat baked pasta such as lasagne: allow the pasta to thaw first then reheat, covered, at 180°C/350°F/gas mark 4 until bubbling hot throughout.
- To reheat baked pasta in the microwave: thaw, covered, on DEFROST/30% until soft throughout. Reheat, covered, on MEDIUM-HIGH/75% until piping hot throughout.
- Reheated baked pasta dishes should feel very hot to the touch in the centre of the base of the dish. Allow to stand for a few minutes before cutting and serving.

Cappelletti with Ham and Cream

SERVES 3–4

- 350 g/12 oz fresh cappelletti with any filling
- 1 medium onion
- 25 g/1 oz butter
- 150 ml/¼ pint double cream
- 5 ml/1 teaspoon coarse grain mustard
- 100 g/4 oz sliced smoked ham
- freshly milled pepper
- freshly grated Parmesan

Add the cappelletti to a large saucepan of boiling water and gently stir until the water has come back to the boil. Reduce the heat to a simmer and cook the pasta for 12–15 minutes. It will rise to the surface of the water when ready.

Meanwhile, peel and finely chop the onion. Melt the butter in a frying pan. Add the onion and gently cook until very soft – about 5 minutes. Stir frequently and do not allow to brown. (M 3 minutes.) Stir in the cream and the mustard and heat until just bubbling around the edges. Draw off the heat. (M 2 minutes.) Finely shred the ham and add to the pan.

Drain the cappelletti, shaking well to remove all the water. Tip into a warmed serving bowl and add the cream mixture and a good seasoning of pepper. Lightly stir to coat the pasta with the sauce.

Pass the Parmesan separately.

Pasta Quills with Stir-fried Asparagus

SERVES 4 V

- 4 eggs
- 700 g/1½ lb asparagus
- 175 g/6 oz penne (pasta quills)
- 60 ml/4 tablespoons olive oil
- 45 ml /3 tablespoons vegetable stock
- 30 ml/2 tablespoons tarragon or white wine vinegar
- 5 ml/1 level teaspoon Dijon mustard
- 30 ml/2 tablespoons chopped fresh tarragon

Place the eggs in a pan of cold water and bring quickly to the boil. Reduce the heat and simmer for 6 minutes. Drain and immediately cover with cold water.

Snap off and discard the woody ends of the asparagus. Line up several spears at a time and cut on the diagonal into 2.5 cm/1 inch pieces.

Cook the pasta according to the packet directions in a large pan of boiling salted water (or M).

Meanwhile, place a 25 cm/10 inch frying pan (use one with a lid) over a medium heat. Add 15 ml/1 tablespoon of the oil. Add the asparagus and stir-fry for 1 minute, then add the stock. Cover with the pan lid and simmer for 3 minutes or until the asparagus pieces are tender but crisp. Draw off the heat.

Whisk together the remaining olive oil with the vinegar, mustard and cut-up tarragon leaves. Pour over the asparagus and lightly stir.

Drain the pasta well and tip into a large bowl. Add the stir-fried asparagus with its dressing and toss to mix. Season with freshly milled pepper. Turn on to a large warm serving platter.

Carefully peel the eggs – remember they are still soft in the middle – cut in half and arrange on top of the dish. Scatter over the tarragon leaves and serve immediately.

freshly milled pepper
a few whole tarragon leaves

Spaghetti with Seafood Sauce and Anchovy Crumbs

Illustrated on Plate Six

SERVES 4

Gradually add the spaghetti to a large pan of boiling water, pushing the strands until they are under the water. Stir until the water comes back to the boil. Cook for 8–10 minutes.

Meanwhile, cover the tomatoes with boiling water and leave to stand a few minutes. When the skins begin to split, remove from the water. Peel off the skins and cut each tomato into thick slices, discarding the stem end. Peel and crush the garlic.

Heat the oil in a large frying pan and add the tomatoes and garlic. Cook over a low heat for 10 minutes, stirring once or twice and adding the cooked shellfish for the last 5 minutes.

Tip the contents of the can of anchovies into a processor or blender. Tear the bread into quarters and add to the anchovies. Buzz until you have anchovy-flavoured crumbs. Quickly fry until golden brown.

450 g/1 lb spaghetti
450 g/1 lb ripe tomatoes
2 cloves of garlic
30 ml/2 tablespoons olive oil
350 g/12 oz cooked and shelled prawns or mussels
2 slices white bread
1 (50 g) can anchovies

Drain the spaghetti and turn into a large warmed serving bowl. Add the seafood sauce and toss lightly to coat the pasta. Serve topped with the anchovy crumbs.

ALMOST INSTANT SAUCES

Quick meals for 2 people – just cook 225 g/8 oz pasta of any shape, drain well and add one of the following sauces:

Smoky Tomato and Garlic [V] Tip a 285 g jar of sun-dried tomatoes packed in oil into a blender or processor with 3 peeled smoked (or fresh) cloves of garlic and 150 ml/¼ pint hot water. Buzz until the tomatoes and garlic are finely chopped. Pour into a small saucepan and heat, stirring constantly, until bubbling hot. Season with freshly milled pepper and add to the pasta.

Pimento and Parmesan [V] Drain a 185 g tin of pimentos and cut into slivers. Peel and finely chop 1 small onion and 1 clove of garlic. Cook the onion and garlic in 15 ml/1 tablespoon oil until soft, then add the pimentos and 150 ml/¼ pint hot vegetable stock. Heat until bubbling hot. Stir into the pasta and serve sprinkled with 45 ml/3 tablespoons grated Parmesan.

Butter and Herbs [V] Heat 100 g/4 oz garlic or herb butter until bubbling hot. Toss with the pasta and sprinkle generously with chopped fresh herbs such as parsley or chives.

Pesto and Cream [V] Gently heat a 190 g jar of pesto with 150 ml/¼ pint single cream. Pour over the pasta and toss lightly.

Mushroom and Bacon Finely chop 4 rashers of smoked streaky bacon and cook with 125 g/4 oz sliced mushrooms until golden brown. Add 30 ml/3 tablespoons dry sherry and cook until the liquid has almost evaporated. Stir in 150 ml/¼ pint whipping cream and heat through. Season to taste and add to the pasta.

Tomato and Black Olives [V] Whisk together a 230 g can chopped tomatoes, 30 ml/2 tablespoons pesto sauce and 150 ml/¼ pint crème fraîche. Gently heat until bubbling. Add a seasoning of salt and freshly milled pepper and 25 g/1 oz pitted and sliced black olives. Spoon over the pasta.

Bacon and Sour Cream Finely chop 100 g/4 oz smoked streaky bacon and cook until golden brown. Add 100 g/4 oz thinly sliced ripe tomatoes and 2 crushed cloves of garlic. Cook until soft. Stir in 150 ml/¼ pint soured cream, 30 ml/2 tablespoons mayonnaise and 30 ml/2 tablespoons chopped fresh thyme. Gently heat until the mayonnaise has melted, then spoon over the pasta.

SIMPLE PASTA SIDE SALADS

Pasta plus a well-flavoured dressing and a few other ingredients makes a very good side dish to serve with cold meats or cheeses. Pasta shapes are better for salads than noodles or spaghetti because the curves and twists hold the dressings best – shells, spirals and bows are especially pretty. Cook 225 g/8 oz pasta to package directions. While the pasta is cooking, make the chosen dressing in a large salad bowl. Drain the pasta, taking particular care to remove all the water, to avoid diluting the dressing. Add the pasta to the dressing, lightly turning it to coat with the dressing. Serve at room temperature soon after making. Each recipe serves 4 as a side salad.

Indonesian Pasta Salad [V] Combine, in a large salad bowl, 30 ml/2 level tablespoons smooth peanut butter, 30 ml/2 tablespoons lemon juice, 15 ml/1 level tablespoon soft brown sugar, 30 ml/2 tablespoons soy sauce and 45 ml/3 tablespoons olive oil. Whisk until smooth, then add a seasoning of salt and freshly milled pepper and 15 ml/1 tablespoon sesame oil. Add the hot pasta and gently stir to coat with the dressing. Stir in any of the following: chopped spring onions, grated carrot, toasted sesame seeds, beansprouts or sliced water chestnuts.

Tex-Mex Pasta Salad [V] Combine, in a large salad bowl, 30 ml/2 tablespoons white wine vinegar, 5 ml/1 level teaspoon sweet chilli sauce, 5 ml/1 level teaspoon soft brown sugar, 1 crushed clove of garlic and 75 ml/3 fl oz olive oil. Whisk until smooth, then add a seasoning of salt and freshly milled pepper and 5 ml/1 level teaspoon crushed dried chilli flakes. Add the hot pasta and gently stir to coat with the dressing. Stir in any of the following: chopped spring onions, de-seeded and chopped red peppers, diced avocado or sweetcorn kernels.

Curried Pasta Salad Turn the hot pasta into a large bowl, add 15 ml/1 tablespoon olive oil and toss. Allow to cool slightly. Meanwhile, whisk together 100 ml/4 fl oz mayonnaise, 100 ml/4 fl oz natural yogurt, 10 ml/2 level teaspoons curry paste, 5 ml/1 level teaspoon tomato purée, 15 ml/1 tablespoon mango chutney (chop up any large pieces of fruit) and 15 ml/1 tablespoon lemon juice. Add to the cooled pasta and gently toss. Stir in any of the following: cooked peeled prawns, de-seeded and chopped red pepper, diced red-skinned apples, salted peanuts.

Pesto Pasta Salad In a large salad bowl whisk together 45 ml/3 tablespoons prepared pesto (page 118), 60 ml/3 tablespoons olive oil, 15 ml/1 tablespoon fresh lemon juice, a seasoning of salt and freshly milled pepper and 15 ml/1 tablespoon coarsely chopped fresh parsley. Add the hot pasta and gently toss. Stir in any of the following: halved cherry tomatoes, nuggets of feta cheese, slivers of Italian salami, black or green olives.

SUN-DRIED TOMATOES

Sun-dried tomatoes in their 'raw' state are dark red, shrivelled and dry as a bone, but they have a deliciously intense tomato flavour. To use, put them into a tomato sauce, vegetable soup or meat casserole (where there is plenty of liquid) and they will soften and swell during cooking. Or soak them for two minutes in hot water, then add to any dish for a rich tomato flavour. If using on top of a dish such as a pizza, add for the last few minutes of cooking as they have a tendency to burn because of their high sugar content.

Sun-dried tomatoes packed in oil are ready to spoon into a dish or salad. Serve with mozzarella and crusty bread as a quick meal. For a speedy pasta sauce, tip the tomatoes and oil into a blender or processor and buzz until smooth. Toss with hot pasta. A spoonful added to an oil and vinegar dressing makes a delicious tomatoey salad dressing. Store opened jars of tomatoes in oil or unused puréed tomatoes in the fridge.

Sun-dried tomato paste should not be confused with concentrated tomato purée. The paste has a sweeter, fruitier flavour. Stir it into risotto, hot pasta, mayonnaise or oil and vinegar dressings. After spooning the paste from the jar, add a little olive oil to seal the surface and it will last for ages, stored in the fridge.

Fusilli Salad with Parma Ham

SERVES 4

2 slices white bread
1 clove of garlic
75 ml/5 tablespoons olive oil
1 bunch (6–8) spring onions
100 g/4 oz fresh or frozen green peas
4 slices *prosciutto* (Parma ham)
175 g/6 oz fusilli (pasta spirals)
100 ml/4 fl oz vegetable stock
30 ml/2 tablespoons sherry vinegar
freshly milled pepper
2 Little Gem lettuces

Trim the crusts from the bread and cut into neat dice. Peel and crush the garlic. Heat 30 ml/2 tablespoons of the oil in a frying pan and add the garlic and diced bread. Cook over a medium heat, stirring constantly, until golden brown. Drain on absorbent kitchen paper.

Trim and shred the celery. Trim the spring onions and finely slice all the white and some of the green stems. If using frozen peas, place in a strainer and pour boiling water through. When thawed, rinse with cold water and dry on kitchen paper. Cut the *prosciutto* into bite-sized pieces.

Cook the pasta according to the packet directions in a large pan of boiling salted water (or [M]).

Meanwhile, pour the stock into a 25 cm/10 inch frying pan (use one with a lid), add the celery and bring to a simmer. Cover and simmer for 4 minutes to tenderize the celery. Add the onions and peas and cook a further 2 minutes. Draw off the heat. Add the vinegar and remaining oil.

Drain the pasta and turn into a large bowl. Add the vegetable mixture and the dressing from the pan. Season with freshly milled pepper.

Trim away the outer coarse leaves of the lettuces, cut into wedges and arrange on a serving platter. Spoon over the pasta salad, add the *prosciutto* and sprinkle with the *croûtons*. Serve immediately.

Tortelloni Salad with Artichokes and Broccoli

SERVES 4 [V]

- 450 g/1 lb trimmed broccoli florets
- 1 (400 g) can artichoke hearts
- 100 ml/4 fl oz olive oil
- 30 ml/2 tablespoons red wine vinegar
- 15 ml/1 level tablespoon coarse grain mustard
- 5 ml/1 level teaspoon Dijon mustard
- 15 ml/1 level tablespoon soft brown sugar
- salt and freshly milled pepper
- 250 g/8 oz fresh spinach and cheese tortelloni
- 75 g/3 oz pitted green olives
- shavings of Parmesan

Divide the broccoli florets into bite-sized pieces and thinly slice the stems. Drain the artichoke hearts and cut each one in half through the centre.

Combine the olive oil, vinegar, mustards, sugar and a seasoning of salt and pepper in a small bowl and whisk together.

Cook the tortelloni according to the directions on the packet in a large pan of boiling salted water. (Or [M].) Tip the broccoli pieces on top of the pasta to steam for the last 2–3 minutes of the cooking time.

Drain the pasta and broccoli well and turn them into a large bowl. Add the dressing and gently mix to coat the pasta. Add the artichoke hearts and olives and turn to mix.

Spoon the tortelloni salad on to a serving platter. Pare shavings of Parmesan (with a vegetable peeler) and scatter over the top. Serve immediately.

CHAPTER EIGHT

Grains, Beans and Pulses

Grains, beans and pulses have an important place in today's healthy diet. Used imaginatively they overcome their previous poor image, as recipes with surprising variety and wide appeal.

GRAINS, BEANS AND PULSES FROM A – Z

Grains, beans and pulses are among some of the earliest foods known to have been eaten by man. Along with potatoes, rice and pasta they form the basis of most traditional and ethnic diets. Many are a rich source of protein and are valuable in a vegetarian diet. With the popularity of the Mediterranean style of diet and new processing methods which have reduced the lengthy cooking time of many of these foods, they are rapidly gaining in popularity in our own recipes today.

We have given the methods we like to use. However, we recommend taking a look at the packaging instructions of the brand you have bought as they do vary. Where a microwave cooking method has not been given, it indicates that little time is saved. The use of a pressure cooker may reduce the cooking time.

Barley

Pot (or Scotch) barley needs soaking overnight. Pearl barley doesn't, as it has been steamed and polished to remove the outer husk, thus eliminating the need for soaking and at the same time reducing the cooking time. Traditionally used in stews and soups, barley can also be used in place of rice in recipes or as a side dish.

Basic method Soften a small onion, finely chopped, in 15 ml/1 tablespoon oil. Stir in 225 g/8 oz pearl barley and cook for 2 minutes. Stir in 600 ml/1 pint hot stock, cover and cook for 30–40 minutes, stirring once or twice. Season before serving. Serves 4.

Beans

Dried beans must be soaked in cold water for at least 8 hours or overnight before cooking. After soaking, drain the beans and rinse thoroughly before covering with cold water and bringing to the boil. Boil hard for 10 minutes, then cover, lower the heat to a simmer and cook for up to 1–1¼ hours until tender. Do not overcook them, as they will break up. Beans need a minimum length of time to rehydrate, and microwave cooking is not very much quicker than conventional. Using a pressure cooker, however, will shorten the cooking time. Canned beans are the ultimate time-saver. Tip the beans into a sieve and rinse under cold running water before use. Beans absorb flavours better when they are hot. When making a bean salad, cover the rinsed beans with fresh cold water, bring just to the boil, then drain well before tossing in the dressing.

Bulgar

Bulgar is produced from wholewheat grains which have been steamed, dried and then broken into tiny pieces. It can be served simply soaked and added to other ingredients, as in Bulgar Salad with Fruits and Nuts (page 136), or cooked and served like rice. Some people find bulgar salads more digestible if the grain is cooked, cooled and then added to a dressing.

Basic method If wished, first soften a finely chopped onion or leek in 30 ml/2 tablespoons olive oil. Stir in 225 g/8 oz bulgar and 300 ml/½ pint stock or water. Bring to a simmer, stirring. Cover and cook over a low heat for 15 minutes until the liquid is absorbed. Draw off the heat and allow to stand for 10 minutes. Streaky bacon could be frizzled in the pan first and chopped herbs added at the end of the cooking time. Serves 4.

Microwave cooking Cook a small finely chopped onion in 15 ml/1 tablespoon oil on HIGH/100% for 2 minutes. Stir in 225 g/8 oz bulgar and 300 ml/½ pint boiling water or stock. Cook on HIGH/100% for 6 minutes. Cover and allow to stand 5 minutes.

CORNMEAL

This is ground corn, called cornmeal in the USA and polenta in Italy. It may be finely or coarsely ground and can vary in colour from pale cream to bright yellow. It can be used in baking, is the staple ingredient of one variety of gnocchi, and, as polenta, may be served in place of potatoes, rice or pasta.

Basic method Bring 1.7 litres/3 pints half water/half milk to the boil. Slowly add 300 g/10 oz cornmeal, stirring constantly and briskly. Continue to cook, stirring rapidly, until smooth and thickened. Reduce the heat to low and simmer for 20 minutes, stirring frequently to avoid the mixture catching on the base of the pan. Season to taste, and stir in a good knob of butter and some grated Parmesan. Serves 4–6.

Microwave cooking Pour 600 ml/1 pint cold water into a large bowl. Stir in 100 g/4 oz cornmeal. Cook on HIGH/100% for 12 minutes, stirring once or twice. Stir in a knob of butter and some salt and pepper, cover, and allow to stand 3 minutes. Serves 2–3.

Serve freshly cooked as a side dish, or spread the cooked cornmeal in a shallow buttered baking dish and allow to cool completely before cutting into squares for making Gnocchi with Pancetta and Tomato Ragù (page 139). Alternatively, cut into fingers, brush with butter or olive oil, and grill until golden brown on both sides. Serve with grilled meats or casseroles.

COUSCOUS

Couscous is actually very minute pellets of semolina. It needs to be cooked, traditionally by steaming, and is served with stews of meat or vegetables in a sauce. Cold cooked couscous can be made into a salad.

Basic method Measure 450 ml/¾ pint cold water and 2.5 ml/½ level teaspoon salt into a saucepan. Bring to the boil. Remove from the heat and stir in 225 g/8 oz couscous. Cover and let stand for 5 minutes. Add a knob of butter or 15 ml/1 tablespoon olive oil and lightly fork through to separate the grains. Serves 4. A stock cube or the zest and juice of a lemon may be added to the water.

Microwave cooking Place 75 g/3 oz couscous in a medium bowl and pour over 300 ml/½ pint boiling water or stock. Stir then cook on HIGH/100% for 5 min. Cover and allow to stand 2–3 minutes. Add a knob of butter or a little olive oil and fork to separate the grains before serving. Serves 2.

FLAKES

A wide variety of flaked grains can be found in wholefood shops and supermarkets. Use in baking or choose a combination to make muesli (see page 142).

LENTILS AND SPLIT PEAS

No need to soak. Split red lentils and green and yellow split peas cook to a soft purée to serve as a side dish such as the Indian dish called Dhal or in thick, satisfying soups. Whole lentils are cooked until soft to the bite but retain their shape. They readily absorb added flavours, such as the dressing in the Green Lentil and Pepperoni Salad (page 147). We find canned green lentils an excellent item to have in the cupboard for quick salads. Like beans, they absorb the dressing more readily if they are brought just to the boil first.

OATMEAL

There are various grades of oatmeal, defined by the degree of cutting or milling applied to the whole oat grains. Coarse pinhead oatmeal can be used in place of rolled oats to make a very coarse porridge. Other grades of oatmeal include medium, used in the recipe for Oatmeal Bread (page 148).

Quinoa

Quinoa is a highly nutritious golden-coloured grain from South America which has recently become available in our shops. It is an important addition to vegetarian diets. A few minutes toasting in a non-stick frying pan will enhance the golden colour and give a rich flavour. It is then cooked in stock or water until it has absorbed all the liquid. Serve as a side dish or add to dishes such as casseroles towards the end of the cooking time. Check the packaging for preparation and cooking times.

Bulgar and Sweet Pepper Salad

SERVES 4 [V]

- 175 g/6 oz bulgar
- 1 large lemon
- 1 vegetable stock cube
- 2 medium onions
- 2 yellow peppers
- 30 ml/2 tablespoons olive oil
- 5 ml/1 level teaspoon sugar
- 50 g/2 oz seedless raisins
- 50 g/2 oz toasted pine-nuts
- 30 ml/2 tablespoons sesame oil
- salt and freshly milled pepper

Tip the bulgar into a large bowl. Finely grate the lemon rind and extract the juice, and add to the bowl. Dissolve the stock cube in 450 ml/¾ pint boiling water, add to the bulgar and lightly mix together. Cover with a folded teatowel and leave to stand 20–30 minutes to allow the grains to absorb all the liquid.

Peel and thinly slice the onions. Cut the peppers into quarters, removing and discarding the stems and seeds. Cut into chunks.

Heat the oil in a large frying pan and add the onions. Sprinkle with the sugar and cook over a medium heat, stirring frequently, until soft and pale golden brown. Add the pepper pieces and continue to cook until they begin to colour. Add to the bulgar with the raisins, pine-nuts and sesame oil. Season with salt and pepper and lightly mix together.

Leave for 1–2 hours at room temperature to allow the flavours to blend.

Bulgar with Chicken and Brazil Nuts

SERVES 4

75 g/3 oz brazil nuts
50 ml/2 tablespoons olive oil
1 large lemon
2 large onions
2 red peppers
4 large boneless chicken breasts, skinned
freshly milled black pepper
10 ml/2 teaspoons dried cinnamon
15 ml/1 tablespoon clear honey
100 g/4 oz ready-to-eat dried apricots
175 g/6 oz bulgar
1 vegetable stock cube

Cover the brazil nuts with boiling water and leave to stand for 5 minutes. Drain well and cut into slices. Heat 15 ml/1 tablespoon of the oil in a large frying pan, add the nuts and cook over a high heat until golden brown, stirring constantly. Remove from the pan with a slotted spoon and drain on kitchen paper.

In a small pan cover the whole lemon with cold water. Bring just to the boil, then reduce the heat to low and simmer for 5 minutes.

Remove from the water, cool a minute or two, then put on a plate to avoid losing any juice and cut into 8 wedges. Discard any pips.

Peel and finely slice the onions. Cut the peppers into chunky pieces, discarding the stem and seeds. Cut each chicken breast into 3 and season with pepper.

Add the remaining oil to the frying pan, add the chicken pieces and quickly cook over a high heat until golden brown on all sides. Remove from the pan.

Add the onion to the hot pan drippings and cook for 5 minutes, stirring frequently, until it begins to brown. Sprinkle with the cinnamon and add the honey. Add the red pepper chunks, apricots, lemon wedges with any juice, and the bulgar.

Dissolve the stock cube in 600 ml/1 pint boiling water and add to the pan. Stir well and bring just to the boil. Add the chicken pieces, gently pushing them into the pan. Cover and cook over a low heat for 20 minutes, until the chicken is cooked through and the bulgar has absorbed the stock.

Serve sprinkled with the brazil nut chips.

Bulgar Salad with Fruits and Nuts

SERVES 4

V

100 g/4 oz ready-to-eat dried apricots
75 ml/3 fl oz orange juice
225 g/8 oz bulgar
1 vegetable stock cube
30 ml/2 tablespoons olive oil
1 bunch (6–8) spring onions
salt and freshly milled pepper
finely grated rind and juice of 1 lemon
15 ml/1 tablespoon hazelnut oil
50 g/2 oz toasted pine-nuts

Using scissors, cut the apricots into fine slivers into a bowl. Add the orange juice and leave to soak for 1 hour until the apricots are plump and soft.

Measure the bulgar into a large serving bowl. Dissolve the stock cube in 300 ml/½ pint boiling water and pour over the bulgar. Cover with a teatowel and leave to stand until the liquid is absorbed – 20–30 minutes. Lightly mix in the olive oil and leave to cool.

Trim the spring onions, and chop all the white and some of the green stems. Add to the bulgar along with the apricots and any juices in the bowl. Season to taste with salt and freshly milled pepper. Add the lemon rind and juice and the hazelnut oil. Gently turn with a large spoon to combine the ingredients. Just before serving fork in the pine-nuts.

Marinated Peppers with Bulgar Stuffing

SERVES 6

V

175 g/6 oz bulgar
1 vegetable stock cube
2 medium onions
100 ml/4 fl oz olive oil
5 ml/1 level teaspoon caster sugar
15 ml/1 tablespoon fresh thyme
3 lemons
salt and freshly milled pepper
50 g/2 oz seedless raisins
50 g/2 oz pine-nuts
6 yellow or red peppers

Measure the bulgar into a large bowl. Dissolve the stock cube in 225 ml/8 fl oz boiling water and stir into the bulgar. Leave to soak for 20–30 minutes until the stock is absorbed.

Peel and finely slice the onions. Heat 30 ml/2 tablespoons of the oil in a frying pan, add the onions and sprinkle with the sugar. Cook gently, stirring occasionally, until the onions are soft and beginning to take a golden colour. Stir in the thyme. Draw off the heat. Add the finely grated rind and juice of 1 lemon and a seasoning of salt and pepper. Add to the bulgar and mix through. Stir in the raisins and pine-nuts.

Heat the oven to 180°C/350°F/gas mark 4.

Slice the top off each pepper, keeping the stalk intact, and reserve. If necessary, shave the base of each pepper so that it stands level – do not pierce the base – and remove the seeds from inside. Pack the peppers close together in a deep-sided baking dish or casserole.

Spoon the filling into the peppers up to the brim, pressing the stuffing in gently. Cover with the reserved pepper lids. Add 60 ml/4 tablespoons water to the dish and cover with foil or a lid (make sure the foil/lid isn't touching the peppers). Bake for 45 minutes, until the peppers are tender. Remove from the oven.

Whisk together the remaining olive oil, the juice from the remaining 2 lemons and a good seasoning of salt and pepper. Spoon over the peppers. Cover and leave to stand at room temperature until cold.

Lift the stuffed peppers on to a serving platter. Stir the dressing that remains in the baking dish and spoon over the peppers before serving.

Polenta with Chestnut Mushrooms and Smoked Cheese

SERVES 4 [V]

- 1 small onion
- 15 ml/1 tablespoon olive oil
- 1 vegetable stock cube
- 100 g/4 oz cornmeal
- salt and freshly milled pepper
- 450 g/1 lb chestnut mushrooms
- 25 g/1 oz butter
- 100 g/4 oz smoked Cheddar

Finely chop the onion. Heat the oil in a medium-sized saucepan and stir in the onion. Cover and cook over a medium heat until soft and translucent. Dissolve the stock cube in 600 ml/1 pint boiling water and add to the onion. Bring to the boil. Gradually whisk in the cornmeal and cook, stirring constantly, until the mixture boils and is thick, about 10 minutes. (Or [M].) Season.

Line a baking sheet with non-stick baking parchment or lightly oiled foil. Spoon on the polenta, spread level, and shape to approximately 23 cm/9 inches square. Refrigerate until cold and firm – about 2 hours.

Remove the polenta from the refrigerator on the parchment/foil. Lightly oil the baking sheet. Cut the polenta into 4 squares and return to the baking sheet. Lightly brush with oil. Grill the polenta until golden brown, then turn and grill the other side.

Meanwhile, halve the mushrooms if large. Heat the butter in a frying pan, add the mushrooms and cook over a high heat until golden brown. Pile the mushrooms on top of the grilled polenta and cover with thinly sliced cheese. Return to the grill until golden brown. Serve immediately.

Cheese Cornbread

CUTS INTO 8–10 SLICES [V]

150 g/5 oz plain flour
45 ml/3 level teaspoons baking powder
5 ml/1 level teaspoon mustard powder
2.5 ml/½ level teaspoon salt
150 g/5 oz cornmeal
45 ml/3 tablespoons chopped chives
100 g/4 oz mature Cheddar
1 egg
350 ml/12 fl oz milk
30 ml/2 tablespoons grapeseed oil

Heat the oven to 200°C/400°F/gas mark 6.

Oil a 22.5 × 12.5 × 5 cm (9 × 5 × 2 inch) loaf tin and line the base with a strip of greaseproof paper.

Sift the flour, baking powder, mustard powder and salt into a medium mixing bowl. Add the cornmeal and chives. Finely grate the cheese, add to the bowl and mix well. In a smaller bowl combine the egg, milk and oil and whisk with a fork to break up the egg. Add the liquid to the dry ingredients and stir until evenly blended. Turn into the tin and level the top.

Bake for 20–25 minutes or until well risen and browned. Let the cornbread cool in the tin for about 2 minutes before loosening the sides and turning out. Leave on a wire rack until quite cool before cutting into thick slices for serving.

Cornbread is also great toasted.

Gnocchi with Pancetta and Tomato Ragù

SERVES 4–6

Pour the milk into a large saucepan and bring just to the boil over a medium heat. Slowly add the cornmeal, stirring constantly. Cook for 10–15 minutes, stirring to mix in the thickening mixture from the bottom and sides of the pan. When fully cooked, the mixture is very dense and comes cleanly away from the sides of the pan. Remove from the heat and quickly beat in two-thirds of the Parmesan, the egg yolks and a good seasoning of salt and pepper.

Lightly oil a large baking sheet and, using a wet palette knife, spread the cornmeal mixture to a thickness of about 2.5 cm/1 inch. Leave until quite cold, overnight if preferred.

Meanwhile make the ragù. Peel the onion and carrot and very finely chop with the celery. Roughly chop the *pancetta*. Heat the oil in a large saucepan and add the *pancetta*. Cook over a medium heat, stirring frequently, until it begins to brown. Stir in the chopped vegetables and continue to cook until they are soft. Add the tomatoes, vermouth, sugar, tomato purée and sage. Bring to a simmer and cook gently for 20–25 minutes to make a thick tomato sauce.

Heat the oven to 180°C/350°F/gas mark 4.

Cut the cornmeal gnocchi into 5 cm/2 inch squares.

Lightly oil a 1.7 litre (3 pint) rectangular casserole dish. Spoon half the ragù sauce over the base. Arrange the gnocchi squares in overlapping rows like roof tiles. Combine the remaining Parmesan and the breadcrumbs with the melted butter and sprinkle over the top.

Bake until it is very hot and the top is crisp and browned – about 40 minutes. Leave to stand for 5 minutes before cutting into portions. Gently heat the remaining ragù and serve with the gnocchi.

600 ml/1 pint milk
200 g/7 oz cornmeal
75 g/3 oz grated Parmesan
2 egg yolks
salt and freshly milled pepper
1 medium onion
1 carrot
1 stalk celery
100 g/4 oz *pancetta* or streaky bacon
15 ml/1 tablespoon olive oil
2 (397 g) cans chopped tomatoes
45 ml/3 tablespoons dry white vermouth or white wine
15 ml/1 tablespoon sugar
15 ml/1 tablespoon tomato purée
30 ml/2 tablespoons chopped fresh sage
25 g/1 oz fresh white breadcrumbs
25 g/1 oz butter, melted

Couscous with Tomatoes and Blackened Peppers

SERVES 4

V

4 red, yellow or orange peppers
2 medium onions
3 cloves of garlic
15 ml/2 tablespoons oil
5 ml/1 level teaspoon soft brown sugar
30 ml/2 tablespoons crumbled fresh thyme
1 (230 g) can chopped tomatoes
15 ml/1 level tablespoon tomato purée
salt and freshly milled pepper
1 lemon
225 g/8 oz couscous

Quarter the peppers lengthwise and remove the seeds. Arrange the pepper pieces skin side uppermost on the rack of the grill pan. Grill until the skins are charred and blistered. Peel and thinly slice the onions, and peel and crush the garlic.

Heat half the oil in a large frying pan and add the onions. Sprinkle with the sugar and cook over a medium high heat until soft and golden brown. Stir in the garlic and thyme and cook a minute or two. Add the tomatoes, tomato purée and 100 ml/4 fl oz water. Season with salt and pepper. Cook for 10 minutes until the mixture is slightly thickened. Add the peppers to the sauce and heat through. Keep hot.

Meanwhile, measure 450 ml/$^3/_4$ pint water and 2.5 ml/$^1/_2$ level teaspoon salt into a medium saucepan. Finely grate the lemon and add along with the lemon juice. Bring to the boil. Remove from the heat and stir in the couscous. Cover and let stand for 5 minutes. (Or M.) Add the remaining oil and lightly fork through to separate the grains.

Serve the couscous topped with the sauce.

Couscous Salad with Grilled Vegetables

SERVES 6

V *Illustrated on Plate Seven*

2 yellow peppers
2 large onions
2 medium aubergines
olive oil
3 sprigs thyme

Quarter and de-seed the peppers. Peel the onions and cut into thick slices – do not separate the rings. Cut across the aubergines into 1 cm/$^1/_2$ inch slices. Arrange the vegetables on one or more foil-lined baking trays and very lightly brush with olive oil.

Place the vegetables under a preheated grill about 7.5 cm/3 inches from the heat. Grill until brown and tender, then turn the vegetables over, brush with oil and brown the other side. As the vegetables are cooked, transfer them to a shallow platter. Add the sprigs of thyme.

Whisk together 90 ml/6 tablespoons olive oil, the vinegar, mustard and sugar. Peel and crush the garlic and add with a good seasoning of salt and pepper. Spoon half the dressing over the vegetables and leave to marinate for at least 30 minutes or until serving time.

Measure 450 ml/¾ pint water and 2.5 ml/½ level teaspoon salt into a medium saucepan. Finely grate the lemon rind and squeeze the juice. Add to the pan. Bring to the boil. Remove from the heat and stir in the couscous. Cover and let stand for 5 minutes (or [M]). Spoon over the remaining dressing and lightly fork through to separate the grains. Leave to cool.

Pile the couscous in the centre of a large platter and arrange the marinated vegetables around the sides. Sprinkle with the pine-nuts.

- 30 ml/2 tablespoons balsamic or red wine vinegar
- 15 ml/1 level tablespoon wholegrain mustard
- 5 ml/1 level teaspoon muscovado sugar
- 1 clove of garlic
- salt and freshly milled pepper
- 1 large lemon
- 225 g/8 oz couscous
- 50 g/2 oz toasted pine-nuts

Barley, Mushroom and Spinach Pilaff

SERVES 4 [V]

Peel and finely chop the onion. Heat half the butter in a large frying pan and add the onion. Cook over a medium high heat until soft and golden brown. Finely grate the lemon rind and squeeze the juice. Stir into the onions with the barley and stock. Bring to the boil, cover, and reduce the heat to medium low. Cook gently for 30–40 minutes, until the barley is tender and has absorbed the stock. Season with salt and freshly milled pepper.

Just before the barley is cooked, thickly slice the mushrooms and cook in the remaining butter until golden brown. Rinse the spinach in plenty of cold water

- 1 medium onion
- 25 g/1 oz butter
- 1 lemon
- 150 g/6 oz pearl barley
- 625 ml/1¼ pints vegetable stock
- salt and freshly milled pepper
- 225 g/8 oz button mushrooms
- 225 g/8 oz young leaf spinach
- 75–100 g/3–4 oz freshly grated Parmesan

and dry on a teatowel. Roll up the spinach leaves and cut into thin ribbons.

Lightly fork the hot mushrooms and the spinach into the cooked barley and replace the lid for a minute or two to wilt the spinach.

Serve immediately, topped with Parmesan.

Crunchy Apricot Muesli

SERVES 6–8 V

- 225 g/8 oz cereal grains such as oat, barley or wheat flakes
- 50 g/2 oz wheatgerm
- 50 g/2 oz chopped almonds
- 30 ml/2 tablespoons sesame seeds
- 30 ml/2 tablespoons sunflower seeds
- 30 ml/2 tablespoons grapeseed oil
- 60 ml/4 tablespoons clear honey
- 100 g/4 oz ready-to-eat dried apricots

Combine the cereal grains with the wheatgerm, nuts and seeds in a large mixing bowl. Heat the oil and honey in a saucepan until warm and runny. Add to the cereals, lightly tossing together until everything is well mixed.

Heat the oven to 180°C/350°F/gas mark 4.

Turn the muesli mixture into a large roasting tin and spread into an even layer. Bake for 25–30 minutes, stirring once or twice, until an even golden brown.

Cut up the apricots finely and add to the muesli. Let cool completely before storing in an airtight container. Will keep up to 1 month.

Serve with milk or yogurt for breakfast or dessert.

Healthy Flapjacks

MAKES 18 V

- 225 g/8 oz clear honey (see recipe)
- 225 g/8 oz butter
- 350 g/12 oz rolled oats
- 50 g/2 oz chopped almonds
- 50 g/2 oz sunflower seeds
- 30 ml/2 tablespoons sesame seeds

Heat the oven to 180°C/350°F/gas mark 4.

Stand a medium saucepan on the scales and return the scales to zero. Pour in the honey. (Remember to return the scales to zero after removing the saucepan.) Add the butter and set over a low heat to melt.

Measure the oats, almonds, sunflower seeds and sesame seeds into a large mixing bowl. Finely chop the dates and add to the bowl. Pour the melted butter and honey into the dry ingredients and mix well.

75 g/3 oz stoned dates

Turn the mixture into a lightly greased baking tin about 30 × 25 cm/12 × 9 inches and press level, using wet fingers. Set in the preheated oven and bake for 20–25 minutes or until golden.

Leave to cool in the tin and, when half cold, mark into neat divisions with a knife. When quite cold, turn out and break into pieces.

Mixed Bean Salad

SERVES 8 V

- 1 (440 g) can red kidney beans
- 1 (440 g) can chick peas
- 1 (430 g) can borlotti beans
- 1 (430 g) can cannellini beans
- 1 (330 g) can broad beans
- 15 ml/1 level tablespoon tahini
- 30 ml/2 tablespoons sherry vinegar
- 15 ml/1 tablespoon clear honey
- 60 ml/4 tablespoons grapeseed oil
- 30 ml/2 tablespoons soy sauce
- 15 ml/1 tablespoon walnut or sesame oil
- 1 (400 g) can artichoke hearts
- 1 red sweet onion
- 3–4 stalks celery

Tip the contents of each can of beans into a sieve and rinse under cold running water. Place all the beans together in a large saucepan and cover with cold water. Bring to the boil, then drain well and turn into a big serving bowl.

Measure the dressing ingredients into a small bowl and whisk until well combined (or shake in a covered jar). Pour the dressing over the hot beans and stir gently to combine.

Drain the artichoke hearts, cut each in half, and add to the beans. Peel and slice the onion into thin rings. Trim and chop the celery. Add the onion and celery to the bean salad and mix gently.

Cover and marinate for at least 2 hours in the refrigerator before serving. The bean salad can be kept in the refrigerator for 3–4 days, just keep covered, and stir well before serving to distribute the dressing.

White Bean Niçoise

SERVES 4 AS A MAIN DISH

---

1 lemon
5 ml/1 teaspoon Dijon mustard
15 ml/1 tablespoon coarse ground mustard
120 ml/6 tablespoons olive oil
salt and freshly milled pepper
1 (430 g) can cannellini beans
1 bunch (6–8) spring onions
3 stalks celery
30 ml/2 tablespoons chopped parsley
1 large beefsteak tomato
2 (198 g) cans tuna steak
100 g/4 oz black olives

Finely grate the lemon rind and extract the juice. Place the rind and juice in a large bowl. Add both the mustards, the oil and a good seasoning of salt and pepper.

Tip the beans into a strainer and rinse under cold running water. Turn into a saucepan and cover with cold water. Bring to the boil, drain, and add the hot beans to the dressing. Set aside to cool.

Trim the spring onions and finely slice the white and some of the green stems. Scrub and string the celery, then finely slice. Add the spring onions, celery and half the parsley to the beans and lightly mix. Let stand until serving time.

Thinly slice the tomato, discarding the stem, and arrange around the edge of a flat platter. Drain the tuna and break into bite-sized pieces. Spoon the beans into the centre of the platter and top with the tuna and olives. Sprinkle with the remaining chopped parsley.

Broad Bean and Bacon Pan-fry

SERVES 4

---

1 medium onion
6 streaky bacon rashers
15 ml/1 tablespoon olive oil
2 (283 g) cans broad beans
salt and freshly milled pepper
5 ml/1 level teaspoon sugar
10 ml/2 teaspoons white wine vinegar

Peel the onion and slice into thin rings. Trim the bacon and cut into 2.5 cm/1 inch pieces. Using a large frying pan, cook the bacon in the oil over a medium heat to draw out the fat and crisp the bacon pieces – about 8 minutes. With a slotted spoon, transfer the bacon to a plate.

Add the onion rings to the hot pan drippings and cook until soft and golden brown. Meanwhile, drain and rinse the beans. When the onion rings are tender, add the beans and the crisp bacon pieces. Season with salt and pepper, sugar and the vinegar. Heat gently for 2–3 minutes, stirring to ensure the beans heat through thoroughly.

Serve hot as a vegetable – it's particularly good with sausages – or cool to room temperature and serve as a salad with hot garlic bread.

Boston Baked Beans

SERVES 6–8

450 g/1 lb dried haricot beans
225 g/8 oz smoked streaky bacon rashers
1 onion
2 cloves
25 g/1 oz light muscovado sugar
30 ml/2 tablespoons black treacle
15 ml/1 tablespoon tomato purée
15 ml/1 level tablespoon Dijon mustard
5 ml/1 level teaspoon salt
freshly milled pepper
2 (227 g) smoked sausages
squeeze of lemon juice

Put the beans in a large bowl, cover generously with cold water and leave to soak overnight.

Drain the beans and put them in a large saucepan with fresh cold water to cover, about 1.1 litres (2 pints). Bring just to the boil, cover with the pan lid and simmer gently for 1 hour. Roughly chop the bacon, removing any rind.

Heat the oven to 140°C/275°F/gas mark 1.

Transfer the beans and the cooking liquid to a large casserole and add the bacon. Peel the onion and stick the cloves into it. Add to the pan, pushing it under the beans.

In a small bowl, blend the sugar, treacle, tomato purée, mustard, salt and a seasoning of pepper with a ladleful of the bean liquid, then stir into the beans. Cover the casserole, set in the oven and cook for 2–3 hours.

Remove the skin from the sausages and slash the meat in several places with a sharp knife (it looks more attractive). Add to the casserole about 20 minutes before the end of the cooking time. Before serving, check the taste, adding a squeeze of lemon juice to sharpen the flavour if necessary.

BEAN SPREADS

Quick bean spreads make a snack into a nutritious light meal. With the aid of a processor they take minutes to make and will keep, covered, for 2 days in the refrigerator. The variations are numerous: beans will happily marry with tuna, smoked mackerel, crisp bacon – the following two are our favourites.

Serve with hot toast or fresh bread plus simple salad additions – wedges of lettuce, sliced tomatoes, celery or cucumber fingers.

Chick Pea and Anchovy Turn the contents of a 397 g can chick peas into a sieve and rinse under cold water. Drain well and tip into a processor. Add a 50 g can of anchovies, lifting them out of the can with a fork so that a little of the oil goes in with them, freshly milled pepper and the juice of 1/2 a lemon. Blend to a purée. Check whether the mixture needs any additional salt, then spoon into a serving bowl. Lightly stir in 8 sliced pitted black olives.

Butter Bean and Peanut [V] Turn the contents of a 415 g can butter beans into a sieve and rinse under cold water. Drain well and tip into a processor. Blend to a smooth purée. Add 50 g/2 oz salted peanuts, 45 ml/3 tablespoons olive oil, freshly milled pepper and the juice of 1 lemon. Blend to a chunky purée. Taste and add salt if needed.

CHILLIES

Chillies are the pungent members of the large and varied capsicum family, which also includes the more familiar sweet and mild red, yellow and green peppers. Only in recent years have fresh chillies become available here and even then only a few of the many varieties – the Jalapeño chilli is the most common. Chillies vary considerably in size and heat intensity – as a general rule, the smaller the chilli the more fiery the flavour. Red chillies are green chillies which have been allowed to ripen, which makes them sweeter in flavour but hotter too.

Chillies have to be handled with care. Take care not to touch the eyes or mouth when preparing them, and always wash your hands well after handling them – the astringent juices are very irritating.

To use in a recipe, split the pod lengthwise, remove and discard the seeds, then shred or finely chop the flesh. Chopped fresh chillies are used in curries and spiced dishes to pep up the flavour. You can add them to stuffings, relishes or salads. Use small quantities at first and add to taste.

Chilli powder is an aromatic blend of spices with chilli powder as the basic ingredient. Choose a mild or hot blend depending on your taste.

Cayenne pepper is pure ground hot red chillies – it's very hot, so use only a pinch.

Dried chilli flakes (sometimes called crushed chillies) are coarsely ground chilli pods and seeds and are also hot.

Tabasco sauce is a hot pepper sauce in a bottle with a shaker top so that it comes out a drop at a time. Use as a seasoning.

Hot chilli sauce and **sweet chilli sauce** are made from crushed chillies, vinegar and sugar and are used to add a fiery flavour to stir-fries or marinades.

Green Lentil and Pepperoni Salad

SERVES 4

Peel and thinly slice the onion. Heat 15 ml/1 tablespoon olive oil in a large frying pan, add the onion and sprinkle with the sugar. Cook over a medium high heat until the onion is soft and golden brown, stirring frequently. Stir in the garlic.

Roughly chop the sausages, add to the pan and cook a minute or two. Add the remaining oil, the vinegar, soy sauce and a seasoning of salt and pepper.

Drain the lentils and tip into the pan. Gently stir and bring just to the boil. Spoon into a serving bowl. Leave to marinate for at least 1 hour in a cool place (cover and keep in the refrigerator if leaving overnight).

Halve, peel and thickly slice the avocados. Arrange on individual plates and spoon the lentil salad on top. Serve immediately.

1 medium onion
60 ml/4 tablespoons olive oil
10 ml/2 level teaspoons sugar
2 cloves of garlic
100 g/4 oz chorizo sausages
30 ml/2 tablespoons red wine vinegar
30 ml/2 tablespoons soy sauce
salt and freshly milled pepper
1 (432 g) can green lentils
2 ripe avocados

Lentil, Bacon and Apple Soup

SERVES 4 AS A MAIN DISH

Peel and finely chop the onion and carrots. Peel and core the apple and cut into chunks. Snip off any rind from the bacon and cut the rashers across into 1 cm/½ inch strips.

Fry the bacon in a large saucepan until crisp and brown. Remove with a slotted spoon and reserve. Add the butter and onion to the hot bacon drippings, cover with the pan lid and cook over a low heat until soft but not brown.

Return half the reserved bacon to the pan. Add the carrots, apple, lentils, stock and bay leaf. Bring to the boil, then lower the heat and simmer gently, covered, for

1 medium onion
2 carrots
1 large cooking apple
100 g/4 oz smoked streaky bacon
15 g/½ oz butter
175 g/6 oz split red lentils
1.1 litres/2 pints vegetable stock
1 bay leaf
freshly milled pepper

45 minutes or until the lentils and vegetables are quite tender. Discard the bay leaf.

Purée until smooth. Return the soup to the saucepan and reheat to serve. Season to taste with freshly milled pepper.

Serve in warm bowls, sprinkled with the reserved crisp bacon bits.

Oatmeal Bread

MAKES 1 LOAF V

150 g/5 oz medium oatmeal
150 ml/¼ pint natural yogurt
350 g/12 oz plain flour
30 ml/2 level tablespoons baking powder
5 ml/1 level teaspoon salt
extra oatmeal for sprinkling

Measure the oatmeal into a large mixing bowl. Whisk the yogurt into 300 ml/½ pint water and stir into the oatmeal. Leave to soften the oatmeal for at least 1 hour.

Heat the oven to 190°C/375°F/gas mark 5.

Place a sieve over the mixing bowl. Measure in the plain flour, baking powder and salt and sift over the softened oatmeal. Using a table knife, stir and cut through the ingredients to make a soft dough. Turn the dough on to a floured surface and knead about 3 times, just to remove the cracks. Shape into a round and cut a deep slash across the centre.

Place the dough in a greased 20.5 cm/8 inch round deep cake tin and sprinkle generously with extra oatmeal. Bake for 25–30 minutes, or until well risen and brown. Turn on to a wire cooling rack and leave until cold. Oatmeal bread is best 24 hours after baking; it is also delicious toasted. Serve cut in thick slices.

PLATE SEVEN
Couscous Salad with Grilled Vegetables (page 140)

PLATE EIGHT

Fragrant Rice with Summer Garden Vegetables (page 158)

Crunchy Topping

SERVES 6–8 [V]

Heat the oven to 190°C/375°F/gas mark 5.

Combine the oat flakes, sugar, nuts and cinnamon in a bowl. Melt the butter and add to the bowl, stirring well so that everything is thoroughly mixed.

Spread the mixture in a large roasting tin. Bake for 15–20 minutes, stirring about every 5 minutes, until the mixture is golden brown.

As the topping cools, it becomes crisp and crunchy. When quite cold, store in an airtight container for up to 3 months.

Serve sprinkled on poached fruits, yogurt, fresh fruit salads or ice-cream.

- 100 g/4 oz oat flakes
- 50 g/2 oz soft brown sugar
- 25 g/1 oz chopped toasted almonds
- 2/5 ml/½ level teaspoon ground cinnamon
- 75 g/3 oz butter

CHAPTER NINE

Rice

Be adventurous in your choice of rice – today none of the varieties is hard to find. Rice readily absorbs any flavour, to make a wide variety of recipes, hot or cold. Combine with spices, herbs, vegetables, fruit, seafood or chicken to make simple yet imaginative dishes.

GLOSSARY OF RICES

White rice has been polished to remove the outer layer of bran. Some rice, even when polished, may still be quite a creamy or golden colour.

Brown rice (also called wholegrain rice) is unpolished and retains the layers of bran so that it is brownish in appearance. It has a firm chewy texture and a nutty flavour. Brown rice takes a little longer to cook.

Long-grain rice (also called Patna) has slim grains that cook up light, dry and fluffy. It is a good choice when rice is to be served as an accompaniment. Basmati rice is a particularly fine-quality long-grain rice with a distinctive flavour that blends well with spices. To promote the aromatic flavour, soak basmati rice in water for 1 hour before cooking.

Easy-cook rice (may also be labelled pre-cooked or pre-fluffed) has been steamed under pressure before milling. This process hardens the grains and helps to keep them well separated and whole during cooking. It doesn't necessarily mean the cooking time is shorter than ordinary long-grain rice, but it does make it a good choice for anyone who is hesitant about cooking rice.

Quick-cook rice has already been cooked and then dried. Check the packet instructions for cooking times.

Arborio rice (also called risotto rice) has round plump grains which swell and cling together when cooked and become tender and creamy. This rice is very good at absorbing liquids and is traditionally used to make the classic Italian risotto. Other varieties are Avorio or Superfino, which are a yellow colour but become white when cooked.

Glutinous rice (or sticky or sweet rice) is used in Chinese or Japanese dishes. The creamy-coloured medium-sized round grains cook to a sticky soft texture suitable for eating with chopsticks. It is sold in Oriental food stores. Jasmine rice is a particularly aromatic glutinous rice with a delicate flavour. At a pinch pudding rice could be used in place of glutinous rice.

Wild rice is not actually a rice. The slim dark grains are the seeds of an aquatic grass grown in North America, and it has a distinctive flavour that is popular with gourmets. Wild rice is usually combined with long-grain rice, either brown or white, to make an attractive combination that looks good on the dinner party table.

Pudding rice (or short-grain rice) has small rounded or oval grains which become very soft and creamy on cooking. It is used for traditional sweet rice puddings.

Boil-in-the-bag rice is packed in two-portion-sized bags. The rice is already cooked and the bags are simply added to the pan of boiling water for the specified reheating time.

Canned or frozen rice is ready-cooked white or brown long grain-rice. Useful for fast meals, single portions, or recipes that call for pre-cooked rice.

Chickpea, Mango and Basmati Salad

SERVES 4 [V]

Peel and finely chop the onion. Peel the ginger root and grate the flesh. Tip the rice into a strainer and rinse under cold running water. Drain well.

Heat 15 ml/1 tablespoon of the oil in a large saucepan, add the onion and ginger and cook over low heat until soft. Stir in the rice and stock and bring just to the boil. Cover and simmer for 45 minutes, until the rice is tender and the stock absorbed. Drain and rinse the chick peas and add to the hot rice.

To make the dressing, whisk together the remaining 45 ml/3 tablespoons oil, the soy sauce, sugar and the finely grated rind and juice of the lemon. Add a good seasoning of salt and pepper.

Add the dressing to the hot rice and fork through gently to avoid breaking the rice grains. Leave to cool at room temperature. Just before serving the salad, peel and dice the mango and add, with the cashew nuts.

1 medium onion
5 cm/2 inches fresh ginger
225 g/8 oz brown basmati rice
60 ml/4 tablespoons grapeseed oil
600 ml/1 pint vegetable stock
1 (432 g) can chick peas
30 ml/2 tablespoons soy sauce
15 ml/1 tablespoon soft brown sugar
1 large lemon
salt and freshly milled pepper
1 large mango
100 g/4 oz toasted cashew nuts

Brown Basmati with Lamb and Ginger

SERVES 4

Heat the oven to 180°C/350°F/gas mark 4.

Peel and finely chop the onions. Peel and coarsely grate the ginger. Drain the pineapple and reserve the juice. Cut the pineapple into chunky pieces.

Heat the oil in a 1.1–1.7 litre/2–3 pint flameproof casserole. Add the onion, cover and cook gently for about 5 minutes to soften the onion. Add the lamb pieces and stir to seal the surfaces of the meat. Stir in the grated ginger and the rice.

Add the stock, the reserved pineapple juice and the soy

2 medium onions
2.5 cm/1 inch fresh ginger
1 (432 g) can pineapple spears
45 ml/3 tablespoons oil
450 g/1 lb lean cubed lamb
225 g/8 oz brown basmati rice
600 ml/1 pint vegetable stock
30 ml/2 tablespoons soy sauce
100 g/4 oz cashew nuts

sauce. Bring to the boil, stirring once or twice, then cover with the casserole lid and set in the heated oven. Cook, undisturbed, for 1 hour.

Meanwhile, spread the cashew nuts on a baking tray and toast under the grill, or place in the oven with the casserole for 10–15 minutes, until golden.

When the lamb and the rice grains are tender and the liquid in the casserole absorbed, add the pineapple pieces and the nuts. Re-cover to warm the pieces of fruit for 1–2 minutes, then fork through the ingredients and serve.

Spiced Yellow Rice with Chicken Brochettes

SERVES 4

2.5 cm/1 inch fresh ginger
1 small green chilli
6 cardamom pods
10 ml/2 teaspoons oil
225 g/8 oz basmati rice
25 g/1 oz currants
5 ml/1 level teaspoon turmeric
4 cloves
1 cinnamon stick
600 ml/1 pint vegetable stock
2 cloves of garlic
100 g/4 oz butter
60 ml/4 tablespoons chopped fresh parsley
salt and freshly milled pepper
8 boned chicken thighs

Remove the brown outer skin of the ginger and finely chop the flesh. Split the chilli and remove the seeds. Finely chop the flesh (wash your hands afterwards as chillies can irritate the skin). Take the black seeds out of the cardamom pods.

Heat the oil in a large pan over a medium heat. Add the ginger and cook for 30 seconds. Stir in the chilli, cardamom seeds, rice, currants, turmeric, cloves and cinnamon and cook, stirring, for 1 minute. Add the stock and bring to the boil. Reduce the heat to low, cover, and simmer for about 15 minutes until the rice has absorbed the stock and is tender.

Meanwhile, peel and crush the garlic cloves and blend into the butter together with the parsley. Season with a little salt and plenty of black pepper. Open out the chicken thighs and spread each with a little of the butter. Roll up (with the skin on the outside) and thread on to 4 long skewers. Melt the remaining garlic butter. Arrange the chicken on a rack (lined with foil) and brush with the melted butter. Place under a preheated grill 7.5 cm/

3 inches from the heat source. Grill until golden brown and cooked through, turning frequently and basting with the pan juices – about 15 minutes.

Remove the cinnamon stick from the rice and pile on to a serving dish. Arrange the chicken brochettes on top. Combine the buttery pan juices with any remaining melted garlic butter and spoon over the chicken.

Aubergines Stuffed with Cajun Rice

SERVES 4

- 4–5 streaky bacon rashers
- 1 medium onion
- 2 cloves of garlic
- 2 medium aubergines
- 15 ml/1 tablespoon olive oil
- 100 g/4 oz long-grain rice
- 1 (397 g) can chopped tomatoes
- 15 ml/1 tablespoon caster sugar
- salt and freshly milled pepper
- dash of Tabasco sauce
- a little extra oil
- 50–75 g/2–3 oz smoked Cheddar

Trim the streaky bacon and cut in small pieces. Peel and finely chop the onion. Peel and crush the garlic. Halve the aubergines lengthwise and scoop out the flesh, leaving the aubergine shells intact. Coarsely chop the aubergine flesh.

Heat the oil in a 25 cm/10 inch frying pan (use one with a lid). Add the bacon and fry gently to draw the bacon fat. Add the onion to the pan and fry until the onion is softened and the mixture is lightly browned. Stir in the rice and the garlic and mix into the onion and bacon.

Add 150 ml/¼ pint water, the tomatoes, the cut-up aubergine flesh, the sugar, a seasoning of salt and pepper and a dash of Tabasco. Bring to a simmer, cover, and cook gently for 20–30 minutes or until the rice grains are tender and the liquid absorbed. Draw off the heat. (This rice filling could be made ahead.)

Heat the oven to 180°C/350°F/gas mark 4.

Blanch and soften the aubergine shells by putting them in a colander and pouring over boiling water from the kettle. Arrange the shells in a 1.1 litre/2 pint shallow baking dish and brush the insides of each one with a little oil. Spoon the rice filling into the shells. Add 30–45 ml/3–4 tablespoons water to the baking dish and cover with foil.

Set in the heated oven and bake for 40 minutes. Then remove the foil and cover each aubergine with very thin slices of the smoked cheese. Return to the oven for a further few moments to melt the cheese before serving.

Mixed Rice with Chicken and Citrus Fruits

SERVES 4

---

4 boneless chicken thighs
4 chicken drumsticks
2 yellow peppers
1 large onion
15 g/½ oz butter
30 ml/2 tablespoons oil
225 g/8 oz wild and long-grain rice mix
900 ml/1½ pints chicken stock
salt and freshly milled pepper
150 ml/¼ pint double cream
1 orange
1 lemon

Trim the chicken pieces and remove the skin, if you like. Halve, de-seed and coarsely cut up the yellow peppers. Peel and thinly slice the onion.

Heat the butter and oil in a 25 cm/10 inch frying pan (use one that has a lid). Add the chicken pieces and fry to brown, turning frequently. Remove the chicken pieces from the pan.

Add the onion to the pan drippings and fry gently until softened. Add the rice mix and stir through the onions. Stir in the stock, add the peppers and arrange the chicken pieces on top. Bring to a simmer, cover with the pan lid and cook gently for 30–40 minutes until the chicken is tender and the rice grains have absorbed the liquid. Season with salt and freshly milled pepper.

Meanwhile pour the cream into a small bowl. Add the finely grated rind of the orange and the lemon. With a sharp knife cut away the pith and peel from both the fruits (round and round like an apple), then slice into the flesh and lift out the segments. When the rice and chicken are ready, pour over the cream and add the fruit segments. Lightly fork through before serving.

SIMPLE ADDITIONS TO RICE

The addition of just a few simple ingredients, either before cooking the rice or just after, adds colour, flavour and crunch and makes it more appetizing, especially when serving it as an accompaniment. All varieties of rice can be used – just add extra liquid if using a brown rice. Each recipe serves 4.

Before cooking the rice . . .

Green Herb Rice Soften a finely chopped medium onion in a little butter. Stir in 225 g/8 oz rice, 600 ml/1 pint vegetable stock and the finely grated rind of 1 lemon. Cook to basic method (page 160). Finely chop 6–8 spring onions and 30 ml/2 tablespoons parsley. Fork into the hot rice. Serve with chicken or fish.

Minted Butter Rice Soften a finely chopped medium onion in a little butter. Stir in 225 g/8 oz uncooked rice, 5 ml/1 teaspoon dried mint and 600 ml/1 pint vegetable stock. Cook to basic method (page 160). Fork in a little extra butter and some finely chopped fresh mint. Good with lamb.

Herb and Garlic Rice Soften a finely chopped medium onion and 1–2 crushed cloves of garlic in a little butter. Stir in 225 g/8 oz uncooked rice and 600 ml/1 pint vegetable or chicken stock. Cook to basic method (page 160). Fork in 15–30 ml/1–2 tablespoons chopped fresh herbs such as chives or parsley. Serve with grilled chops or steaks.

Golden Rice Soften a finely chopped medium onion in a little butter or oil. Stir in 10 ml/2 teaspoons turmeric and cook a minute longer. Add 225 g/8 oz rice and 600 ml/1 pint vegetable or chicken stock. Cook to basic method (page 160). Fork in 25 g/1 oz toasted flaked almonds and raisins. Good with curries.

Chilli Rice Soften a finely chopped onion and 1–2 crushed cloves of garlic in a little butter or oil. Stir in 225 g/8 oz rice, 600 ml/1 pint tomato juice and 15–30 ml/1–2 tablespoons sweet chilli sauce. Cook to basic method (page 160). Good with hamburgers, sausages or gammon steaks.

After cooking the rice . . .

Coconut Rice Add 50 g/2 oz creamed coconut, finely chopped, and a knob of butter to 450 g/1 lb hot rice (225 g/8 oz uncooked weight). Cover and allow to stand for 5 minutes before lightly forking through. Serve with a chicken or fish curry.

Woodland Mushroom Rice Quickly cook 225 g/8 oz thickly sliced brown cap or button mushrooms in a little butter. Add 30 ml/2 tablespoons dry sherry, toss to combine, then fork into 450 g/1 lb hot cooked wild rice mix. Top with a few toasted sliced brazil nuts. Good with steaks.

Spiced Rice Add 5ml/1 teaspoon each fennel and yellow mustard seeds to 25 g/1 oz hot melted butter. Cook 1 minute then add 5 crushed black peppercorns. Fork into 450 g/1 lb hot cooked basmati rice. Serve with curries.

Speckled Garlic Rice Flake 50 g/2 oz garlic butter on to 450 g/1 lb hot cooked rice. Cover and allow to stand 5 minutes. Add 30 ml/2 tablespoons finely snipped chives and lightly fork through. Serve with white meats or fish.

Fragrant Rice with Summer Garden Vegetables

SERVES 2 V

- 100 g/4 oz Thai Fragrant rice
- 450 ml/¾ pint vegetable stock
- 1 clove of garlic
- 1 bunch spring onions
- 2 small courgettes
- 100 g/4 oz mangetout
- 3 medium-sized ripe tomatoes
- 15 ml/1 tablespoon olive oil
- 30 ml/2 fl oz dry white vermouth
- 30 ml/2 tablespoons chopped fresh tarragon

Rinse the rice under cold running water and drain well. Bring the stock to the boil in a saucepan and stir in the rice. Bring back to the boil, then reduce the heat to low. Cover and cook for 10–12 minutes, until the rice is tender and has absorbed the stock.

Meanwhile, peel and crush the garlic clove. Trim the spring onions and chop all the white part and some of the green stems. Trim the courgettes and cut into thin slices. Blanch the mangetout by placing them in a colander and pouring over boiling water from the kettle. Halve the tomatoes, scoop out the seeds and cut the flesh into chunks.

Heat the oil in a large wok or frying pan and add the crushed garlic, spring onions, courgettes and mangetout. Cook, stirring constantly, over a high heat for 3–4 minutes. Add the tomatoes, vermouth and tarragon. Continue to heat until bubbling hot, then spoon in the hot rice and very gently turn to combine with the vegetables. Serve piping hot.

MOULDED RICE

Rice looks very smart moulded into a ring, which can be filled with a curry or with meat, poultry or fish in a sauce, or into individual sized portions unmoulded straight on to the dinner plate.

Simply add 50 g/2 oz butter in flakes to 450 g/1 lb freshly cooked hot rice and fork through. Spoon evenly into a buttered ring mould or 4 teacups and press down gently.

To unmould, place the serving plate upside down on the ring mould. Turn the right way up and gently remove the mould. Turn individual servings out on to hot dinner plates.

Any of the suggestions in Simple Additions to Rice (see page 157) could be served this way, as could a rice salad (see page 165).

Chestnut Mushroom Risotto

SERVES 4 [V] *Illustrated on Plate Eight*

Place the eggs in a pan of cold water and quickly bring to the boil. Reduce the heat and simmer for 6 minutes, then drain the eggs and plunge them into cold water to arrest the cooking.

Peel and finely chop the onions. Heat the oil in a 25 cm/10 inch frying pan, add the onion and cook gently over a medium heat to soften. Add the rice, stirring to coat the grains with the oil and onion, and cook for a further 2 minutes. Stir in 300 ml/½ pint of the hot vegetable stock and allow the risotto to cook gently, uncovered. As the liquid is absorbed by the rice, add the remaining stock and the wine, about 150 ml/¼ pint at a time, and the chopped parsley. Stir the mixture frequently to loosen the rice grains – they will be tender by the time the liquid is absorbed – about 25–30 minutes.

Meanwhile, trim the mushrooms, slicing any large ones in half. Melt the butter in a separate frying pan, add the mushrooms and cook over a high heat until golden brown. Shell and halve the eggs.

Turn the risotto on to a hot serving dish and spoon the mushrooms on top. Arrange the eggs around the edge of the plate and serve immediately.

4 eggs
2 medium onions
30 ml/2 tablespoons olive oil
225 g/8 oz Italian risotto rice
450 ml/¾ pint vegetable stock
150 ml/¼ pint dry white wine
30–45 ml/2–3 tablespoons chopped fresh parsley
350 g/12 oz chestnut mushrooms
50 g/2 oz butter

HOW TO COOK BETTER RICE

- Choose the right rice for your recipe – see the Glossary of Rices (page 152). Don't just use one rice, enjoy them all.
- Fragile basmati is the only rice that may need to be washed before cooking – check the packet instructions. If necessary, in a strainer under running water is the best way to remove the starchy residue from the rice grains.
- Soaking any brown rice before cooking will shorten the cooking time, as the outer bran layers begin to soften. Combine the rice and measured cooking water in the saucepan about 30 minutes before cooking.
- Cooking rice by the absorption method, where all the cooking liquid is absorbed by the rice grains, is the most foolproof way. Measure 225 g/8 oz long-grain white rice, a

pinch of salt and 600 ml/1 pint cold water into a medium saucepan. Bring to the boil, stirring once or twice, then cover with the pan lid. Reduce the heat to medium low and simmer for 10–15 minutes (do not lift the lid or stir). When cooked the rice will have absorbed all the liquid and will be tender. If the rice is still firm but all the liquid has gone, it has been cooked too quickly. Add a dash of water and reduce the heat. Cover and continue to cook a little longer. When the rice is cooked, draw the pan off the heat and leave undisturbed for 5–10 minutes while it absorbs the steam. Fluff up with a fork before serving.

For brown rice use 1¼ pints water and cook for 30–40 minutes.

❦ Or you can cook rice in the oven, where it will simmer gently undisturbed. Heat the oven to 180°C/350°F/gas mark 4. Measure 225 g/8 oz long-grain white rice and a pinch of salt into a casserole with a tight-fitting lid. Pour over 600 ml/1 pint boiling water and stir. Cover with the casserole lid, place in the heated oven, and bake undisturbed for 30–40 minutes. When cooked the rice will have absorbed the liquid and will be tender. Fluff with a fork and serve.

For brown rice use 750 ml/1¼ pints water and cook for about 1 hour.

❦ The microwave oven is ideal for cooking rice. Put 225 g/8 oz long-grain white rice in a large casserole. Add 600 ml/1 pint boiling water and stir well. Cook, uncovered, on HIGH/100% for 9 minutes. Cover and leave to stand (in or out of the oven) for 5–10 minutes until all the liquid has been absorbed. Fluff with a fork and season to taste before serving.

For brown rice use 750 ml/1¼ pints water and cook for 18 minutes. Leave to stand for 10 minutes until the water is absorbed and the rice tender. Fluff with a fork and season before serving.

❦ The best way to test whether rice is fully cooked is to bite a grain between your teeth. It should be quite tender but still have a slight bite or firmness to it.

Courgette and Lemon Risotto with Chive Butter

SERVES 4 V

75 g/3 oz butter
freshly milled pepper
25 g/1 oz fresh chives
1 medium onion
10 ml/2 teaspoons olive oil
225 g/8 oz risotto rice
600 ml/1 pint vegetable stock

Cream the butter with a generous seasoning of pepper until light and fluffy. Finely chop the chives and stir in. Set aside.

Peel and finely chop the onion. Heat the oil in a large frying pan (with a lid), stir in the onion and cook, covered, over a low heat until soft but not browned. Add the rice and stir to mix. Add the stock and allow to cook gently, covered, for 15 minutes.

Trim the courgettes and cut into thin slices. Tip into a saucepan of boiling water and quickly bring back to the boil. Turn into a colander and drain well. Finely grate the lemon rind and squeeze the juice.

Stir the vermouth, lemon rind and juice into the partly cooked rice. Place the courgettes on top, cover with the pan lid and cook for a further 10–15 minutes or until the vegetables and rice are tender and the liquid completely absorbed.

Spoon into warm shallow bowls and serve piping hot, topped with a spoonful of chive butter.

225 g/8 oz small courgettes
1 large lemon
100 ml/4 fl oz dry white vermouth

FRESH GINGER

Those extraordinary-shaped, pale-coloured knobbly roots (or more properly rhizomes) that lie along with the more exotic vegetables in vegetable displays are hands of fresh ginger. It has a zesty, clean-tasting and pleasantly spicy flavour. A decent-sized piece will keep a couple of weeks in the salad drawer of the refrigerator.

To use, pare off the brown skin with a vegetable peeler or knife. Our recipes usually call for 2.5 cm/1 inch ginger, which gives you a guide for the quantity. Then grate the root on a kitchen grater, using the coarse side so that the pieces are less likely to clump together when added to a recipe. For a milder flavour, cut the ginger into wafer-thin slices.

The warmth of cooking draws out the essential oils in fresh ginger, which is why it is so good in stir-fries. Heat some oil in a wok or frying pan and add the grated or chopped ginger, spring onions and garlic. Stir for a moment or two to flavour the oil before adding the other ingredients.

For a deliciously aromatic flavour, heat slivers of fresh ginger in the sugar syrup when poaching fruits – this is especially good with pears. For a stylish fruit salad, dice 2 or more different-coloured melons and marinate in a ginger-flavoured syrup. Serve well chilled.

If you don't want to bother with the peeling and grating required for fresh ginger, look for the jars of unsweetened ginger purée, usually among the Oriental ingredients in the supermarket. This is fresh ginger finely puréed and mixed with a little lemon juice or oil to keep it smooth and soft. Store the opened jar in the refrigerator. Add a little to hot apple sauce to serve with pork, or to the dressing for a brown rice salad.

REHEATING RICE

To refrigerate cooked rice Place the leftover cooked rice in a bowl and cover tightly to prevent drying out. It will keep for up to 2 days but should be reheated only once. Reheat for serving as an accompaniment (see below) or use for salads (page 165) or stir-fry (page 25).

To reheat cooked rice Place the cooked rice in a saucepan with a tight-fitting lid. Sprinkle over a little cold water – about 30 ml/2 tablespoons for 225 g/8 oz cooked rice. Cover and set over a low heat for 6–8 minutes or until hot. Resist the temptation to lift the lid. Fluff up with a fork to avoid breaking the rice grains.

Alternatively, turn the cooked rice into a buttered casserole, cover and reheat at 180°C/350°C/gas mark 4 for 15–20 minutes or until hot. Fluff with a fork before serving.

To reheat cooked rice in a microwave Place the rice in a casserole and sprinkle with cold water – 30 ml/2 tablespoons to 225 g/8 oz cooked rice. Cover and cook on HIGH/100% for 2–4 minutes until piping hot, stirring once. Fluff with a fork before serving.

To freeze and reheat cooked rice Freeze the cooked rice in covered freezer containers. To use, thaw and reheat as above. Or freeze in sturdy plastic bags and reheat by placing the bag of still frozen rice in a pan of simmering water until piping hot. Be sure to keep the tightly closed opening of the bag above the water. To reheat in the microwave, remove the metal tie and fold under the open end of the bag. Place the bag of rice on a plate and heat on HIGH/100% – 225 g/8 oz cooked rice will take 2–2½ minutes. Gently shake the bag half-way through the heating time.

Seafood Saffron Rice

SERVES 4

- 1 medium onion
- ½ teaspoon saffron strands
- 25 g/1 oz butter
- 225 g/8 oz risotto rice
- 600 ml/1 pint vegetable stock
- 100 ml/4 fl oz dry white vermouth
- 225 g/8 oz prepared green vegetables – trimmed mangetout, small broccoli florets, asparagus tips or cut green beans
- 450 g/1 lb raw king prawns (see recipe)
- 50 g/2 oz garlic or herb butter

Peel and finely chop the onion. Place the saffron strands in a small cup, add 30 ml/2 tablespoons boiling water and leave to infuse for 10 minutes.

Heat the butter in a 25 cm/10 inch frying pan (use one that has a lid), add the onion and fry gently to soften. Add the rice and stir through the onion and butter. Stir in half the vegetable stock and allow the rice to cook gently, uncovered, for 15 minutes.

Place the vegetables in a colander and blanch them by pouring over boiling water from the kettle. Stir the remaining stock and the vermouth into the rice, and the saffron infusion and the vegetables. Cover with the pan lid and allow the mixture to cook gently for a further

10–15 minutes or until the vegetables and rice are tender and the liquid absorbed.

Meanwhile break off the raw prawn shells. Melt the garlic or herb butter in a second frying pan. Add the prawns and sauté gently for 2–3 minutes until they are pink and cooked through. (Ready-cooked and peeled king prawns can be used, in which case toss them in the hot butter just to heat them through.) Draw the pan of saffron rice and vegetables off the heat, add the prawns and flavoured butter from the pan, gently fork up the ingredients and serve.

Paella Salad

SERVES 6–8

- 4 chicken breasts
- 25 g/1 oz melted butter
- 900 ml/1½ pints vegetable stock
- 225 g/8 oz sliced garlic sausage
- 12 large prawns in their shells
- 225 g/8 oz cooked mussels with shells
- 1 small onion
- 75 ml/5 tablespoons olive oil
- 225 g/8 oz long-grain rice
- 12 sun-dried tomatoes
- 3–4 strands saffron
- pinch of granulated sugar
- 45 ml/3 tablespoons white wine vinegar
- 15 ml/1 tablespoon clear honey
- 1 lemon
- salt and freshly milled pepper

Heat the oven to 180°C/350°F/gas mark 4.

Arrange the chicken breasts in a deep baking dish which holds them closely packed. Brush the skins with the butter, then pour in 300 ml/½ pint of the vegetable stock – enough to keep the chicken moist, but not cover them. Bake uncovered for 30–35 minutes, until the chicken is tender and golden. Let cool in the stock. Refrigerate the chicken, sausage, prawns and mussels until serving time.

Peel and finely chop the onion. Heat 30 ml/2 tablespoons of the olive oil in a large saucepan, add the onion and soften over a medium heat for 5 minutes. Stir in the rice. Add the remaining 600 ml/1 pint vegetable stock, stir as the mixture comes to a simmer, then cover the pan and cook gently over a low heat until the rice grains are tender and the stock is absorbed.

Meanwhile, pour boiling water over the sun-dried tomatoes, just to cover them. Let stand 5 minutes, then drain. Cut the tomatoes in half.

To make the saffron dressing, pound the saffron in a medium-sized bowl with the sugar (sugar acts as an abrasive). When the saffron is powdered, add a tablespoonful of boiling water and leave to infuse for 5 minutes. Then add the vinegar, honey, the finely grated rind and juice of the lemon, the remaining 45 ml/3 tablespoons olive oil and a seasoning of salt and pepper.

Turn the cooked rice into a large bowl, add the saffron dressing and the tomatoes and fork through – the rice will take the golden colour from the saffron. Cool to room temperature. (This salad is best served at room temperature, but making it ahead the rice must be refrigerated.)

Mound the rice in the centre of a large platter. Lift the chicken out of the stock and slice thinly. Arrange it around the rice salad with the sliced garlic sausage and the prawns and mussels in their shells.

Savoury Rice with Bacon and Banana

SERVES 2

- 100 g/4 oz smoked streaky bacon
- 1 small onion
- 10 ml/2 teaspoons oil
- 125 g/4 oz long-grain and wild rice mix
- 450 ml/$^{3}/_{4}$ pint vegetable stock
- 1 (198 g) can sweetcorn kernels
- freshly milled pepper
- 25 g/1 oz butter
- 1 large firm banana
- 25 g/1 oz toasted flaked almonds

Roughly chop the bacon, discarding any rind. Using a large frying pan (with a lid), cook over a medium heat until golden brown. Remove with a slotted spoon and keep hot.

Peel and finely chop the onion, add with the oil to the bacon fat, and cook over a medium heat until soft and golden brown, stirring frequently. Stir in the rice mix and cook for 1 minute. Add the stock and stir well. Cover and cook over a low heat for 20 minutes, until the rice is tender and has absorbed the stock.

Return the bacon to the pan together with the drained sweetcorn. Cook for a minute or two until heated through. Season with pepper.

Meanwhile, heat the butter in a small frying pan until foamy. Add the banana, peeled and cut into thick slices. Cook over a high heat until just browned. Lightly fork the bananas through the rice and top with the almonds.

RICE SALADS

Freshly cooked hot rice quickly absorbs a well-seasoned salad dressing to form the base of a substantial salad. Serve with sliced cold meats or poultry, hard-boiled eggs or cheeses. Choose long-grain white or brown rice or easy-cook American for a rice salad, as these rice grains will remain separate when cooked. Add vegetables, fruits or nuts for extra colour and to introduce texture.

You can make these salads ahead. Always keep in the refrigerator and serve within 24 hours of making. Rice salads look very attractive shaped in a ring mould – see page 158.

Basic method Cook 225 g/8 oz long-grain rice (see page 160). While the rice is cooking, make the chosen dressing in a large salad bowl. If necessary, drain the cooked rice well. Immediately add to the dressing and turn the grains with a fork to coat them. As the mixture cools the grains will absorb the flavour. Then add the extra ingredients just before serving so that they retain their freshness and texture. Each recipe serves 4 as a side salad.

Saffron Rice with Sun-dried Tomatoes [V] In a small bowl pound 3–4 saffron strands with a pinch of granulated sugar, using a wooden spoon. Add 15 ml/1 tablespoon boiling water and leave to infuse for 5 minutes. Tip the saffron strands and water into a large salad bowl. Stir in 45 ml/3 tablespoons white wine vinegar, 15 ml/1 tablespoon clear honey, the finely grated rind and juice of 1 lemon, 45 ml/3 tablespoons olive oil and a seasoning of salt and freshly milled pepper. Lift 12 sun-dried tomatoes in oil out of their jar with a fork, cut each in half and add to the dressing. Add the hot rice and mix with a fork.

Brown Rice and Mango [V] Combine 45 ml/3 tablespoons grapeseed oil, 30 ml/2 tablespoons soy sauce, the finely grated rind and juice of 1 lemon, 15 ml/1 level tablespoon soft brown sugar, 2.5 cm/1 inch fresh ginger, peeled and grated, and a seasoning of salt and freshly milled pepper in a large salad bowl. Add the hot rice and mix together with a fork. Leave until quite cold. Slice 2 ripe mangoes by cutting either side of the stone, then slice the halves lengthways, remove the skin and cut the flesh into bite-sized pieces. Fork the diced mango and 100 g/4 oz toasted cashew nuts into the rice salad just before serving.

Curried Rice with Apricots [V] Combine 30 ml/2 tablespoons lemon juice, 30 ml/2 tablespoons mango chutney (chop up any large pieces of fruit), 45 ml/3 tablespoons grapeseed oil, 5 ml/1 level teaspoon curry paste and a seasoning of salt and freshly milled pepper in a large salad bowl. Add the hot rice and mix with a fork. Leave until cold. Meanwhile coarsely chop 12 ready-to-eat dried apricots. Fork the chopped apricots and 100 g/4 oz toasted flaked almonds into the rice salad just before serving.

Crunchy Vegetable Rice [V] Turn the hot rice into a large salad bowl and fork through 30 ml/2 tablespoons Fresh Herb Dressing or Vinaigrette (see page 50). Leave until cold. Meanwhile trim and chop 1 bunch (6–8) spring onions. Halve and de-seed 1 red and 1 yellow pepper, then chop finely. Trim 2 stalks of celery and thinly slice. Whisk 5 ml/1 teaspoon Dijon mustard and a good seasoning of salt and freshly milled pepper into 30 ml/2 tablespoons mayonnaise and stir into the rice just before serving. Mix in the prepared vegetables and 30 ml/2 tablespoons chopped fresh parsley.

Fried Rice with Shredded Omelette

SERVES 4

150 g/5 oz long-grain rice
2 eggs
salt and freshly milled pepper
30 ml/2 tablespoons chopped fresh chives
30 ml/2 tablespoons oil
100 g/4 oz ham, in one slice if possible
100 g/4 oz frozen peas
1 bunch (6–8) spring onions
30 ml/2 tablespoons soy sauce
freshly milled pepper
100 g/4 oz cooked and peeled prawns

Measure the rice into a medium saucepan and add a pinch of salt and 450 ml/¾ pint cold water. Bring to the boil, stirring once or twice, then cover with the pan lid. Reduce the heat to medium low and simmer for 15–20 minutes, or until the liquid has been absorbed and the rice is tender. ([M] Use 450 ml/¾ pint boiling water and cook, uncovered, on HIGH/100% for 10 minutes. Leave to stand for 5 minutes.) Spread the cooked rice on a large plate to cool.

Crack the eggs into a bowl and add 30 ml/2 tablespoons cold water, a seasoning of salt and pepper and the chopped chives. Beat with a fork until well combined. Heat 10 ml/2 teaspoons of the oil in a large frying pan and add the eggs. Cook over a high heat, frequently lifting the cooked edges to allow the uncooked egg to run underneath. When the omelette is fully cooked and pale golden brown on the underside (do not turn over), roll up swiss-roll fashion and slide out on to a plate. Keep hot.

Cut the ham into small cubes. Tip the peas into a strainer and pour boiling water over to thaw them. Drain well. Trim the spring onions and cut into 1.25 cm/1 inch pieces.

Heat the remaining oil in a wok or large frying pan. Gradually add the cooled rice, stirring with a fork to separate the grains. Sprinkle with the soy sauce and stir until blended in. Season with pepper. Add the spring onions, ham, peas and prawns. Cook, stirring constantly, over a high heat until piping hot.

Cut the omelette into thin ribbons. Spoon the fried rice on to warmed plates and top with the shredded omelette.

OLD-FASHIONED RICE PUDDING

A good rice pudding is wonderful. It should be baked slowly in the oven until the grains of rice are soft and tender. The secret of the creamy consistency is to stir in the first 3 skins as they form on the surface of the pudding and before they have time to brown. This recipe will not fail you if you carefully follow the instructions.

Heat the oven to 160°C/325°F/gas mark 3.

Start by generously buttering a 900 ml/1½ pint baking dish. Measure 600 ml/1 pint creamy milk into a saucepan and heat gently. Sprinkle 40 g/1½ oz pudding (or short-grain) rice into the buttered dish and add 15 g/½ oz butter in flakes. Allow the milk to come to the boil, then pour over the rice and stir gently to mix.

Place the dish in the oven and cook until the rice is tender and the mixture creamy, about 2 hours. The pudding will form a skin about every 15 minutes. Stir in the first 3 skins, then mix in 30–45 ml/2–3 tablespoons double cream and leave the pudding to brown. Serve hot with some very cold double cream (unwhipped) to trickle over each portion.

CHAPTER TEN

Cheese and Eggs

With very little time or effort cheese and eggs can be made into tasty lunch or supper dishes. They combine well with other foods, both sweet and savoury. In fact, it doesn't take much to smarten cheese and eggs into something really grand.

BUYING AND STORING CHEESE

❦ Cheese keeps best whole – which really means that when you buy a piece of cheese, you should eat it quickly. Cheese bought from a counter where it is freshly cut is best – and you can often ask for a taste before you buy. Look for an exciting range and the more unusual cheeses in one of the many new specialist cheese shops.

❦ Along the supermarket shelves cheese will be prepacked. Look out for those with the Farmhouse label. These are actually made in the traditional, natural manner and allowed to mature before they are cut and packed. There will be handy vacuum packs of grated cheese but you will get a better flavour if you freshly grate your own – and it's less expensive.

❦ An old-fashioned larder temperature is the ideal one for keeping good cheese fresh and happy. For most of us, however, the refrigerator is the only alternative, although it is really too cold and airless.

❦ Seal only the cut surface of a piece of cheese with clingfilm or foil, then wrap the whole piece in greaseproof paper which is porous and lets the cheese breathe through the rind. Put the cheese, carefully wrapped, in the salad drawer of the refrigerator.

❦ Fresh, soft cheeses such as cream, curd or ricotta are perishable and should always be kept refrigerated.

❦ Allow about 1 hour to bring cheese back to room temperature and regain its full flavour before serving. Vacuum-packed cheese should be opened up at least half an hour prior to consumption to let the cheese breathe.

❦ Hard and semi-hard cheese, carefully wrapped, will store for 1–2 weeks; blue-vein cheeses also have a reasonable life if well protected against drying up; soft ripened cheeses (such as Camembert or Brie) are delicate and perishable. They have to be eaten at the correct stage of ripeness, which means they do not keep well and should be eaten within 1–2 days. If they are not fully ripe when bought (they should give slightly when pressed), let them sit at room temperature. Processed cheeses are made by melting and mixing natural cheeses. They usually taste mild but have good keeping qualities. Soft unripened cheeses have no ageing period and are eaten fresh. These include cream cheese, often flavoured with herbs, garlic and seasoning, curd or cottage cheese, mascarpone and ricotta. They are very perishable – observe the 'use by' date on the pack.

Cheese and Leek Bake

SERVES 6–8 [V]

450 g/1 lb leeks
150 ml/¼ pint vegetable stock
100 g/4 oz butter
25 g/1 oz plain flour
425 ml/¾ pint milk
salt and freshly milled pepper
grated nutmeg
350 g/12 oz mature Cheddar
225 g/8 oz pasta shapes
6 slices fresh white bread

Trim and rinse the leeks, then cut across into 1 cm/½ inch slices. Place the leeks in a large frying pan (use one that has a lid), add the stock and bring to a simmer. Cover and cook over a medium heat until the leeks are tender – about 5–6 minutes.

Meanwhile place half the butter, the flour and the milk in a large saucepan. Cook over a medium heat, whisking continuously, until the sauce is smooth and thickened. ([M] Combine half the butter, the flour and the milk in a large bowl. Cook for 4–5 minutes, stirring frequently, until the sauce comes to a boil and thickens.) Remove from the heat and season with salt, pepper and a grating of nutmeg. Stir in 225 g/8 oz of the cheese.

Cook the pasta according to the package directions. Drain well and add to the sauce, together with the leeks and any stock remaining in the frying pan. Gently mix together.

Heat the oven to 190°C/375°F/gas mark 5.

Melt the remaining butter. Trim the crusts from the bread, lightly brush with butter and cut each slice in half diagonally. Arrange the bread slices around the edge of a lightly buttered 1.4 litre (2½ pint) shallow baking dish. Spoon in the pasta mixture and sprinkle with the remaining grated cheese.

Bake for 15–20 minutes or until golden brown and bubbling.

Leek and Potato Frittata

Illustrated on Plate Nine

SERVES 3

225 g/8 oz potatoes
225 g/8 oz leeks
25 g/1 oz butter
50 g/2 oz smoked ham
50 g/2 oz Double Gloucester
6 eggs
salt and freshly milled pepper
freshly grated nutmeg

Peel the potatoes and cut into thin slices. Add to a pan of boiling salted water and cook until just tender – about 6 minutes. Drain.

Trim the leeks and clean thoroughly. Cut into 2.5 cm/1 inch slices. Melt the butter in a large frying pan (preferably non-stick, and use one that has a lid) and stir in the leeks. Cover and cook over a medium heat until the leeks are tender but not brown, about 10 minutes.

Meanwhile, cut the ham into thin strips and grate the cheese. Break the eggs into a bowl and add 30 ml/2 tablespoons cold water. Season with salt, pepper and a grating of nutmeg. Beat with a fork until well combined.

Add the potatoes to the leeks and gently mix together. Pour over the beaten eggs and cook over a medium high heat. As the egg sets around the edge, lift with a spatula to allow the uncooked egg to run on to the hot base of the pan. Once the mixture is set, but still moist on the surface, sprinkle with the ham and grated cheese. Set under a hot grill until golden brown. Serve immediately.

QUAIL'S EGGS

Quail's eggs have only recently begun to be farmed, and supplies are regularly available in the larger supermarkets. These eggs are tiny, and boiling is the most satisfactory method of cooking them.

Place the eggs in a saucepan of cold water to cover and bring to the boil. Reduce the heat and simmer for 3 minutes, then plunge them into cold water. Shelled and sliced they make a pretty addition to a salad or starter.

Mushroom and Spinach Frittata

SERVES 4 [V]

---

225 g/8 oz chestnut mushrooms
100 g/4 oz fresh small leaf spinach
6 eggs
salt and freshly milled pepper
45 ml/3 tablespoons olive oil
30 ml/2 tablespoons grated Parmesan

Wipe the mushrooms with a damp cloth and trim the stalks. If very large, halve or thickly slice. If not using the packed pre-washed variety, rinse the spinach thoroughly and roll in a teatowel to dry. Stack the leaves and roll up into bundles. Slice across into ribbons. Shake apart.

Crack the eggs into a bowl, add 30 ml/2 tablespoons water and a good seasoning of salt and pepper. Mix lightly.

Preheat the grill.

Heat the oil in a 25 cm/10 inch frying pan (preferably non-stick). Add the mushrooms and turn in the hot oil for 1–2 minutes. Add the spinach and cook until shiny but not wilted – about 1 minute. Pour over the egg mixture. Cook over a medium high heat and, as the egg sets around the edge, lift with a spatula to allow the uncooked egg to run on to the hot base of the pan. Once the mixture is set, but still moist on the surface, sprinkle with the Parmesan and grill until golden brown. Serve immediately.

Celeriac and Potato Gratin

SERVES 2 [V]

---

225 g/8 oz celeriac
225 g/8 oz potatoes
100 g/4 oz Gouda
150 ml/¼ pint single cream
1 clove of garlic

Heat the oven to 190°/375°F/gas mark 5.

Cut off the tough skin of the celeriac and peel the potatoes. Cut both into very thin slices (this is most quickly done using the slicing blade of a processor) and tip into a pan of boiling salted water. Bring back to the boil and cook for 2–3 minutes. Drain well.

Grate the cheese. Heat the cream with the peeled and crushed clove of garlic until just bubbling around the edges, using the pan the potatoes and celeriac were cooked in. When the cream is hot, return the vegetables to the pan and gently stir to coat them with the cream.

Lightly butter a shallow ovenproof dish and spoon in half the vegetables. Sprinkle with half the cheese and top with the remaining vegetables and any cream left in the pan. Evenly cover with the remaining cheese.

Bake for 25–30 minutes until the vegetables are soft throughout when tested with a fork and the top is golden brown. Serve on its own as a light meal, or add some slices of cold ham or grilled bacon.

Scalloped Potatoes with Two Cheeses

SERVES 4

- 700 g/1½ lb potatoes
- 2 large onions
- 100 g/4 oz smoked back bacon rashers
- 1 clove of garlic
- 30 ml/2 tablespoons olive oil
- salt and freshly milled pepper
- 15 ml/1 tablespoon white wine vinegar
- 100 g/4 oz curd cheese
- 1 (225 g) carton Greek-style yogurt
- 2 eggs
- 100 g/4 oz Cheshire cheese

Peel and thinly slice the potatoes – this is most quickly done using a processor. Add to a saucepan of cold salted water and bring to the boil. Simmer for 2 minutes, then drain.

Meanwhile, peel and thinly slice the onions. Trim and chop the bacon, peel and chop the garlic. Heat the oil in a large frying pan, add the onion, garlic and bacon and cook gently to soften the onion and draw the fat from the bacon – about 5 minutes. Season with salt and pepper, add the vinegar and then the potato slices. Gently turn to blend together, then spoon the mixture into a 1.1 litre/2 pint baking dish and spread level.

Heat the oven to 190°C/375°F/gas mark 5.

Beat the curd cheese with the yogurt and eggs until smooth. Season to taste and grate in the Cheshire cheese. Stir well then spoon evenly over the potatoes. Bake for 25 minutes. Serve hot.

FROMAGE FRAIS

Fromage frais deserves a special mention, as it is half-way between cream and soft cheese, with a lightness of taste that makes it ideal for use in both sweet and savoury dishes. Fromage frais is available with varying fat levels: 1% natural fromage frais is virtually fat free, 4% fromage frais is very low fat and 8% fromage frais has an added touch of fresh cream which makes it slightly richer tasting. Even so, it still has less than half the fat content of single cream.

Spoon fromage frais as a topping on desserts; stir into bowls of soup for a finishing touch; add black pepper and chopped herbs and pile on top of baked potatoes or serve as a dip with crudités. We've found it works well in savoury mousses, either completely or partly replacing the more calorie-laden mayonnaise. When used in place of cream in dessert mousses you will get a softer set than when the richer cream is used. You will get a better result using half fromage frais, half cream.

Tuna Cheese Casserole with Pimento Sauce

SERVES 4

- 6 slices fresh white bread
- 1 (198 g) can tuna steak in brine
- 175 g/6 oz mature Cheddar
- 45 ml/3 tablespoons chopped fresh chives
- 50 g/2 oz melted butter
- 3 eggs
- 600 ml/1 pint milk
- 5 ml/1 level teaspoon mustard powder
- salt and freshly milled pepper
- 1 (400 g) can pimentos in water
- 15 ml/1 tablespoon sherry vinegar
- pinch granulated sugar

The day before serving: trim the crusts from the bread if very crusty then cut into small cubes. Drain the tuna and flake. Grate the cheese.

Butter a 1.7 litre/3 pint casserole or soufflé dish and arrange the breadcubes, tuna, cheese and chives in layers, finishing with cheese. Pour over the butter.

Whisk together the eggs, milk and mustard powder with pepper to taste. Strain over the layers, then cover and refrigerate overnight.

Heat the oven to 180°C/350°F/gas mark 4.

Uncover the casserole and cook for 1¼–1½ hours, until puffy and golden brown. Serve immediately.

While the casserole is cooking, drain the pimentos and buzz with the vinegar and sugar in a blender or processor to a slightly chunky consistency. Gently warm to serving temperature. Season with salt and freshly milled pepper and serve with the casserole.

CHEESE SPREADS

Being bland in flavour but with an excellent soft texture, curd and cream cheese, along with added flavours, make tempting spreads for hot breads, toast or crackers.

Blend the ingredients together in a bowl with a wooden spoon. Alternatively buzz the soft ingredients until creamy in a processor, but stir in herbs or nuts by hand for the best texture.

Pack the spread in an attractive pot, cover and store in the refrigerator ready for a quick snack. Add a side salad to extend it to a light meal. Or pile on to melba toast for nibbles with drinks.

Garlic Herb Cream 50 g/2 oz soft butter with 225 g/8 oz curd cheese until smooth. Beat in 1–2 crushed cloves of garlic, a seasoning of salt and freshly milled pepper, and 30 ml/2 tablespoons single cream to get a soft spreading consistency. Add a squeeze of lemon juice and 15 ml/1 tablespoon each of chopped chives and parsley.

Stilton Cream Cut away the rind from 100 g/4 oz Stilton then break the cheese into small pieces. Add 30 ml/2 tablespoons single cream and beat until soft. Add 100 g/4 oz cream cheese and mix until smooth. Season with salt and freshly milled pepper and add 30 ml/2 tablespoons finely chopped fresh sage.

Potted Cheese with Walnuts Beat 100 g/4 oz grated mature Cheddar or Cheshire cheese with 50 g/2 oz butter, a seasoning of salt and freshly milled pepper and a grating of nutmeg. Beat in 30 ml/2 tablespoons dry sherry and 25 g/1 oz finely chopped walnuts.

Twice-baked Cheese Soufflés

SERVES 6 [V]

40 g/1½ oz butter
45 ml/3 level tablespoons plain flour
225 ml/8 fl oz milk
50 g/2 oz grated mature Cheddar
6 slices wholemeal bread
3 eggs
salt and freshly milled pepper
freshly grated nutmeg
150 ml/5 fl oz double cream
25 g/1 oz grated Parmesan

Heat the oven to 180°C/350°F/gas mark 4.

Thoroughly grease 6 individual ramekins with butter. Melt the remaining butter in a medium saucepan, stir in the flour and cook gently for a few minutes. Gradually stir in the milk, beating well to make a smooth sauce. Bring to a simmer and cook for 2–3 minutes. Draw the pan off the heat, add the Cheddar and stir until melted. ([M] Combine the butter, flour and milk in a medium bowl. Cook for 2–3 minutes, stirring frequently, until the sauce comes to the boil and thickens. Add the cheese and stir until melted.)

Toast the bread and cut out 6 circles, using the top of a ramekin as a pattern.

Separate the eggs. Put the whites in a mixing bowl and beat the yolks into the sauce. Season the sauce with salt, pepper and a little grated nutmeg. Beat the egg whites to stiff peaks and carefully fold into the sauce. Spoon the mixture into the greased ramekin dishes and level the top.

Set the dishes in a roasting tin and add boiling water to a depth of 2.5 cm/1 inch. Bake for 15–20 minutes or until firm. Remove the soufflés from the oven. Increase the oven heat to 200°C/400°F/gas mark 6. Cool the soufflés for 10 minutes, then loosen the sides and turn out each soufflé on to a toast circle. Arrange in a heatproof gratin dish and pour over the cream, taking care to coat each soufflé. Sprinkle with the Parmesan and return to the oven for 10–15 minutes or until the sauce is bubbling hot and the soufflés lightly browned.

Cheese and Mushroom Soufflé

SERVES 2–3 [V]

- 350 g/12 oz open-cup mushrooms
- 1 small onion
- 2 cloves of garlic
- 50 g/2 oz butter
- salt and freshly milled pepper
- 40 g/1½ oz grated Parmesan
- 30 ml/2 level tablespoons plain flour
- 200 ml/7 fl oz milk
- freshly grated nutmeg
- 50 g/2 oz grated Gruyère
- 3 eggs
- 1 extra egg white
- 5 ml/1 level teaspoon sugar

Discard the mushroom stalks and chop the caps finely. Peel and finely chop the onion. Peel and crush the garlic.

Melt half the butter in a large frying pan, add the onion and cook gently until soft. Add the garlic and mushrooms and continue to cook gently until the mushrooms are soft and any liquid has evaporated. Season with salt and pepper and draw off the heat.

Lightly grease a 1.1 litre/2 pint soufflé dish and sprinkle with 15 ml/1 tablespoon of the grated Parmesan.

Melt the remaining 25 g/1 oz butter in a saucepan. Stir in the flour and cook gently for 1 minute. Gradually stir in the milk, beating well to make a thick sauce. Bring to a simmer, season with salt, pepper and a grating of nutmeg. Turn the mixture into a large bowl. ([M] Combine the remaining 25 g/1 oz butter, the flour and milk in a large bowl. Cook for 2–3 minutes, stirring frequently, until the sauce comes to the boil and thickens. Season with salt, pepper and a grating of nutmeg.) Stir in the Gruyère and remaining Parmesan.

Separate the eggs, beating the yolks into the sauce. Whisk the egg whites, including the extra one, to stiff peaks. Sprinkle in the sugar and whisk again until glossy. Fold a little of the whites into the cheese mixture, then carefully fold in the remainder.

Spoon the mushrooms into the base of the prepared soufflé dish. Spoon the soufflé mixture on top and spread level. Refrigerate until serving time – no longer than 24 hours.

Heat the oven to 190°C/375°F/gas mark 5.

Bake the soufflé for 30–35 minutes or until well risen and golden brown. Serve immediately.

CHEESE FOR COOKING

- Choose mature cheese with a good strong flavour for cooking. A Farmhouse Cheddar grates easily and melts deliciously – smoked Cheddar adds a new dimension to a cheese sauce. Try crumbly Cheshire, creamy-flavoured Double Gloucester or Lancashire. Nutty-tasting Gruyère is one of the finest cheeses for cooking, Emmental is less expensive. Parmesan and Pecorino are good, too. Mature cheeses melt more quickly and have a depth of flavour that means you can use less to get more taste.
- Small pieces of cheese melt and blend faster in a soup or sauce. If the cheese is firm, use a coarse grater which ensures long flakes of grated cheese. Often you can simply crumble a cheese – Stilton or Lancashire, for example.
- Some cheeses brown better than others. Gruyère tops the list and will grill to a beautiful colour in any sauce-topped dish. A generous sprinkling of grated Parmesan will also ensure a golden crust. Low fat cheeses do not brown well, though they can be encouraged with a dusting of paprika which turns golden under the grill.
- Use a low heat for cooking – cheese should be cooked gently and only for a short time. For sauces, take the pan off the heat, then add the cheese and stir until melted – the heat of the pan will usually be sufficient to do this.
- A mild-flavoured cheese used in a sauce can be enhanced by adding a little prepared mustard or mixing in a tablespoon of grated Parmesan.
- For a crunchy cheese topping on made-up dishes, combine dry white breadcrumbs and grated cheese in equal parts. Under the heat of the grill the cheese melts, the breadcrumbs absorb the oil in the cheese and the whole topping goes delightfully crunchy.

Sunflower Cheese Crisps

MAKES ABOUT 6 DOZEN

V

Sift the flour and salt into a mixing bowl. Add the butter, cut into pieces, and rub in with the fingertips. Alternatively, blend the ingredients in a food processor and tip into a bowl. Press the cottage cheese through a sieve into the bowl. Add the sunflower seeds. Stir to blend, then, with floured fingertips, draw the mixture together to make a dough. Turn on to a floured board and divide the dough in half.

Heat the oven to 160°C/325°F/gas mark 3.

Roll one half of the dough on a lightly floured surface to a rectangle about 3 mm/1/8 inch thick – so thin that you can feel the sunflower seeds making the dough bumpy. Cut the dough into 5 cm/2 inch squares, prick each square several times with a fork, and place on ungreased baking trays. Bake for 20–25 minutes until lightly browned and crisp. Cool on a wire rack. Repeat with the second half of the dough.

150 g/5 oz plain flour
1.25 ml/1/2 level teaspoon onion or celery salt
50 g/2 oz chilled butter
1 (225 g) carton natural cottage cheese
25 g/1 oz sunflower seeds

Toasted Caerphilly with Pears

SERVES 4

V

Peel the pears, then halve and scoop out the cores with a teaspoon. Slice each pear half thinly. Thinly slice the cheese.

Toast the bread on one side only under a hot grill. Lightly butter the untoasted side and top with the pear slices. Arrange the cheese on top to cover the pears. Place under the grill until the cheese is melted and bubbling hot. Serve immediately.

2–3 firm ripe dessert pears
100 g/4 oz Caerphilly
4 thick slices granary bread
butter

CUTTING IT FINE

A handsome cheese board can be the mainstay of a lunch or something to linger over after dinner. Whatever the occasion, give your cheese board the attention it deserves. Here are some worthwhile do's and don'ts:

- Don't feel obliged to have a 'board' for your cheese – some of the nicest presentations we've seen have set the cheeses on a large old-fashioned plate or platter.
- Avoid too much choice – it's better to have 2 or 3 good-sized pieces of cheese than a confusion of smaller bits. It looks impressive and the cheese keeps better.
- A hard cheese, something semi-soft and a blue cheese could be a guide but there are no rules – have what you like. Or, go for a theme such as British cheeses only – there's a wide variety to choose from.
- Give cheese space. There is no need for them all to be on the same plate – it's a good idea to put a blue cheese on a separate plate with its own knife.
- Fresh leaves look very pretty tucked under a cheese – especially a soft variety such as a fresh goat's cheese. Polish some vine or bay leaves with a soft cloth and sit the cheese on top. Or tuck a sprig of fresh herb such as sage or thyme between hard cheeses.
- Fresh fruit goes well with cheese. It is much more stylish to pass a bowl of polished apples, pears, plums, nectarines or fresh figs than to add bunches of grapes to the actual cheese board.
- There's nothing like a plum or pear chutney to accompany a bread and cheese lunch. Or an old-fashioned fruit cheese, cut in slices – quince cheese is wonderful.
- For lunch a simple crusty bread is best with cheese. Ring the changes with an unusual bread – a mixed grain loaf, a poppy-seed plait or a thinly sliced walnut or raisin bread. Or serve with our superb Oatmeal Bread (page 148). Thin oat cakes go extremely well with a soft goat's cheese, while matzo crackers which are crisp and plain are excellent with hard or blue cheese. For after dinner, crisp water biscuits or your own home-baked Sunflower Cheese Crisps (page 179) would be delicious.

PLATE NINE
Leek and Potato Frittata (page 172) with Coleslaw (page 51)

PLATE TEN

Lemon Curd Tartlets (page 190) with Red Raspberry Sauce (page 208)

HOW TO COOK BETTER EGGS

- Let eggs come to room temperature (this takes about 30 minutes) before using them. If they are cold, they will crack when boiled, give less volume when whisked and be more likely to curdle in cake mixes.
- Another way to help stop boiled eggs cracking is to prick the rounded end with a pin or egg pricker before putting them into the water.
- Drain boiled eggs as soon as the time is up. Immediately plunge them into cold water to stop further cooking – this way you won't have any dark rings around the yolks.
- Have the courage to take scrambled eggs, or an omelette, off the direct heat just before they finish cooking – they will continue to cook to perfection in the heat of the pan.
- An easy way to separate eggs is to crack an egg on to a plate then, with an upturned eggcup or small glass, hold the yolk back while you allow the white to slide off. If a speck of yolk slips in with the white, scoop it out with a piece of the egg shell.
- When whisking egg whites, make sure the mixing bowl you use is completely grease-free. Either rinse the bowl in hot water and dry again or rub round the inside of the bowl (before putting in the egg whites) with a cut lemon. Not only will it be grease-free but the acidity of the lemon juice will produce a better volume in the beaten mixture.

Scrambled Eggs Croustade

SERVES 4

- 4 soft baps
- 75 g/3 oz butter, melted
- 100 g/4 oz smoked salmon pieces or finely chopped smoked ham
- 8 eggs
- 50 ml/2 fl oz single cream or milk
- freshly milled pepper
- 50 g/2 oz soft cheese with herbs
- 30 ml/2 tablespoons chopped chives

Cut a slice from the top of each bap and scoop out the soft crumbs, leaving just a thin wall of bread. Lightly brush the insides and outer surfaces of both the base and tops with melted butter. Divide the smoked salmon or ham between the baps. Place on a baking sheet and warm through in a 160°C/325°F/gas mark 3 oven while cooking the eggs.

Break the eggs into a mixing bowl, add the cream or milk, and season with pepper. Heat the remaining butter in a 25 cm/10 inch frying pan and, when hot and frothing, pour in the egg mixture. Cook over a moderate heat, drawing the mixture up in folds as the eggs begin to thicken.

When the mixture is set, remove from the heat and add the herb cheese in flakes – the heat of the eggs will melt it. Spoon the scrambled eggs into the warm bread cases, top with chopped chives and serve immediately.

Ham and Eggs in Peppers

SERVES 4

1 thick slice white bread
25 g/1 oz butter
15 ml/1 tablespoon olive oil
2 large red or yellow peppers
4 slices dry cured smoked ham
4 eggs
salt and freshly milled pepper

Trim the crusts from the bread and cut into neat dice. Melt half the butter with the oil in a frying pan. When it is hot add the bread and fry, stirring constantly, until golden brown. Drain on kitchen paper.

Heat the oven to 190°C/375°F/gas mark 5.

Cut the peppers in half lengthways right through the stem. Scoop out the seeds and membrane. Add the peppers to a pan of boiling water and simmer for about 5 minutes or until tender when tested with a knife tip. Take care not to overcook. Remove from the pan and drain, cut side down, on kitchen paper.

Arrange the pepper halves in a buttered shallow baking dish. Fold a slice of ham inside each and break in an egg. Sprinkle with salt and pepper and add a flake of the remaining butter to each yolk. Scatter over the *croûtons*.

Bake until the eggs are just set – about 12–15 minutes. Serve immediately.

Egg and Anchovy Mousse

SERVES 4 AS A LIGHT MAIN COURSE, 8 AS A STARTER V

6 eggs
1 (50 g) can anchovies
150 ml/¼ pint double cream
200 ml tub fromage frais

Place the eggs in a pan of cold water and bring to a simmer. Cook for 6 minutes to hard-boil, then drain and cover with cold water to arrest the cooking. Shell while still slightly warm, then submerge in fresh cold water. Lift the anchovies out of the can and drain on kitchen paper to remove excess oil, then finely chop.

Tip the fromage frais and curd cheese into a large bowl and add the mayonnaise. Whisk together until smooth. Season with pepper. Finely chop the eggs and add to the cheese with the chopped anchovies. Lightly and evenly mix together. Cover and chill for about 30 minutes to allow the flavours to blend.

Spoon the chilled mousse on to plates and serve with hot unbuttered toast as a starter or with salad and crusty bread as a light meal. It is also good spooned into split soft baps with sprigs of watercress.

100 g/4 oz curd cheese
60 ml/3 tablespoons mayonnaise
freshly milled pepper

Cinnamon Toasts with Fresh Raspberry Compote

SERVES 4

Whisk together the eggs and milk then pour into a shallow dish large enough to hold the slices of bread in a single layer. Trim the crusts from the bread if very thick, then slide the bread into the milk mixture. Turn the bread over and set aside for 5–10 minutes to allow it to absorb the egg and milk.

Meanwhile, place the raspberries in a serving bowl. Gently heat the redcurrant jelly with the lemon juice until just melted. Pour over the fruit and lightly mix together. Combine the sugar and cinnamon. Using a large frying pan, heat half the butter and add 2 of the bread slices. Cook over a medium high heat until golden brown on both sides. Turn carefully to avoid breaking the bread. When cooked, slide on to warm serving plates and sprinkle with the spiced sugar. Keep hot. Repeat with the remaining butter and bread slices.

Serve very hot, with the raspberry compote spooned over the top and crème fraîche or Greek-style yogurt.

2 eggs
300 ml/½ pint milk
4 thick slices fresh bread
225 g/8 oz fresh raspberries
1 (227 g) jar redcurrant jelly
15 ml/1 tablespoon fresh lemon juice
60 ml/4 level tablespoons demerara sugar
1.25 ml/¼ level teaspoon ground cinnamon
25 g/1 oz butter
crème fraîche or Greek-style yogurt

WHAT YOU SHOULD KNOW ABOUT EGGS

Eggs were in the news a lot after the risk of salmonella food poisoning was linked to them being eaten raw. High temperatures destroy salmonella, for example when eggs are baked in a cake or pudding, or boiled or fried until they are hard cooked. However, you can't always do that with an egg when texture and flavour is what you are after. Now British egg producers are registered with the Government, flocks are regularly tested for salmonella and chickens are fed on a controlled grain diet. Even so, taking heed of the Government health warning on the use of raw eggs in recipes for those who are at most risk – the young and elderly – is sensible. Neither of these groups should consume recipes made with raw eggs. For the rest of us, common sense, a clean cool kitchen and refrigeration are timely precautions.

- Eggs marked 'free range' imply that the hens have continuous daytime access to outdoor runs; those marked 'barn' or 'perchery' are from hens that are permanently kept indoors and unmarked eggs are from battery hens which are caged. Don't be confused by eggs labelled 'Direct from the Farm' or 'Farm Fresh' – these are not necessarily free range.
- Eggs are graded according to size and labelled from size 1 (the largest) to size 7. The recipes in this book are based on size 2 eggs, the best size for most purposes.
- Chilling keeps eggs fresh longer, so put in the refrigerator as soon as possible. Store in their own egg boxes to protect them.
- Keep eggs away from fresh meat or strong smelling foods such as cheese or fish – remember egg shells are porous.
- Buy only as many eggs as you reasonably require and use them within 2 weeks of purchase. Put new boxes of eggs underneath older ones so that you use them in the order bought.
- Check inside the cartons and, if there are any cracked eggs, discard them – just in case.
- Keep mixing bowls and work surfaces very clean. Hands too – remember thumbtips are pressed into eggs when you separate them.
- Never let prepared egg dishes stand around in a warm kitchen or on a buffet table, for example. Where dishes are not for immediate consumption, keep refrigerated until serving time.

CRÊPES

Wafer-thin crêpes can be wrapped around unlimited fillings, both sweet and savoury. Simple to make, they have the added virtue of being suitable for successfully storing in the refrigerator for up to 3 days or, frozen, for up to 3 months. Cool each freshly made crêpe on absorbent kitchen paper. When quite cold, stack and pack in a freezer bag.

Make the crêpes in a 15 cm/6 inch heavy omelette or crêpe pan. It takes a minute or two for the pan to heat up and for you to determine the right temperature, but once heated, the cooked crêpes will slip out easily. Keeping the hot surface very lightly greased is simple using a pad of kitchen paper and a saucer of oil. Dip the pad into the oil and rub over the hot pan before each crêpe.

A crêpe batter is usually made with white flour, but use a mixture of wholemeal and white if preferred. A good pinch of chopped fresh herbs adds a pretty speckled effect for savoury crêpes. The following recipe makes enough batter for about 12 crêpes:

300 ml/½ pint milk
1 egg
1 egg yolk
15 ml/1 tablespoon melted butter or oil
100 g/4 oz plain flour
pinch of salt

Put the milk, egg and egg yolk, butter or oil, flour and salt into a processor or blender (in that order). Buzz for a few seconds, scrape the sides of the container and buzz again. Alternatively, sift the flour and salt into a mixing bowl. Make a well in the centre and break in the egg and egg yolk and half the milk. Using a wooden spoon, stir from the centre, gradually drawing in the flour. When the ingredients are blended, beat to a smooth batter and stir in the remaining milk and the butter or oil. Whichever method you use, strain the batter into a jug and it will be easier to pour when making the crêpes.

Heat a 15 cm/6 inch crêpe or omelette pan and grease lightly (see above). Pour in a very thin layer of batter (about 30 ml/2 tablespoons) and tip the pan to spread evenly over the base. When browned on the underside, loosen the crêpe with a spatula, turn it over and cook the other side. Slide out on to kitchen paper.

Sweet Cheese Crêpes

SERVES 4

12 crêpes (see above)
finely grated rind and juice of ½ a large lemon
100 g/4 oz golden sultanas
375 g/12 oz curd cheese
1 egg
1.25 ml/½ level teaspoon cinnamon
30 ml/2 level tablespoons caster sugar
150 ml/¼ pint single cream

Combine the lemon rind and juice with the sultanas in a small bowl and leave to 'plump up' for 15 minutes.

Turn the curd cheese into a large bowl and add the egg, cinnamon and sugar. Beat until smooth then stir in the sultanas and lemon.

Divide the filling between the crêpes, spooning it on to the paler side of the crêpes and spreading it almost to the edge, then lightly fold up swiss-roll fashion. Arrange in a single layer in a shallow buttered dish. Pour over the cream.

Bake at 190°C/375°F/gas mark 5 for 15–20 minutes, until golden brown. Serve very hot.

Coffee Crêpes

SERVES 4

- 8 crêpes (see pages 184–5)
- 375 g/12 oz curd cheese
- 15 ml/1 tablespoon coffee essence
- 75 g/3 oz soft brown sugar
- 15 ml/1 tablespoon rum
- 1 pack (40) ratafias
- 25 g/1 oz butter
- icing sugar for dusting

Heat the oven to 200°C/400°F/gas mark 6.

In a medium mixing bowl, combine the curd cheese, coffee essence, soft brown sugar and rum, and stir to blend. Lightly crush the ratafias (the easiest method is to put them in a freezer bag and gently crush with a rolling pin) and fold them in – the ratafias should remain in crunchy bits.

Melt the butter and use a little of it to brush round the inside of a 1.1 litre/2 pint shallow baking dish. Separate the crêpes and, on to one half of each, place a spoonful of the filling. Fold over the other half to make half-moon shapes.

Tuck the filled crêpes in the baking dish, slightly overlapping. Brush with the remaining melted butter. Bake for 10 minutes to heat through. Dust with icing sugar and serve hot.

CHAPTER ELEVEN

Puddings

Old-fashioned hot puddings updated to use modern methods; pies and tarts made with press-in pastry; unlimited chocolate sauces and hot baked fruits. With such a choice, you can't fail to please.

PRESS-IN SHORTCRUST PASTRY

Measure 175 g/6 oz plain flour, a pinch of salt, 1.25 ml/¼ level teaspoon baking powder and 45 ml/3 level tablespoons caster sugar into the food processor. Cover and buzz to mix. Add 75 g/3 oz chilled butter, cut in small pieces, and process to fine crumbs. Tip into a bowl and add 1 beaten egg. Mix in with a fork – the mixture will be crumbly. Or sift the flour, salt and baking powder into a bowl and stir in the sugar. Add the butter (at room temperature) in pieces and rub in with the fingertips. Mix in the beaten egg.

To make a 20 cm/8 inch tart shell Evenly distribute the crumbly dough over the base of an ungreased 20 cm/8 inch (2.5 cm/1 inch deep) round metal tart tin, preferably one with a loose bottom. With lightly floured fingers, press the dough evenly and firmly into the sides and base of the tin. Chill.

To make 6 10 cm/4 inch tartlets Divide the crumbly dough evenly between 6 10 cm/4 inch fluted metal tartlet tins. With lightly floured fingers press the dough evenly and firmly into the sides and base of each tin. Chill.

To bake blind Heat the oven to 190°C/375°F/gas mark 5 (remember to put in the baking sheet). Place the tart or tartlet shells on the hot baking sheet and bake until golden brown – about 12–15 minutes. Let the baked shells cool for 1 minute, then remove from the tins and leave to cool completely on a wire rack.

Yorkshire Curd Tart

SERVES 6

1 prepared 20 cm/8 inch tart shell, chilled (see above)
3 eggs
225 g/8 oz curd cheese
50 g/2 oz caster sugar
finely grated rind of 1 lemon
30 ml/2 tablespoons currants
15 ml/1 tablespoon melted butter
freshly grated nutmeg

Heat the oven to 200°C/400°F/gas mark 6 (remember to put in the baking sheet).

Separate the eggs, cracking the whites into a medium bowl and the yolks into a second bowl. Beat the egg whites to stiff peaks. Add the curd cheese to the egg yolks with the sugar and beat until soft and creamy – no need to wash the beaters. Blend in the lemon rind, currants, melted butter and a grating of nutmeg (about 1.5 ml/½ level teaspoon). Fold in the beaten egg whites using a metal spoon. Spoon the mixture into the tart shell and spread evenly.

Stand the tart on the heated baking sheet. Bake for 10 minutes then reduce the heat to 180°C/350°F/gas mark 4 and bake for a further 20 minutes. Serve warm or at room temperature – it is usual for the top of a curd tart to crack during baking or when cooling.

For a special but very untraditional treat, serve the Yorkshire Curd Tart with Black Cherry and Kirsch Sauce (page 208).

Apple and Cheese Tart

SERVES 6

- 1 prepared 20 cm/8 inch tart shell, chilled (page 188)
- 100 g/4 oz caster sugar
- 30 ml/2 level tablespoons cornflour
- 5 ml/1 level teaspoon ground cinnamon
- 1.25 ml/¼ level teaspoon ground cloves
- 700 g/1½ lb dessert apples
- 150 ml/5 fl oz double cream
- 50–75 g/2–3 oz grated mature Cheddar

Heat the oven to 190°C/375°F/gas mark 5 (remember to put in the baking sheet).

In a large bowl combine the sugar, cornflour, cinnamon and cloves. Quarter, peel and core the apples and thinly slice into the bowl of spiced sugar. Toss to coat in the mixture.

Arrange the apple slices in layers in the tart shell – take a little time over this, packing them in neatly. Pour over the cream. Stand the tart on the heated baking sheet. Bake for 40–45 minutes, or until the apples are tender. Remove the tart from the oven and cool on a wire rack for 10 minutes. Ease the tart from the tin and slide it back on to the baking sheet.

Sprinkle the cheese around the edge of the tart. Place briefly under a preheated grill until the cheese is golden – if the tart is already well browned, protect the top of it with a small square of kitchen foil. Serve warm with warm Real Custard Sauce (page 190) or pouring cream.

REAL CUSTARD SAUCE

Making a real custard sauce is no problem if you give it your whole attention and do not stint on the ingredients. There is no room for economizing here – egg yolks, sugar and rich milk or cream are the vital ingredients, plus the flavourings of your choice. Use real vanilla extract or vanilla sugar (see page 198). If you use low-fat or skimmed milk the result will be thin and disappointing. Cornflour is sometimes used as a thickener but that's another recipe altogether. Real custard is smooth and creamy and as good as cream when you serve it chilled. Serve this special sauce with pride – to accompany fruit pies or tarts, poached fruits, or to top a superb trifle.

Warm Custard Sauce In a mixing bowl blend 3 egg yolks and 25 g/3 level tablespoons caster sugar to a cream. Heat 300 ml/$^{1}/_{2}$ pint single cream (or equal parts whole milk and cream) in a saucepan, then stir the hot liquid into the eggs and sugar and blend well. Strain the custard back into the rinsed saucepan. Set the pan over a medium heat and stir for 6–8 minutes, until the custard coats the back of a metal spoon. Remove the pan from the heat and immediately pour the custard into a cold bowl to lower the temperature quickly. Stir in 5 ml/1 teaspoon vanilla extract and pour into a jug for serving.

To keep custard warm, set the jug in a bowl of warm (not boiling) water. Stir occasionally to prevent a skin forming.

Chilled Custard Sauce Immediately after the cooked custard has been poured into the cold bowl, place the bowl in a larger bowl of iced water. Stir continuously until the custard is cold. The ice speeds up the process, and stirring prevents a skin forming. Once the custard is quite cold, cover the bowl and chill until required.

Lemon Curd Tartlets

Illustrated on Plate Ten

SERVES 6

- 6 prepared 10 cm/4 inch tartlets, chilled (page 188)
- 3 eggs
- 175 g/6 oz caster sugar
- finely grated rind and juice of 2 lemons
- 50 g/2 oz butter
- icing sugar

Heat the oven to 190°C/375°F/gas mark 5 (remember to put in the baking sheet).

Place the tartlet shells on the hot baking sheet and bake until pale gold – about 12 minutes. Remove from the oven and stand the baking sheet on a wire rack.

Meanwhile, combine the eggs, sugar, lemon rind and butter in a medium bowl. Set the bowl over a pan a quarter filled with simmering water on a low heat. Using a wooden spoon, stir until the sugar has dissolved and the butter melted. Remove from the heat and stir in the lemon juice. Pour the hot mixture into a jug and then carefully fill each tartlet shell just to the rim.

Reduce the oven heat to 180°C/350°F/gas mark 4. Return the baking sheet with the tartlet shells to the oven and bake for 15 minutes or until the filling has set. Cool for 5 minutes, then with a knife tip loosen each one and slide from the baking tins. Dust lightly with icing sugar and serve warm or cold.

DESSERT SAUCES

As a change from custard or cream, treat the family to a special dessert sauce. We've suggested our favourite combinations, but we are sure you will come up with many more.

Butterscotch Cream Measure 75 g/3 oz soft brown sugar, 175 g/6 oz golden syrup and 50 g/2 oz butter into a small saucepan. Stir over a low heat until softened and blended – do not boil. Stir in 150 ml/¼ pint double cream and 15 ml/1 tablespoon lemon juice and remove from the heat. If wished, add 50 g/2 oz chopped walnuts. This sauce thickens on standing but will thin when gently heated again.

Serve warm or cold, with sliced bananas and a scoop of vanilla ice-cream, with Espresso Chocolate Chunk Yogurt Ice-cream (see page 217), or with brown bread ice-cream.

Caramel Measure 225 g/8 oz granulated sugar into a clean, dry frying pan. Stir over a moderate heat until the sugar has melted and has become a golden caramel syrup. Draw the pan off the heat and gradually add 75 ml/3 fl oz boiling water down the side of the frying pan, stirring all the time – carefully because the mixture will bubble and steam. Stir to a smooth caramel sauce, add 15 ml/1 tablespoon white wine vinegar and cool. Serve with chilled orange slices or scoops of coffee ice-cream.

Sharp Lemon Measure 100 g/4 oz caster sugar, 15 ml/1 level tablespoon cornflour, a pinch of salt and the finely grated rind of 1 lemon into a small saucepan. Stir in 225 ml/8 fl oz cold water and mix until the cornflour is completely blended in. Set over a medium heat and bring to a simmer, stirring constantly. Simmer for 2–3 minutes then remove from the heat. Stir in the juice of 2 lemons and 5 ml/1 teaspoon butter.

Serve soon after making (either hot or warm as it won't reheat), over sugared pancakes or hot gingerbread or with apple pie.

Rum and Jam Measure 225 g/8 oz thick fruit jam (any flavour) into a small saucepan and add the juice of 1 lemon. Stir over a low heat to melt the jam. Press the mixture through a sieve, crushing the fruit pulp, and return to the pan. Add 75 ml/3 fl oz water and bring to a simmer, stirring. Remove from the heat and stir in 15 ml/1 tablespoon rum.

Serve with baked puddings and baked or poached fruits.

Butterscotch Apple Pudding

SERVES 4–6

175 g/6 oz self-raising flour
5 ml/1 level teaspoon baking powder
pinch of salt
5 ml/1 level teaspoon ground ginger
100 g/4 oz soft tub margarine
100 g/4 oz caster sugar
2 eggs
30 ml/2 tablespoons chopped stem ginger
30 ml/2 tablespoons milk
2 dessert apples
25 g/1 oz butter
25 g/1 oz soft brown sugar

Heat the oven to 190°C/375°F/gas mark 5.

Butter a 1.1 litre/2 pint pudding basin. Sift the flour, baking powder, salt and ground ginger into a medium bowl. Add the margarine, sugar, eggs, chopped stem ginger and milk. Stir with a wooden spoon to blend the ingredients, then beat to a soft cake mixture.

Peel, quarter and core the apples, then slice them thickly. Melt the butter and brown sugar in a frying pan, add the apple slices and turn them in the butterscotch mixture to glaze. Spoon the apple slices and butterscotch glaze into the base of the prepared basin.

Spoon the cake mixture on top and spread level. Lightly butter a square of foil and place over the basin, tucking the foil securely around the edge of the basin. 'Oven steam' for 1 hour. (Or M.)

NUTTY SHORTCAKE PASTRY

Adding finely chopped hazelnuts to a shortcake pastry recipe adds subtle flavour and an extra richness. We recommend roasting the nuts first to bring out their flavour. Simply spread the hazelnuts in a single layer in a baking tin and bake until golden brown – about 15 minutes – at 200°C/400°F/gas mark 6. Alternatively, grill or dry-fry until browned. Rub off the flaky outer skins. Leave to cool before very finely chopping by hand or in a processor or blender using the pulse switch. Whole or chopped roasted nuts may be kept for 2–3 weeks in an airtight jar.

Nutty Shortcake Pastry Place 200 g/7 oz plain flour, a pinch of salt, 150 g/5 oz butter cut in cubes and 75 g/3 oz sifted icing sugar in a processor. Buzz to fine crumbs. Add 50 g/2 oz finely chopped toasted nuts. Beat 10 ml/2 teaspoons water with 1 egg yolk in a cup. Switch on the processor and gradually add to the dry ingredients through the lid. Buzz just to a soft dough. Wrap the dough in clingfilm and refrigerate at least 1 hour or overnight before use.

Fresh Fruit Shortcake

SERVES 8–10

1 recipe Nutty Shortcake Pastry (page 192)
150 ml/¼ pint double cream
1 (200 ml) tub Greek-style yogurt
450–700 g/1–1½ lb fresh fruit – strawberries, raspberries, kiwis
75 ml/6 tablespoons strawberry conserve
juice of ½ a lemon

Heat the oven to 190°C/375°F/gas mark 5.

On a lightly floured surface roll out the pastry to a 20.5 cm/8 inch circle. Slide the pastry on to a baking tray (invert and use the base if your tray has a rim). Pinch the edges of the pastry into an attractive rim with lightly floured fingertips, then prick all over with a fork. Let the pastry rest at room temperature for 10 minutes.

Bake the shortcake for 25–30 minutes until golden brown. Meanwhile, whip the double cream to soft peaks and fold in the yogurt. Prepare the fruit, slicing the strawberries if large, and peeling and slicing the kiwi fruits.

Allow the shortcake to cool for 10 minutes on the baking sheet, then carefully slide on to a flat serving plate. Spread two-thirds of the strawberry conserve over the shortcake almost to the rim. Evenly spoon on the cream mixture and arrange the fruit attractively on top. Warm the remaining conserve with the lemon juice and drizzle over the fruit to glaze. Best served within 30 minutes.

HOT BAKED FRUITS

Tangy flavours mellow into a natural sweetness when fruits are heated for serving. Additions such as soft brown sugar or sweet wine help the transformation, and the end result is a delicious syrup for spooning over. Serve hot fruits with well-chilled cream or thick Greek-style yogurt for a complete contrast. Each recipe serves 4–6.

Basic method Pack the fruit in a shallow casserole dish large enough to take them in a single layer. Add the other ingredients and cover with the casserole lid or with foil. Heat the oven to 180°C/350°F/gas mark 4. Bake the fruit for 25–30 minutes until tender. Serve warm straight from the casserole, spooning the syrup over each portion.

Pears with Sugared Cream Peel 6 firm ripe dessert pears, cut in half, and scoop out the cores. Pack into the casserole, cut sides uppermost. Sprinkle with 45 ml/3 tablespoons soft brown sugar and 25 g/1 oz butter, cut into flakes. Cover and bake as above. Immediately pour over 150 ml/¼ pint double cream and serve at once.

Fresh Figs in Port Rinse 12 ripe fresh figs and with a sharp knife cut a cross in the flesh of each fig at the stalk end. Pack into the casserole cut side up, and pour over 175 ml/6 fl oz port. Sprinkle with 30 ml/2 tablespoons soft brown sugar, cover and bake.

Pineapple with Buttered Rum Trim off the leaves and stem end of a medium-sized ripe pineapple. Cut off the skin and cut the flesh lengthwise into 4–6 spears. Pack into the casserole and sprinkle with 60 ml/4 tablespoons rum and 45 ml/3 tablespoons soft brown sugar. Flake over 25 g/1 oz butter, cover and bake.

Apple Wedges with Lemon Peel and core 6 large eating apples and cut into wedges. Generously butter the casserole and pack with the apples. Sprinkle with the finely grated rind and juice of 1 large lemon and 100 g/4 oz demerara sugar. Flake over 25 g/1 oz butter, cover and bake.

Spiced Bananas Peel 6 firm ripe bananas and pack into the casserole. Combine the finely grated rind and juice of 1 lemon with 75 g/3 oz soft light brown sugar, 1.25 ml/½ level teaspoon each of ground cinnamon and nutmeg, and a pinch of ground cloves. Sprinkle evenly over the bananas and flake over 25 g/1 oz butter. Cover and bake.

PERFECT PASTRY CRUSTS

A tart with any kind of sweet filling will always get a warm welcome from family and friends alike – and fast requests for a repeat performance! We know some people, even experienced cooks, find making pastry a problem, but take heart. With this no-fail shortcrust recipe there is no time-consuming rolling out of the dough. Instead, the sweet crumbly mixture is pressed into the baking tin using lightly floured fingertips, and because the dough is mixed with an egg, the crust bakes up crisp and golden every time.

- When switching on the oven, slip in a baking sheet to heat up. When the tart tin is filled, slide it on to the hot baking sheet and bake. This ensures a crisp brown base to the tart.
- Loose-bottomed metal tart tins are better than heatproof glass or china flan dishes. Metal conducts heat more efficiently, and with a loose base you can remove the baked tart completely and let it cool on a rack. (Let the freshly baked tart cool for 10 minutes, then stand the tart tin on an unopened can. The sides of the tart tin will drop to the countertop. Loosen the base of the tart tin with a metal spatula and slide the tart on to a wire rack.)
- We have given you both the food processor and the fingertip method (see page 188). When using a processor, use chilled butter and, after buzzing to fine crumbs, tip the mixture into a bowl and add the egg with a fork. This avoids over-mixing the pastry. When mixing with the fingertips, use butter at room temperature.
- Once you have shaped the pastry shell, pop it into the refrigerator while you are making the filling. Slip the unbaked pastry shell into a large freezer bag if you wish to chill it for several hours or overnight.

OLD-FASHIONED PUDDINGS UPDATED

It is perfectly easy to cook some of our much-loved traditional puddings using updated recipes and methods. These delicious recipes are good examples. No need for the old-fashioned saucepan of simmering water that needed constant topping-up. Nowadays puddings can be 'oven steamed' in a roasting tin of boiling water with a covering of kitchen foil. A microwave cooks excellent 'steamed' puddings too. Pudding mixtures are feather-light made by the all-in-one method where all the ingredients are quickly mixed together in one bowl. Serve the puddings with a sauce where recommended, with Real Custard sauce (see page 190) or just with spoonfuls of clotted cream.

'Oven steaming' method Heat the oven to 190°C/375°F/gas mark 5. Place the filled and covered pudding basin(s) in a roasting tin and pour in boiling water from the kettle to a depth of 2.5 cm/1 inch. Cut a piece of kitchen foil large enough to completely cover the roasting tin and basin. Place over the top and carefully tuck under the edge of the roasting tin. Bake for the time suggested in the recipe. Lift the roasting tin out of the oven and carefully remove both the layers of foil. Turn the pudding(s) on to a warmed serving plate.

Microwave method Use non-metallic pudding basin(s). Stand the pudding(s) on a microwave rack and cook, following the oven manufacturer's guidelines. Leave to stand for a few minutes before turning out on to a warmed serving plate.

Orange Marmalade Pudding with Marmalade Sauce

SERVES 4–6

- 60 ml/4 tablespoons orange marmalade
- 175 g/6 oz self-raising flour
- 5 ml/1 level teaspoon powder
- pinch salt
- finely grated rind of 1 orange
- 100 g/4 oz soft tub margarine
- 75 g/3 oz caster sugar
- 2 eggs
- 30 ml/2 tablespoons milk

Heat the oven to 190°C/375°F/gas mark 5.

Well butter a 1.1 litre/2 pint pudding basin and put 15 ml/1 tablespoon of the marmalade in the bottom. Sift the flour, baking powder and salt into a medium-sized bowl. Add the grated orange rind, margarine, sugar, eggs, milk and remaining marmalade. Stir with a wooden spoon to blend the ingredients, then beat to a soft cake mixture.

Turn the mixture into the prepared pudding basin. Lightly butter a square of foil and place over the basin, tucking the foil securely around the edge of the basin. 'Oven steam' for 1 hour (see above). (Or [M].)

For the sauce
5 ml/1 level teaspoon cornflour
25 g/1 oz caster sugar
50 ml/2 fl oz water
100 g/4 oz orange marmalade
juice of 1 orange

Meanwhile make the sauce. Put the cornflour, sugar and water into a saucepan and mix well. Add the marmalade (cut up any large pieces of fruit) and the orange juice. Cook, stirring, until the marmalade has melted and the sauce comes to the boil. Cool slightly before serving with the pudding.

CHOCOLATE SAUCE UNLIMITED

Everyone's favourite, chocolate sauce should be served warm, when the texture is thin and shiny. As chocolate thickens as it cools, simply place the jug of sauce in a saucepan of warm water for a few minutes, stirring until smooth. Each sauce makes 4 servings.

Basic Warm Chocolate Sauce Place 50 g/2 oz caster sugar and 60 ml/4 tablespoons water in a small saucepan and place over medium heat. Stir until the sugar has dissolved, then bring to a rolling boil. Draw off the heat and add 100 g/4 oz plain chocolate, broken in pieces. Allow the chocolate to melt in the warmth of the pan, then stir with a whisk until smooth. Finally stir in 15 ml/1 tablespoon butter.

Vanilla Stir in 2.5 ml/½ teaspoon vanilla extract with the butter.

Rum Add 30 ml/2 tablespoons rum with the butter.

Mocha Use strong black coffee in place of the water.

Chocolate Nut Add 25 g/1 oz chopped nuts (any kind) to any of the recipes.

Any of the above can be served with warm baked chocolate puddings or with Espresso Chocolate Chunk or White Chocolate Hazelnut Yogurt Ice-cream (page 217).

Dark Cocoa Sauce Measure 150 ml/¼ pint water and 100 g/4 oz caster sugar into a small saucepan. Stir over a low heat until the sugar has dissolved and the syrup is boiling. Add 50 g/2 oz cocoa powder and whisk until smooth.

Serve chilled with Chocolate Terrine (page 233) or with chocolate or vanilla cheesecakes.

Chocolate Espresso Measure 15 ml/1 level tablespoon instant espresso coffee granules into a measuring jug and add 175 ml/6 fl oz boiling water. Stir to blend. Pour the hot coffee into a food processor or blender and add 100 g/4 oz caster sugar and 113 g/4 oz packet plain chocolate chips. Buzz until quite smooth. Pour into a jug and serve warm or cold.

Serve poured over poached pears, profiteroles or coffee mousse.

Chocolate Cream Heat 300 ml/½ pint double cream with 100 g/4 oz plain or milk chocolate, broken into small chunks, until the chocolate has melted and the sauce is smooth.

Serve freshly made, poured over rich vanilla or coffee ice-cream or vanilla profiteroles.

Double Chocolate Chip Puddings

SERVES 6

Heat the oven to 190°C/375°F/gas mark 5.

Butter the insides of 6 150 ml/$^{1}/_{4}$ pint pudding moulds (or heatproof cups) and line the base of each with a circle of non-stick baking parchment. Sift the flour, cocoa powder, cinnamon, salt and baking powder into a medium bowl. Add the margarine, sugar, eggs and milk. Stir with a wooden spoon to blend the ingredients, then beat to a soft cake mixture. Stir in the chocolate chips.

Divide the mixture equally between the moulds. Lightly butter 6 squares of foil and place one over each pudding, tucking the foil securely around the edge of each mould. 'Oven steam' for 40 minutes (see page 195). (Or [M].)

Serve with warm Dark Cocoa Sauce (page 196).

- 175 g/6 oz self-raising flour
- 30 ml/2 level tablespoons cocoa powder
- 5 ml/1 level teaspoon ground cinnamon
- pinch of salt
- 5 ml/1 level teaspoon baking powder
- 100 g/4 oz soft tub margarine
- 100 g/4 oz soft brown sugar
- 2 eggs
- 30 ml/2 tablespoons milk
- 50 g/2 oz plain chocolate chips

Chocolate Sauce Pudding

SERVES 4

Heat the oven to 190°C/375°F/gas mark 5.

Start with the cake mixture: butter a 1.1 litre/2 pint baking or pie dish. Sift the flour with 30 ml/2 level tablespoons of the cocoa powder into a medium-sized bowl. Add the margarine, caster sugar, eggs, vanilla extract and milk. Stir with a wooden spoon to blend the ingredients, then beat to a soft cake mixture. Stir in the walnuts.

Spoon the mixture into the prepared dish and spread evenly. In a small bowl combine the soft brown sugar with the remaining cocoa. Stir in the hot (not boiling) water and stir until smooth. Pour the sauce over the top of the cake mixture.

- 100 g/4 oz self-raising flour
- 60 ml/4 level tablespoons cocoa powder
- 100 g/4 oz soft tub margarine
- 100 g/4 oz caster sugar
- 2 eggs
- 2.5 ml/$^{1}/_{2}$ teaspoon vanilla extract
- 15 ml/1 tablespoon milk
- 50 g/2 oz chopped walnuts
- 100 g/4 oz soft brown sugar
- 225 ml/8 fl oz hot water

Bake the pudding for 40 minutes. During baking the sponge cake rises to the surface and the chocolate sauce forms a delicious pool underneath. Serve hot, with chilled single cream or smetana.

Spiced Sugar Plum Cake

SERVES 6

- 175 g/6 oz self-raising flour
- 5 ml/1 level teaspoon baking powder
- 75 g/3 oz caster sugar
- 1 egg
- 90 ml/6 tablespoons milk
- 30 ml/2 tablespoons grapeseed oil
- 450 g/1 lb ripe plums
- 25 g/1 oz butter
- 50 g/2 oz demerara sugar
- 2.5 ml/$^1/_2$ level teaspoon ground cinnamon
- 25 g/1 oz chopped walnuts

Heat the oven to 200°C/400°F/gas mark 6.

Generously butter a baking tin about 27.5 × 17.5 cm/11 × 7 inches. Sift the flour and baking powder into a medium-sized bowl. Add the caster sugar and mix. Crack the egg into a small bowl, add the milk and oil and mix with a fork to break up the egg.

Add the egg mixture to the dry ingredients. Stir with a wooden spoon to blend the ingredients, then beat to a soft cake mixture. Spread evenly in the prepared tin.

Halve the plums and remove the stones. Melt the butter and brush it over the cake batter. Arrange the plum halves in rows over the cake mixture. Combine the demerara sugar, cinnamon and walnuts and sprinkle over the fruit.

Bake for 35 minutes. Let the cake cool for 5 minutes before cutting into squares. Serve with Real Custard Sauce (page 190), chilled cream or natural yogurt.

ALL ABOUT VANILLA

Vanilla is the fruit of a climbing orchid. The slender deep brown pods are cured to make 'vanilla pods' and will keep their flavour for at least 5 years if they are kept in an airtight container. From these pods pure vanilla extract is made. It really is worth searching in specialist food shops, or sourcing a mail order service for the genuine article. Be prepared to pay more – vanilla extract is expensive – but the flavour and aroma is wonderful and you will need to use less of it. Most bottles of so-called vanilla are actually a synthetic vanilla flavour. Only when the label reads 'vanilla extract' or 'pure vanilla' have you got the real thing.

An effective way to get a vanilla flavour (less expensive too) is to use the pods to make your own vanilla sugar. Just add 1 or 2 pods to a jar of caster or granulated sugar and leave for a week or so for the flavour to be taken up by the sugar. Use vanilla sugar in place of unflavoured sugar in dessert sauces, custards, puddings and in baking. As the vanilla sugar is used, top up the container with more unflavoured sugar, cover and shake to blend. Alternatively, the flavour from a vanilla pod can be extracted by steeping it in the milk for a custard or pudding, or in the syrup for poaching fruits. Bring the milk (or syrup) containing the pod to a simmer and leave it to stand for about an hour to infuse. Remove the pod before completing the recipe. After use rinse the pod and dry, then store in an airtight container (or in the sugar jar) until next required.

LITTLE POTS OF CUSTARD

Egg yolks provide the creaminess in a baked custard and the whites help the mixture to set. Simple country-style baked custards are made with whole eggs, but for a really delicious soft texture we use a higher proportion of yolks to whites. A baked custard is richer if you substitute single cream for some of the milk. Custards must be cooked gently, otherwise the texture will not be smooth. This is why they are baked in dishes set in a pan of water, which maintains an even cooking temperature. If custards are overcooked they will be spoilt – when set there should be just the slightest quiver in the centre when gently moved. Set the oven timer so you don't forget about them!

Basic method Heat the oven to 160°C/325°F/gas mark 3. Butter 6 individual ramekin dishes and stand them in a roasting tin. When the custard has been poured into the ramekins, pour cold water into the roasting tin to a depth of 2.5 cm/1 inch. Bake for 20–25 minutes, until the custards are set. Lift the ramekins from the tin. Let cool, then chill at least 4 hours or overnight.

Vanilla Pots de Crème Heat 600 ml/1 pint milk (or milk and cream) until just beginning to bubble around the edges. Whisk together 1 whole egg, 4 egg yolks and 25 g/1 oz caster sugar until creamy. Gradually stir in the hot milk. Add 5 ml/1 teaspoon vanilla extract. Strain the custard into a jug and pour into the ramekins. Bake.

To serve, whip 150 ml/¼ pint whipping cream to soft peaks and spoon on top of each chilled custard. Lightly sprinkle with finely chopped toasted hazelnuts.

Moka Pots de Crème Measure 15 ml/1 level tablespoon instant coffee granules into a medium bowl. Add 30 ml/2 tablespoons boiling water and stir until dissolved. Add 100 g/4 oz plain chocolate, broken in pieces, and set the pan over a saucepan a quarter filled with hot water (off the heat) until the chocolate has melted. Stir until smooth. Stir in 25 g/1 oz caster sugar, 1 whole egg and 3 egg yolks, and mix well. Heat 450 ml/¾ pint milk (or milk and cream) until just beginning to bubble around the edges. Gradually stir into the egg mixture. Strain into a jug and pour into the ramekins.

To serve, whip 150 ml/¼ pint whipping cream to soft peaks and spoon on top of each chilled custard. Sprinkle with grated plain chocolate.

Coffee Walnut Puddings with Coffee Cream Sauce

SERVES 6

75 g/3 oz butter
175 g/6 oz soft brown sugar
50 g/2 oz chopped walnuts
15 ml/1 level instant coffee granules
30 ml/2 tablespoons boiling water
150 g/5 oz self-raising flour
5 ml/1 level teaspoon baking powder
50 g/2 oz golden syrup
100 g/4 oz soft tub margarine
2 eggs

For the sauce
15 ml/1 level tablespoon instant coffee granules
30 ml/2 level tablespoons soft brown sugar
150 ml/$^1/_4$ pint double cream

Heat the oven to 190°C/375°F/gas mark 5.

Melt the butter and use a little of it to brush round the insides of 6 150 ml/$^1/_4$ pint pudding moulds or heatproof cups. To the remaining butter, add 100 g/4 oz of the soft brown sugar and the walnuts. Stir to mix. Spoon the walnut topping into each buttered mould.

In a small bowl combine the coffee granules with the boiling water and stir until the coffee has dissolved. Sift the flour and baking powder into a medium-sized bowl. Add the remaining soft brown sugar, the golden syrup, margarine, eggs and dissolved coffee. Stir with a wooden spoon to blend the ingredients, then beat to a soft cake mixture. Spoon the mixture into each mould, filling them two-thirds full.

Arrange the moulds on a baking tray and bake for 15 minutes or until they are well risen. Loosen the sides of each pudding and turn out on to individual plates.

While the puddings are baking, make the sauce. Put the coffee granules and soft brown sugar into a small saucepan. Add the double cream and stir to blend. Warm gently until the coffee has dissolved, but do not allow to boil.

Serve the puddings with the Coffee Cream Sauce or with single cream.

CHAPTER TWELVE

Desserts

Stylish fruit salads, yogurt ice-creams and creamy blender puddings make refreshing summer desserts. Consider a glamorous dessert cake for that special occasion when you need to impress.

DAIRY CHOICE

Being knowledgeable and selective about your choice of dairy products and fats is important both from a health point of view and for successful cooking. Nowadays there is a wide variety of dairy foods to choose from, both traditional and the new, lower fat alternatives, plus an ever-widening range of non-dairy fats and spreads. In cooking, your choice can affect the flavour or texture of the finished dish. In our recipes we've indicated the dairy product we know will give the best result and have used a low fat alternative wherever suitable.

MILK

Whole milk contains the cream which settles as a layer on the top of the milk or, if the milk has been homogenized, will be evenly distributed throughout. Most whole milk sold through the supermarkets is homogenized. Low fat **semi-skimmed milk** has a proportion of the fat removed; **skimmed milk** is almost fat free. Since reducing the fat also reduces the vitamin content, some low fat milks are sold with added vitamins. Semi-skimmed milk is pleasant to drink (particularly when well chilled) and a sensible choice in a healthy diet. Skimmed milk is too watery for some tastes but invaluable in a calorie-controlled diet.

Buttermilk is made by adding a culture to pasteurized skimmed milk. It has a thick consistency and a tart flavour. Use in baking when sour milk is needed, in creamy salad dressings, soups and as a refreshing low fat drink. If you are unable to find buttermilk, use natural yogurt diluted in equal parts with cold water. As with all fresh milks, keep in the refrigerator and observe the 'use-by' date.

Long life milk is ultra-heat treated (UHT), which means that unopened cartons can be kept for months without refrigeration (see 'best before end' date on carton). Once opened, UHT milk should be treated as fresh milk. UHT milk is excellent for making home-made yogurt as it doesn't have to be boiled first.

CREAM

Cream adds a smooth rich texture to recipes. The type of cream is determined by the amount of fat in it – each has a specified minimum content. For perfect results it is important to use the cream specified in a recipe – they are not interchangeable.

Clotted cream, which is very rich and thick (minimum fat content 55%), is a matured cream which has been scalded over simmering water, which produces the characteristic crusted surface. It is used spooned straight from the pot. **Double cream** (minimum fat content 48%), is the most versatile of all the creams and whips beautifully. **Extra-thick double cream** has the same fat content, but has been homogenized to give a thicker consistency. Use double cream in cooking – it can be boiled without separating and will remain creamy in a sauce or soup; do not thin it down.

Whipping cream (minimum fat content 30%) will whip to a good light volume but will not hold added ingredients without separating and cannot be subjected to heat. Don't substitute it for double cream in hot recipes or when making ice-creams – the lower fat content will give larger ice crystals and a less smooth ice-cream. **Single cream** (minimum fat content 18%) will not whip but is ideal for adding to soups. **Half cream** (minimum fat content 12%) is suitable for serving with cereals or using in place of milk. **Soured cream** (minimum fat content 18%) is single cream commercially soured with a lactic culture. Soured cream cannot be whipped – for the thickest consistency spoon very well chilled straight from the carton without stirring. Soured cream becomes very thin when heated.

Crème fraîche (mimimum fat content 48%) is double cream with a slightly acid taste because it has been soured naturally in much the same way as yogurt. Like double cream it can be heated, even boiled, without separating. **Smetana** (minimum fat content 10%) is a combination of single cream and skimmed milk, homogenized and soured with a culture to give a thick smooth consistency. It can be used in place of soured cream in recipes where it is stirred in at the end of cooking (do not allow the dish to boil).

All creams are very perishable and should be kept refrigerated in their sealed containers. Once the foil seal is broken, keep the carton tightly covered as it can easily pick up the flavour of other foods. Use within the 'use-by' date on the carton.

Yogurt

Yogurt is prepared from whole or skimmed milk, usually cow's milk but ewe's and goat's milk yogurt is available too. The milk is heat treated and a culture added, which works on the milk to produce a set. 'Set' yogurts separate once they are spooned into, 'stirred' yogurts retain their smooth creamy texture. Most commercially produced yogurts, unless pasteurized after preparation (to extend their shelf life) contain living bacteria and are 'live'. Bio-yogurt contains an additional bacterial culture which, it is claimed, is beneficial to health. **Natural whole milk yogurt** has a creamier texture and taste and a higher fat and calorie count than a low fat version made of skimmed milk, but they are interchangeable in recipes. **Greek-style yogurt** is a whole milk yogurt and may have cream added which makes the taste richer but raises the fat content. Even so, Greek-style yogurt is a healthy substitute for fresh cream as a topping and for use in recipes.

When yogurt is added to hot food it will curdle, which looks unappetizing though the flavour is not spoilt. You can get round this by just spooning the yogurt on top of the hot food – such as a curry or soup. Or stir it in just before serving without reheating the dish. Yogurt can be stabilized to prevent it curdling by the addition of cornflour. Stir 5 ml/1 level teaspoon cornflour into 15 ml/1 tablespoon cold water and stir into 300 ml/½ pint yogurt. Stir equal amounts of natural yogurt and cold water together to use in place of sour or buttermilk when making scones or soda breads.

Always buy yogurt from a refrigerated cabinet because the culture is still 'live' and working. Keep refrigerated and eat by the date stamped on the lid.

Butter and Margarine

Originally the choice was simple – between butter or margarine. Now there is a bewildering choice of butters, margarines and dairy or oil-based spreads to choose from. Anything labelled butter or margarine must contain a minimum of 80% fat, which makes them versatile and good for cooking, but it's worth remembering that calorie for calorie, margarine is just as fattening as butter. The health argument between butter and margarine has raged for years but, we maintain, where the flavour counts, butter is best.

Butters vary in flavour, colour and texture depending on the source of the milk. **Traditional butter** is a sweet cream butter, usually lightly salted and packed in greaseproof paper or gold foil. **Continental-style butter** is a lactic butter, paler in colour, usually unsalted and wrapped in silver foil. Flavours vary, so shop around to find the one you like best. When browning meats or fish, the addition of 15 ml/1 tablespoon oil to the butter being used allows the butter to become hotter before it starts to burn.

Hard block margarines can be substituted for butter in cooking. Better-quality hard margarines have an acceptable flavour. **Soft tub margarines** are excellent for quick-mix cake or pudding recipes but should not be used for pastry, crumbles or biscuits as they have a higher water content than block margarines.

Anything with less than a minimum 80% fat content must be called a **spread**. Spreads remain soft when refrigerated but their content limits the use of some of them in cooking – check the packaging. **Full-fat spreads** can be dairy or oil based and usually combine a proportion of cream for a buttery taste with vegetable oil, which prevents them hardening in the fridge. Full-fat spreads may be used in cooking. **Low-fat spreads** usually contain buttermilk and oil and are suitable for spreading only. Keep spreads in the refrigerator, as they are inclined to become oily if left at room temperature for any length of time.

Raspberry and Coffee Cream Cake

SERVES 6–8

30 ml/2 level tablespoons instant coffee granules
225 ml/8 fl oz boiling water
75 g/3 oz caster sugar
450 g/1 lb ricotta cheese
75 g/3 oz sifted icing sugar, plus extra for dusting
16 trifle sponges
450 g/1 lb fresh raspberries

The day before serving: select a 20 cm/8 inch square baking tin or glass dish with straight sides and at least 5 cm/2 inches deep. Line with foil or clingfilm.

Dissolve the coffee granules in the boiling water. Add the caster sugar and stir until dissolved. Leave to cool.

Combine the ricotta cheese with the icing sugar. Slice the sponge cakes in half horizontally. Arrange a layer of sponge slices in the base of the lined mould, sugary sides downwards – this will be the top of the dessert.

Spoon one-third of the coffee syrup evenly over the sponge cakes. Sprinkle with one-third of the raspberries and then half the sweetened ricotta. Cover with a second layer of sponge slices and soak with coffee syrup as before. Add half the remaining raspberries and evenly spoon over the remaining ricotta cheese. Finally top with the remaining sponge cakes and spoon over the rest of the coffee syrup. Cover and chill for 24 hours.

Unmould on to a serving dish and remove the lining paper. Top with the remaining raspberries and add a final dusting of icing sugar.

BUYING AND STORING FRESH FRUITS

Fresh fruits are bright, colourful and endlessly varied. We use them for their delectable sweet or tart flavours and they are the shapes with which we decorate or pretty up our recipes. These days it is possible to buy fruits from all over the world all year round – look at the tags and labels. Get to know where fruits come from, note the varieties and learn to select the ones you like. Remember, for the best value and freshness – not to mention flavour – buy fruits when they are in season.

Bananas and **pineapples** are available all the year round. Bananas are sold by the hand or bunch. When the yellow skins are flecked with brown, bananas are ripe for eating. Choose those with green tips for serving whole or in chunks. Pineapples on sale are ripe and ready-to-eat. They should be dry – any with bruises or soft spots should be passed over. Both of these are fruits to keep at room temperature and use quickly.

Apricots, nectarines, peaches and figs are seasonal summer fruits, delicate and easily bruised. Buy apricots that are bright coloured and fully ripe, when they will have a delicious flavour. Peaches and nectarines are frequently sold under-ripe and will often benefit from a 48-hour sit at room temperature. Before buying, look at the stalk ends – there should be no sign of green. Buy figs that are ripe – they should be soft to the touch – and use them quickly. Of all the imported fruits figs transport the least happily. **English plums** are in sad decline. Where are our superbly flavoured Victoria plums? Instead we have fruits from California and Spain. Late in summer **greengages** make an appearance, a golden amber when ripe, and a delicious flavour for eating raw or cooked. Seek out Victoria plums and greengages in local greengrocers.

Grapes should be plump and on the bunch. The seedless varieties are good for recipes if you dread the thought of taking out the pips. For a real treat look for the large pale green grapes called Muscat. Serve grapes lightly chilled.

Charentais **melons** are small with a peachy flesh and a wonderful flavour; choose them for special occasions. Ogen, Galia and Honeydew melons are general purpose. Plan to buy melons a few days before you want to serve them. Then you can select a melon that is firm and let it stand at room temperature for a day or so to ripen as you like it. To test, press gently at the blossom end – the flesh should give a little. Another sign is the delicious perfume. When a melon is ripe, put it in the refrigerator and eat it as soon as possible. Watermelons are picked ripe, so use them straight away.

Mangoes have a wonderful flavour and colour. Look for fruits that have a golden yellow/green skin, sometimes with a pink blush. A delicious perfume is another sign that your mango is ripe. **Kiwi** fruits have a furry brown skin that you pare off to reveal a bright green flesh. Sadly, they are frequently sold unripe, when they feel hard and have no flavour. Let them stand at room temperature for a few days after purchase. Kiwis have the best flavour when they are beginning to feel soft. Keep exotic fruits cool but out of the refrigerator; chilling does nothing for their delicate flavours.

Berries have a short summer season but they are among the most flavoursome of our fruits. Red- and blackcurrants, raspberries, strawberries and cultivated blackberries are very perishable. Avoid buying punnets that are stained with fruit juices. Green early gooseberries are the ones to buy for cooking, but later in summer sweeter, plump dessert gooseberries are delicious for eating raw. Blueberries make an appearance in summer, sweet, ripe and ready for eating raw or in recipes. Use soft fruit within 24 hours. Chill temporarily in the refrigerator if you have to but, if you plan to serve fresh raspberries or strawberries as they are, make sure you take them out of the cold at least 1 hour before serving so they regain their full sunny flavour.

Apples and **pears** are available all the year round, but our own home-grown varieties ripen in late summer through to autumn. Get to know some of the old-fashioned varieties – Laxton's Fortune, Egremont Russet, Ellison's Orange or Chiver's Delight. Our unique, sour-tasting Bramley Seedling, or cooking apple, is the one to choose for puddings and pies and recipes where you require apple purée. The sweeter dessert apples hold their shape when cooked. Use dessert apples when slices are required for decorative purposes or for slicing into fruit salad. Apples will last only a few days in the fruit bowl, and will keep better stored in a plastic bag in the refrigerator. Pears are picked unripe, which is fine for cooking, but if you want to eat them out of hand, take them home and let them sit in the warmth for a day or so. Conference is our most versatile pear, with an elegant shape; choose it for poaching. Comice or William pears are the ones for eating raw. Occasionally you may see **quinces** for sale. These are as hard as wood, but when pared and cut up they pulp down very quickly. Combine quinces with apples for an old-fashioned taste in a pie.

Citrus fruits should be smooth-skinned, heavy for their size and firm. Get to know the different orange varieties – Valencias are very juicy for squeezing. Shamoutis have a delicious flavour, while Navels have no pips and cut into elegant segments. Yellow grapefruit are tangy while the pink varieties are sweeter – both are a good buy when you want to mix the segments. Easy peelers are the tiny clementines and tangerines (the best flavour but they have pips). Satsumas have no pips but you lose out on flavour. Kumquats are like miniature oranges but the skin is thin and sweet while the centres are tangy. Never be without lemons in the kitchen; they are infinitely versatile and even a small amount of juice can work miracles on a bland dish. Try the occasional lime, the fragrance and flavour is wonderful. Store citrus fruits in the salad drawer of the refrigerator and they will keep well.

WHIPPED CREAM

Double and whipping cream may be whipped straight from the carton. Extra-thick double cream has been homogenized to give it a thicker consistency. Really intended for spooning over desserts, it can be whipped if it is first thinned slightly. To each 150 ml/¼ pint extra-thick double cream stir in 30 ml/2 tablespoons cold milk until smooth, then whip.

For best results have the bowl, beaters and cream in the refrigerator for several hours before whipping. If you keep cream well chilled the fat globules remain firmer and as a result you will get a better whipped volume. Whip the cream just to soft peaks for folding in, it will then blend in smoothly and evenly. If you have slightly overbeaten cream by mistake, quickly beat in a spoonful or two of very cold milk.

Strawberry and Lemon Layer Cake

SERVES 8

- 175 g/6 oz plain flour
- 10 ml/2 level teaspoons baking powder
- 150 g/5 oz caster sugar
- 2 eggs
- 75 ml/3 fl oz grapeseed oil
- 75 ml/3 fl oz milk
- grated rind and juice of 2 lemons
- 100 g/4 oz granulated sugar
- 300 ml/½ pint double cream
- 450 g/1 lb fresh strawberries

Heat the oven to 160°/325°F/gas mark 3.

Grease and line the base of a 22.5 cm/9 inch spring-release tin.

Sift the flour and baking powder into a medium-sized bowl. Stir in the sugar. Separate the eggs, cracking the yolks and whites into different bowls. Add the oil, milk and lemon rind to the yolks and mix with a fork. Pour into the dry ingredients and beat to a smooth batter. Whisk the whites to stiff peaks and fold into the batter with a metal spoon. Pour the batter into the prepared tin and spread level. Bake for 40–45 minutes.

Meanwhile make the lemon juice up to 225 ml/8 fl oz with water and pour into a small saucepan. Add the granulated sugar and stir over a low heat to dissolve the sugar. Prick the surface of the just-baked cake with a fork, then spoon over the hot syrup. Let cool completely – preferably overnight.

Transfer the cake to a flat serving platter. Whip the cream until thick. Spread evenly over the top of the cake. Chill for at least 4 hours, until the cream is firm. Hull the strawberries and perch them upright on top of the cream.

For the final flourish, serve with Red Raspberry Sauce (page 208).

FRUIT SAUCES

The addition of an appropriate sauce can lift the most simple of desserts – store-bought ice-cream – into something really special.

Very simple to make, all our favourite dessert sauces are equally good served hot, warm or cold. Serve freshly made or cover and cool until required. To reheat for serving hot or warm, place the container of sauce over a pan of simmering water and stir until the desired temperature. Or warm in the microwave using MEDIUM/50% power. When serving cold, for the optimum flavour, serve at room temperature rather than chilled. Each sauce makes 4–6 servings.

Red Raspberry Pick over 450 g/1 lb fresh raspberries, put half of them in a saucepan and mash with a fork. Add 45 ml/3 tablespoons redcurrant jelly and stir over a low heat until the jelly has melted. Combine 15 ml/1 tablespoon cornflour with 30 ml/2 tablespoons water to make a smooth mixture and add to the pan. Stir until the mixture thickens and boils, then draw off the heat. Pass the sauce through a sieve and discard the pips. Add 15 ml/1 tablespoon raspberry vinegar or lemon juice and the remaining raspberries.

Serve warm or cold with thick yogurt, spooned over Fresh Lemon or Crushed Strawberry Yogurt Ice-cream (page 217), skinned fresh peaches, or rich chocolate cake.

Black Cherry and Kirsch Strain the liquid from 1 (425 g) can black cherries in juice or syrup. Make up to 300 ml/8 fl oz with red wine. Measure 15 ml/1 tablespoon cornflour into a saucepan, add the liquid and stir to blend. Add 15 ml/1 tablespoon redcurrant jelly. Stir over a moderate heat until thickened and clear. Taste and, if not sweet enough, add a little extra redcurrant jelly. Add the reserved cherries and 15 ml/1 tablespoon Kirsch.

Serve warm or cold with cream-filled meringues, spooned over Tangy Orange Yogurt Ice-cream (page 217) or with Yorkshire Curd Tart (page 188).

Fresh Blackberry Pick over 450 g/1 lb fresh blackberries and place in a mixing bowl. Sprinkle with 100 g/4 oz caster sugar, toss gently, and leave for 2 hours so the juices run. Press the fruits and juice through a sieve and discard the pips. Stir in the juice of 1 lemon.

Serve cold or warm with apple snow, hot apple pie, lemon mousse or sorbet or Fresh Lemon Yogurt Ice-cream (page 217).

Rum and Raisin Measure 50 g/2 oz soft brown sugar and 15 ml/1 level tablespoon cornflour into a saucepan. Add 100 ml/4 fl oz water and stir to mix. Cook, stirring constantly, until the sauce is boiling, then draw off the heat. Add 25 g/1 oz butter, 50 g/2 oz seedless raisins and 45 ml/3 tablespoons dark rum.

Serve warm over coffee or chocolate ice-cream, hot apple pie or chocolate cheesecake.

Ginger and Lemon Measure 15 ml/1 level tablespoon caster sugar and 15 ml/1 level tablespoon cornflour into a saucepan. Add the finely grated rind of 1 lemon and mix. Squeeze and reserve the lemon juice. Stir in 150 ml/¼ pint water and 45 ml/3 tablespoons ginger preserve. Bring to the boil, stirring constantly, then draw off the heat. Add the reserved lemon juice.

Serve warm with baked apples or pears, warm gingerbread or baked vanilla cheesecake.

Strawberry Pick over and hull 450 g/1 lb fresh strawberries. Put in a food processor or blender with 175 g/6 oz caster sugar and the juice of 1 lemon. Cover and blend to a purée – by liquidizing the fruit and sugar together the mixture thickens to a sauce consistency.

Serve cold with thick yogurt, gooseberry mousse or fool, vanilla ice-cream with fresh peach slices, with a light lemon cheesecake or mousse or with Crushed Strawberry Yogurt Ice-cream (page 217).

Chocolate Pastry Cream Cake

SERVES 12–16

---

200 g/7 oz plain flour
50 g/2 oz cocoa powder
150 g/5 oz butter
40 g/1½ oz caster sugar
1 egg yolk
750 ml/1¼ pints double cream
75 g/3 oz icing sugar
cocktail cherries with stalks
grated or flaked plain chocolate

Place the flour, 25 g/1 oz of the cocoa and the butter in a processor and buzz to coarse crumbs. Tip into a bowl. (Alternatively, sift the flour and cocoa into a bowl and rub in the butter with the fingertips.) Stir in the caster sugar. Add 30 ml/2 tablespoons cold water to the egg yolk and mix with a fork. Add to the dry ingredients and mix until just combined. Using your fingertips, lightly knead to a smooth dough. Wrap and chill for 30 minutes.

Heat the oven to 190°C/375°F/gas mark 5.

Cut 7 sheets of non-stick baking parchment to fit your baking tray. On 6 of them, draw a 22.5 cm/9 inch circle in pencil – use a plate as a guide. Divide the dough into 6 portions. Set one piece of dough in a pencilled circle. Cover with the spare sheet of parchment and roll the chocolate pastry to a thin 22.5 cm/9 inch circle. Peel off the covering parchment and trim the edges of the pastry to a neat shape. Slide the pastry (and parchment) on to the baking tray. Bake for 5 minutes until the pastry is just crisp. Slide the pastry and parchment on to a wire cooling rack and leave until cold. Repeat with the remaining 5 portions of dough.

Pour the double cream into a large mixing bowl. Set a sieve over the bowl and measure in the icing sugar and the remaining 25 g/1 oz cocoa powder. Sift over the cream and then whip to soft peaks.

To assemble the cake, carefully peel the baking parchment off the pastry. Set one layer on a flat serving dish and spread with a thin layer of cream. Cover with a second pastry layer. Repeat the layers, finishing with a swirled layer of the cocoa cream on top. Refrigerate for 24 hours.

Just before serving, decorate the top with cocktail cherries and grated or flaked plain chocolate.

Double Chocolate Cheesecake

SERVES 12

50 g/2 oz butter
25 g/1 oz icing sugar
1 egg yolk
25 g/1 oz chopped roasted hazelnuts
75 g/3 oz self-raising flour
175 g/6 oz white chocolate
175 g/6 oz plain chocolate
700 g/1½ lb curd cheese
225 g/8 oz fromage frais
175 g/6 oz caster sugar

Heat the oven to 200°C/400°F/gas mark 6.

Grease the base of a 22.5 cm/9 inch spring-release tin. Put the butter, icing sugar and egg yolk into a food processor and process until soft and creamy. Add the nuts and flour and process to a smooth dough.

Unclip the sides of the spring-release tin. Using a palette knife, spread the dough over the base of the tin. Bake for 10–15 minutes until golden. Allow to cool, then add the spring-release sides. Lower the oven heat to 160°C/325°F/gas mark 3.

Break the white chocolate into a small mixing bowl and the plain chocolate into a medium-sized bowl. Melt both separately by placing the bowls over saucepans quarter filled with hot (not boiling) water (or [M]). Put the curd cheese, fromage frais and caster sugar into a food processor and buzz until smooth.

Spoon half the cheese mixture into the melted plain chocolate and blend together. Add the melted white chocolate to the remaining cheese mixture and blend. Spoon the two mixtures alternately into the spring-release tin. With a knife, stir once or twice to marble the mixture. Bake for 50 minutes until firm to the touch. Cool completely, then refrigerate for 24 hours before removing from the tin and serving.

GELATINE

Some cooks avoid recipes using powdered gelatine, perhaps remembering desserts that were rubbery and unpalatable. If you follow our simple guidelines, we guarantee that will never happen again.

❦ Measure gelatine very accurately. A stiff

and rubbery set is due to using too much gelatine.

The correct proportion is 15 g/½ oz (15 ml/3 level teaspoons) gelatine to 600 ml/1 pint liquid. Gelatine also comes packed in individual packets sufficient to set 600 ml/1 pint. In soufflés and mousses part of the liquid may consist of eggs and cream.

❦ Gelatine must be softened before adding to hot mixtures or dissolved before adding to cold mixtures. Do not allow a mixture containing gelatine, or dissolved gelatine itself, to come to the boil or the setting properties of the gelatine will be greatly reduced.

To soften, sprinkle the gelatine over 30–45 ml/2–3 tablespoons of cold liquid (which may be taken from the measured liquid used in the recipe) in a small bowl. Leave for about 5 minutes until the granules have absorbed the liquid and the gelatine is like a 'cake' or 'sponge'. At this stage it can be stirred into a hot mixture, when it will dissolve quickly and easily.

To dissolve, stand the bowl of gelatine at the 'cake' stage in a saucepan that has about 2.5 cm/1 inch of hot water in it. Gently stir until the gelatine is dissolved and there are no granules visible. Allow to cool slightly and when lukewarm add to the main mixture. (Or M. Heat the gelatine 'cake' on DEFROST/30% for 2–3 minutes, stirring once, until clear.)

❦ Setting time for gelatine mixtures can vary from 2–4 hours in the refrigerator. The more acid the mixture, the longer the time needed. If refrigerating overnight, cover the dish or mould with clingfilm.

❦ To unmould a gelatine mixture, start by loosening the edge of the mould with a knife blade dipped in water. Then dip the mould (up to the rim) in hand-hot water for 10 seconds. Place a serving plate over the top, invert the plate and mould together and give a sharp shake. The mixture should slip out easily. If it doesn't work the first time, give the mould another quick dip and try again.

For individual moulds or ramekins, treat as above, turning each mould on to your wetted fingers, then slide on to the serving plate.

FRUIT PLATTERS

Fresh fruits have such lovely colours and intriguing shapes which can be exploited to good effect if you set them out attractively. Presentation is everything, so be prepared to spend a little time on the arrangement – there is no prettier way to end a meal.

Start with a good-sized platter that will give you space rather than depth so that nothing is overcrowded. Select fruits that are at their best, thinking about the colours and shapes. Do you want one fruit only or lots of contrast? It's worth remembering that if you group fruits, rather than mixing them all up, you will get a bolder impact. Consider adding a few leaves – strawberry or blackcurrant are particularly pretty shapes – slip them under the fruits for background colour. Mint or lemon balm sprigs, fresh and aromatic, look very decorative tucked around the edge of the platter.

Fruits need to be prepared with care, pips and stones removed, segments meticulously freed from membrane and peel, tough outer skins sliced away – on a fruit platter everything should be edible. Then the prepared fruits should be sliced boldly, trying to get a variation in shape, some fruits in halves, others in slices, some left whole or in small bunches. With the exception of those to be marinated, fruit platters should be prepared just before the meal is started so that they remain very fresh. Squeeze a little fresh lemon juice on anything that might discolour.

Pass dessert plates for serving, not bowls. In hot weather it is rather nice to chill the plates well first.

The following fruit platters will serve 6.

Exotic Fruits with Vodka Syrup Make the sauce ahead of time and allow to cool. Dissolve 100 g/4 oz caster sugar in 150 ml/$^1/_4$ pint water and bring to a simmer. Add the juice of 2 limes (save a thin slice off 1 lime for decoration) and leave until cold. Add 30 ml/2 tablespoons vodka (or Cointreau) and pour the syrup into a small serving bowl or jug. Segment 2 pink grapefruit and cut a Galia or Ogen melon into slim wedges: slice 2–3 sharon or star fruits; snip 225 g/8 oz black grapes into small bunches and slice half a fresh pineapple. Arrange on a platter. Add the reserved lime slice to the sauce and stand the bowl on the fruit platter. Let guests select their fruits, then drizzle over a little vodka syrup.

Red Fruits Crush 450 g/1 lb raspberries with 100 g/4 oz sugar and gently warm to make the juices run. Pass through a sieve to extract the seeds and add a squeeze of fresh lemon juice to sharpen the flavour. Hull 900 g/2 lb fresh strawberries and pile them on the platter. Pour over a little of the red raspberry sauce and pass the rest separately. The red sauce on red fruits looks spectacular.

Sugared Berries Take 900 g/2 lb mixed summer fruits – raspberries, redcurrants, strawberries or loganberries. Hull or string the fruits and arrange them on the platter. Shake 50 g/2 oz icing sugar through a sieve over the fruits. Let the fruits stand for 15 minutes before serving – they look very pretty when still a little sugary. Pass a bowl of softly whipped cream or a jug of tangy smetana.

Pineapple with Vanilla Sugar Take a slice from the top and base of 1 large pineapple. Then, using a sharp knife (one with a long blade) and with the fruit standing upright, cut down and around to slice away the outer rind. Using a small vegetable knife, cut out the 'eyes' diagonally around the pineapple. Lay the pineapple on its side and slice the fruit across. Arrange the pineapple slices on the platter. Sprinkle over 50 g/2 oz vanilla sugar (page 198).

Melon with Raspberries Cut 2 Charentais melons (they have a sweet perfumed flesh) in quarters, remove the seeds and cut away the outer rind. Then slice the melon into wedges (like an apple) and arrange the wedges around the edge of the platter. Pile 450 g/1 lb hulled raspberries in the centre. Sprinkle the raspberries with a little caster sugar.

Berries with Soft Cheese Turn 1 (500 g) tub fromage frais into a mixing bowl and stir in 25 g/1 oz caster sugar. Whisk 150 ml/$^1/_4$ pint double cream to soft peaks and beat 2 egg whites until stiff. Fold the cream and egg whites into the sweetened fromage frais. Line a sieve with a generous square of double-thickness butter muslin. Turn the mixture into the centre. Draw opposite sides of the muslin to the centre and tie in a loose knot. Leave undisturbed in the refrigerator for 24 hours. As the moisture drips from the bag, soft curds will form. Carefully untie the muslin bag and turn the soft cheese on to a platter. Surround with 700 g/1$^1/_2$ lb fresh raspberries or strawberries. Pass a bowl of caster sugar for sprinkling.

PLATE ELEVEN

Almost Instant Desserts (page 218), *clockwise from top right:* Raspberry Sundae, Brioche and Apple Croute, Amaretti Custard, White Chocolate Cream Pot and Hot Fruit Salad

PLATE TWELVE
Fruit and Nut Glazed Christmas Cake (page 224) with Rum Punch (page 235)

STYLISH FRUIT SALADS

The most important ingredient of a successful fruit salad is the syrup. Made to a simple basic recipe, it is then flavoured to compliment the fruits you wish to use. The basic syrup can be made ahead and chilled. Stored in the refrigerator it will keep for at least a week – a useful standby in the summer. Taste as you add the flavourings, remembering that the syrup will appear quite sweet until the fruits are added.

Always choose ripe fruits and prepare them as you would for eating. Don't cut them into too small pieces, the most attractive fruit salads have quite large chunks or whole fruit. To appreciate the individual fruit flavours, don't be tempted to combine too many kinds of fruit in one salad – we like to use two or three at the most. The most stylish salads combine fruits of the same colour, such as raspberries, redcurrants and strawberries, or try a green and white combination of kiwi fruits, white-fleshed melon and white grapes. Avoid bananas, which go mushy, and apples, which go brown.

Whatever your choice, let the fruit marinate in the syrup for about 2–3 hours before serving – the sweet syrup will draw the natural fruit juices to achieve the desired balance of flavours.

Basic syrup Put 100 g/4 oz granulated sugar and 150 ml/¼ pint water into a saucepan and stir over a low heat until the sugar has dissolved. Then add the citrus peels or spices suggested in the recipe you have chosen and bring to a simmer. Draw off the heat and leave until cold. Strain the syrup and add the fruit juices, liqueurs or rose or orange flower water suggested in the recipe. Use this amount of syrup with 900 g/2 lb fruit to serve 6.

Aromatic Orange Add 5 ml/1 teaspoon coriander seeds and 2–3 pieces pared orange rind to the hot syrup. After straining, add the juice of 1 orange and ½ a lemon. Delicious with raspberries, strawberries, kiwi fruits, orange and grapefruit segments.

Vanilla Add a vanilla pod and 2–3 strips pared orange rind to the hot syrup. After straining, return the vanilla pod to the cold syrup plus the squeezed juice of the orange. Pour over fresh peaches, dessert pears or plums.

Lightly Spiced Use soft brown sugar instead of granulated in the basic syrup and add 5 cm/2 inches cinnamon stick, 3 cloves and 2–3 pieces pared lemon rind to the hot syrup. After straining add the juice of 1 lemon. Superb with blueberries, blackberries, plums and peaches.

Ginger and Lime Add 2–3 pieces pared lime rind and 5 ml/1 teaspoon grated fresh ginger (could be purėed from a jar see page 161) to the hot syrup. After straining, add the juice of the lime. Adds a real kick to pears, mango, melon, pineapple or papaya.

Liqueur Add 2–3 pieces pared lemon rind to the sugar syrup. After straining, add the juice of the lemon and 30 ml/2 tablespoons Kirsch, Amaretto, Cointreau or Maraschino (miniature bottles are useful for this). Very good with cherries, apricots, raspberries or peaches.

Wine Jelly with Fresh Berries

SERVES 6

1 (75 cl) bottle rosé wine
15 ml/1 level tablespoon gelatine
45 ml/3 tablespoons Crème de Framboise
225 g/8 oz fresh raspberries
225 g/8 oz fresh blueberries

Measure 90 ml/6 tablespoons of the rosé wine into a small bowl, sprinkle the gelatine over the top and allow to soak for 5 minutes. Set in a pan containing 2.5 cm/1 inch hot water and stir until the gelatine has completely dissolved.

Pour the rest of the wine into a large jug and add the Crème de Framboise. Stir in the dissolved gelatine and mix gently together. Pour the wine jelly into 6 wine glasses, filling them at least three-quarters full. Chill until set. Pick over the raspberries and blueberries and chill alongside the jelly.

Before serving, spoon the fresh berries on to each glass of wine jelly. They will gently sink into the jelly.

Rosewater Bavarois

SERVES 6

45 ml/3 tablespoons rosewater
15 ml/1 level tablespoon powdered gelatine
300 ml/$^1/_2$ pint creamy milk
3 egg yolks
50 g/2 oz caster sugar
8 trifle sponges
2 egg whites
300 ml/$^1/_2$ pint double cream
icing sugar and pink sugar (see method) to decorate

Measure the rosewater into a teacup, sprinkle in the gelatine and allow to soak for 5 minutes. In a saucepan heat the milk until almost boiling. In a mixing bowl cream the egg yolks and caster sugar until creamy. Stir in the hot milk and mix well. Strain the custard back into the rinsed saucepan. Set the pan over a medium heat and stir for 6–8 minutes, until the custard coats the back of a metal spoon. Remove from the heat, add the softened gelatine and stir until dissolved. Pour the custard into a mixing bowl and allow to cool.

Slice the sponge cakes in half horizontally. Use to line the base and sides of a 1.1 litre/2 pint pudding basin, cutting to fit and setting the sugary sides towards the outside. Beat the egg whites until stiff and gently whip the cream. Fold both into the cooled custard. Pour into the sponge-lined basin and cover the surface with the rest of the sponge cakes. Chill for at least 4 hours, until firm.

To serve, trim the edges of the sponge cakes level with the rim of the bowl and invert the dessert on to a serving plate. Dust with icing sugar and pink sugar (made by buzzing caster sugar with a few drops of red food colouring in a food processor or blender).

WHIZZ UP A CREAMY DESSERT

Creamy desserts of unbelievable smoothness can be made in minutes with the help of a blender or processor. Buzz the ingredients together, pour into individual dishes and chill until set. We like to ring the changes and use individual porcelain ramekins, small wine glasses, tiny coffee cups and old-fashioned custard cups.

Each recipe makes 6 desserts.

Chocolate Pots Break 150 g/5 oz plain chocolate into pieces and put in a blender or processor. Heat 300 ml/$^1/_2$ pint single cream until almost boiling, then add to the chocolate. Buzz until the chocolate has melted and the mixture is smooth. Add a pinch of salt, 1 egg and 2.5 ml/$^1/_2$ teaspoon vanilla extract. Buzz again until smooth. Pour into individual dishes and chill for at least 24 hours, when the custard will set.

Cappuccino Cups Measure 45 ml/3 tablespoons soft brown sugar and 15 ml/1 tablespoon instant coffee granules into a blender or processor and buzz to a fine powder. Add 450 g/1 lb curd cheese and buzz until smooth. Add 150 ml/$^1/_4$ pint double cream and 45 ml/3 tablespoons coffee-flavoured liqueur and buzz just to combine. Spoon into individual dishes and chill for at least 4 hours or longer. Before serving, top each cup with 10 ml/2 teaspoons Greek-style yogurt in a level layer. Dust with cocoa powder mixed with a pinch of cinnamon.

Banana Fool Spoon 1 (142 ml) carton whipping cream and 1 (142 ml) tub natural yogurt into a blender or processor. Buzz just to combine, then add 4 large ripe bananas, peeled and thickly sliced, 30 ml/2 tablespoons caster sugar and 15 ml/1 tablespoon lemon juice. Buzz until smooth. Spoon into individual dishes and chill for about 30 minutes. Serve topped with grated chocolate.

Marron Mousse Turn 1 (439 g) can unsweetened chestnut purée into a blender or processor. Add 100 g/4 oz sifted icing sugar and 50 ml/2 fl oz rum and buzz until blended. Turn the mixture into a bowl. Fold in 1 (250 g) tub thick Greek-style yogurt and mix to a smooth cream. Spoon into individual dishes and chill for at least 4 hours.

Coffee Creams with Chocolate Caraque Put 1 (225 g) carton curd cheese, 150 ml/$^1/_4$ pint double cream and 45 ml/3 tablespoons coffee essence into a blender or processor. Buzz until blended. Spoon the mixture into individual dishes. Melt 100 g/4 oz plain chocolate, spoon a little on to each coffee cream and tip the dish so that the chocolate runs in a thin layer to cover the cream. Chill for at least 4 hours. Dust with cocoa powder just before serving. The chocolate sets to a crisp topping with the soft coffee cream underneath.

THE PERFECT PAVLOVA

Unlike a baked meringue shell which is crisp throughout, a pavlova has a crisp outside and a soft spongy meringue centre. Like making a meringue, egg whites are stiffly beaten and sugar then folded in. What makes a pavlova different is the addition of vinegar – do use a straight white wine vinegar, not a flavoured one. The resulting thick fluffy meringue is spooned into a circle on non-stick baking parchment. Keep the mixture in a single thick layer by smoothing the meringue level rather than hollowing out the centre. This way each portion will have a good part of the crisp shell and the soft spongy centre. For serving, a pavlova is topped with a generous layer of whipped cream and fresh fruits. Alternatively, use up the egg yolks in a rich lemon cream filling. Add the cream and toppings at least 1 hour before serving; this gives the cream a chance to set firm and make cutting into slices easier.

Basic Pavlova Heat the oven to 150°C/300°F/gas mark 2. Cut a sheet of non-stick baking parchment to fit a baking tray and with a pencil outline a 20 cm/8 inch circle. Place the paper on a baking tray – a little dab of butter on each corner of the tray will hold it flat.

Rub round the inside of a mixing bowl with a cut lemon to ensure the bowl is grease-free. Crack in 3 egg whites and weigh out 175 g/6 oz caster sugar. Whisk the egg whites to stiff peaks, then gradually whisk in half the sugar (1 tablespoon at a time), beating each addition in well before adding the next. Fold in the remaining sugar, using the cutting edge of a tablespoon, and, as the sugar begins to disappear, add 5 ml/1 teaspoon white wine vinegar. Spoon the mixture on to the paper-lined tray, forming a mound of meringue within the pencilled outline. Push the mixture to the edges of the circle and spread the meringue level. Bake for 45 minutes. Turn off the oven heat and leave the pavlova in the oven until cold. Slide the cold pavlova off the baking parchment on to a flat serving plate.

Red Fruit Pavlova Whip 300 ml/½ pint double cream with 5 ml/1 teaspoon vanilla extract to soft peaks and spoon on to the pavlova, spreading it evenly. Pick over 450 g/1 lb red fruits – strawberries, raspberries and redcurrants – and spoon on top of the cream. Chill for at least 1 hour before serving. Serve with Red Raspberry Sauce (page 208).

Lemon Cream Pavlova Combine 3 egg yolks and 75 g/3 oz sugar in a mixing bowl. Stir with a wooden spoon until creamy. Add the finely grated rind and juice of 2 lemons and mix. Set the bowl over a saucepan a quarter filled with simmering water on a low heat. Stir for about 12 minutes, until the mixture has a creamy consistency. Lift the bowl off the water and leave until the filling is quite cold. Spoon on to the pavlova and spread evenly. Whisk 300 ml/½ pint double cream to soft peaks and spoon on top of the lemon filling. Chill for at least 1 hour. Lightly sprinkle with toasted flaked almonds before serving. Serve with one of our Fruit Sauces (page 207).

YOGURT ICE-CREAMS

This selection of superb ice-creams are made with thick Greek-style yogurt yet have the same smooth texture as the richest ice-creams made with egg yolks or custard. In addition, using tangy yogurt results in wonderfully fresh and intense flavours. For the very best results ice-creams should be made and served straight away. You can do this easily with an ice-cream freezer machine – if all the ingredients are chilled before use, the ice-cream will take 20–30 minutes to freeze. These recipes are equally successful made in a domestic freezer and briskly forked through half-way through the freezing time.

Yogurt ice-cream base Prepare all the flavouring ingredients ahead and chill them until you are ready to complete the recipe.

Whisk together 1 (500 ml) tub thick Greek-style yogurt and 150 ml/¼ pint double cream. Add the flavouring ingredients and mix well. Freeze in an ice-cream freezer machine according to the manufacturer's instructions. Alternatively, turn the mixture into a 1.1 litre/2 pint freezer container and freeze uncovered until thick. With a fork turn the thickened mixture at the sides to the middle. Cover and return to the freezer until just firm.

Fresh Lemon Combine 100 ml/4 fl oz fresh lemon juice, 100 ml/4 fl oz water and 225 g/8 oz caster sugar in a small saucepan. Bring to the boil, stirring constantly. Reduce the heat and simmer for 5 minutes. Cool and then chill.

Tangy Orange Thaw 1 (190 g) carton frozen concentrated unsweetened orange juice (do not dilute). Stir in 100 g/4 oz caster sugar until dissolved.

Apricot Brandy Coarsely snip 100 g/4 oz ready-to-eat dried apricots into a medium saucepan and add the finely grated rind and juice of 1 orange and 150 ml/¼ pint water. Bring to a simmer, cover and stew gently for about 30 minutes until very soft. Remove from the heat and, with a wooden spoon, beat to a coarse purée. Stir in 50 g/2 oz caster sugar and 45 ml/3 tablespoons brandy. Chill.

Butterscotch Fudge Measure 45 ml/3 tablespoons golden syrup, 75 g/3 oz soft brown sugar and 50 g/2 oz butter into a medium saucepan. Stir over a low heat until the sugar has dissolved and the butter melted. Draw off the heat, add 15 ml/1 tablespoon lemon juice and leave until cold. Chop 6 pieces soft vanilla fudge and add with the sauce.

Espresso Chocolate Chunk Measure 15 ml/1 tablespoon espresso or dark continental-style instant coffee granules into a medium saucepan. Add 30 ml/2 tablespoons boiling water and stir to dissolve the granules. Add 30 ml/2 tablespoons golden syrup and stir over a medium heat until the syrup has melted and the ingredients are blended. Leave until cold. Chop 50 g/2 oz plain chocolate into small chunks and add with the sauce.

White Chocolate Hazelnut Combine 100 g/4 oz caster sugar with 100 ml/4 fl oz water in a medium saucepan and stir over a low heat until the sugar has dissolved. Draw off the heat and add 2 (100 g) packets white chocolate chips. Stir until they have dissolved. Cool. Add 50 g/2 oz chopped roasted hazelnuts with the syrup.

Crushed Strawberry Stir in a 350 g/12 oz jar strawberry conserve.

ALMOST INSTANT DESSERTS

Everyone enjoys and appreciates a little something sweet at the end of the meal. It need not be anything elaborate, in fact it can just be a simple combination of delicious ingredients – such as we suggest here. These recipes will serve 4 and are illustrated on Plate Eleven.

Raspberry Sundaes Half fill tall pretty glasses with fresh raspberries and spoon over a little fresh orange juice. Softly whip 150 ml/½ pint double cream with 1.25 ml/½ teaspoon vanilla extract then fold in 150 ml/¼ pint natural yogurt. Spoon on top of the fruit and decorate with a fresh sprig of mint.

Hot Fruit Salad Cut the segments from 2 pink grapefruit, 1 white grapefruit and 2 large oranges over a bowl to catch the segments and juice. Squeeze any juice from the pulp before discarding it. Peel and thickly slice 2 large bananas. Drain the citrus fruit juice into a measuring jug and add the finely grated rind and juice of 1 lemon. Add cold water to make 300 ml/½ pint. Pour the juices into a frying pan and stir in 150 g/5 oz caster sugar. Over a medium heat, stir constantly until the sugar has melted. Increase the heat and boil for 3–4 minutes or until syrupy. Add the fruit and cook until bubbling hot. Serve piping hot with a spoonful of thick natural yogurt.

Amaretti Custards Sandwich pairs of Amaretti biscuits with lemon curd or apricot conserve and place each pair in individual custard or coffee cups. Sprinkle each with a little sweet sherry. Whisk together a 350 ml carton of dairy custard and a 200 ml tub Greek-style yogurt. Spoon over the biscuits. If possible leave to stand 30 minutes or so to allow the biscuits to soften. Just before serving sprinkle with toasted flaked almonds and sift over a little icing sugar.

Brioche and Apple Croûtes Finely grate the rind and squeeze the juice from 1 large lemon. Remove the cores from 2 large red-skinned dessert apples with an apple corer and cut each apple across into 4–6 slices. Measure 100 ml/4 fl oz water into a frying pan and add the lemon juice, rind and 100 g/4 oz caster sugar. Cook over a medium-high heat, stirring constantly, until the sugar has melted and the liquid has reduced to a syrup. Add the apple slices, turning to coat with the syrup. Cook, turning gently, until soft and translucent. While the apples are cooking, toast 4 thick slices of brioche. Spoon the apples and syrup over the brioche *croûtes* and serve with a scoop of vanilla ice-cream.

White Chocolate Cream Pots Melt 1 (150 g) bar white chocolate in a medium bowl over hot water (or in the microwave). Remove from the heat and stir in 150 ml/¼ pint soured cream and 15 ml/1 tablespoon rum. Beat 150 ml/¼ pint double cream to soft peaks and fold into the chocolate mixture. Spoon into individual ramekins, coffee cups or glasses and chill for at least 2 hours or (loosely covered with clingfilm) overnight. A sprinkling of grated plain chocolate on top would look pretty.

Cheese and Berry Tartlets

SERVES 6

Turn the cream cheese into a medium-sized mixing bowl. Add the caster sugar and lemon rind and mix until smooth. Beat in sufficient cream to make the filling soft and light. Spoon into the tartlet shells, smoothing the top to a slight dome. Press the chosen fruit gently into the filling. Cover loosely with clingfilm and chill for up to 4 hours. Just before serving, lightly sift over a little icing sugar.

- 225 g/8 oz cream cheese
- 75 g/3 oz caster sugar
- finely grated rind of 1 lemon
- 45–60 ml/3–4 tablespoons double cream
- 6 10 cm/4 inch tartlet shells, baked and cooled (see page 188)
- 225 g/8 oz ripe fruit such as blackberries, raspberries, blueberries
- icing sugar

Lemon Cream Tartlets

SERVES 6

Turn the cream into a bowl and, using a wire whisk, beat to soft peaks. Add the lemon curd and fold through. Spoon into the tartlet shells, mounding the mixture. Cover with the pine-nuts. Cover loosely with clingfilm and refrigerate for up to 4 hours.

Just before serving, generously dust with sifted icing sugar.

- 225 ml/8 fl oz double cream
- 45 ml/3 level tablespoons lemon curd
- 6 10 cm/4 inch tartlet shells, baked and cooled (see page 188)
- 100 g/4 oz toasted pine-nuts
- icing sugar

CHAPTER THIRTEEN

Christmas

Christmas is the time for making something really special – glamorous cakes, special desserts, party foods and gifts. Traditional recipes are a must, and everyone has their own favourites. Here they have been given a new twist.

Golden Celebration Cake

SERVES 10–12

Tastes change, and not everyone enjoys the traditional fruit cake any more. This one combines soft cake layered with fruit-studded buttercream and a fluffy lemon icing. It should be baked and iced up to a week ahead to allow the flavours to mingle. Top with marzipan or glacé fruits, sugared grapes or tiny fresh flowers just before serving. A truly festive cake for any occasion.

The Cake and Glacé Fruit Buttercream

- 225 g/8 oz self-raising flour
- 10 ml/2 level teaspoons baking powder
- 225 g/8 oz caster sugar
- 225 g/8 oz soft tub margarine
- 4 eggs
- 5 ml/1 teaspoon vanilla extract
- 100 g/4 oz soft butter
- 225 g/8 oz icing sugar
- 30 ml/2 tablespoons fine-cut orange marmalade
- 2 slices glacé pineapple or 2 glacé apricots

Heat the oven to 160°C/325°F/gas mark 3.

Lightly butter and flour a 20 cm/8 inch round deep cake tin, tipping out any excess flour. Line the base with a circle of baking parchment. Sift the flour and baking powder into a large mixing bowl. Add the caster sugar, margarine, eggs and vanilla extract. Stir with a wooden spoon until blended, then beat for 1 minute to a smooth cake batter. Turn the mixture into the prepared tin and spread level. Bake for 50–60 minutes. Let the cake cool in the tin for 10 minutes, turn on to a cooling rack and leave until quite cold.

To make the cake filling, cream the butter until fluffy. Sift the icing sugar on to a plate and beat into the butter about one third at a time. (If using an electric mixer all the sugar can be added at one go.) Beat in the marmalade. Finely chop the glacé fruits and gently stir in. Split the cake into three layers by cutting horizontally twice. Divide the buttercream filling equally and use to sandwich the cake layers. Place the cake in the refrigerator to firm up the buttercream, while making the Vanilla Marzipan.

For the Vanilla Marzipan and Apricot Glaze

175 g/6 oz icing sugar
175 g/6 oz ground almonds
1 egg
175 g/6 oz caster sugar
2.5 ml/½ teaspoon vanilla extract
extra sifted icing sugar for kneading
50 g/2 oz granulated sugar
30 ml/2 tablespoons lemon juice
75 ml/5 tablespoons apricot jam
a little extra caster sugar

Makes enough to cover the top and sides of one 20 cm/8 inch cake *or* the top only of one 23 cm/9 inch cake.

Sift the icing sugar on to a square of greaseproof paper, add the ground almonds and set aside. Put the egg and caster sugar into a mixing bowl and set over a saucepan one quarter filled with hot water (off the heat). Whisk until the mixture is light in colour and warm to the touch. Remove the bowl from the saucepan. Whisk in the vanilla extract. Stir in the icing sugar and ground almonds with a wooden spoon and mix to a stiff paste.

Turn the mixture on to a work surface lightly dusted with sifted icing sugar and knead until the marzipan is smooth and pliable. Slip inside a freezer bag and leave to rest at room temperature for at least 1 hour before covering the cake.

Put the granulated sugar and lemon juice in a small saucepan and stir over a low heat until the sugar has dissolved. Sieve the apricot jam into the pan and stir until blended. Bring to the boil, then lower the heat and simmer for 2–3 minutes until the glaze hangs in heavy drops from the spoon.

Gently brush the hot apricot glaze over the top of the cake. Divide the marzipan into 2 portions – one-third for the cake top and two-thirds for the sides. Dust the work surface with caster sugar and roll the smaller portion to a 20 cm/8 inch circle. Turn the cake over on to the marzipan circle and press gently. Leave the cake face down. Roll the remaining marzipan into a rope long enough to coat the sides then, using a rolling pin, flatten the rope to equal the depth of the cake. Trim the edges straight. Brush the sides of the cake with the hot apricot glaze then wrap the marzipan around the sides of the cake, pressing on gently. Turn the cake the right way up and leave uncovered at room temperature for 24 hours before adding the Lemon Frosting.

350 g/12 oz icing sugar
50 ml/2 fl oz lemon juice
25 g/1 oz caster sugar

For the Lemon Frosting

Makes enough for the top and sides of one 20 cm/8 inch cake.

Warm a mixing bowl by either filling with boiling water or popping into a warm oven for a few minutes. Dry well. Sift the icing sugar into the warmed mixing bowl. Put the lemon juice and caster sugar into a small saucepan. Stir over a low heat until the sugar has dissolved. Bring just to the boil and remove from the heat. Pour into the icing sugar and, using a wooden spoon, beat until smooth and shiny. Use while warm – this icing sets quite fast.

Take a silver cake board – about 25.5 cm/10 inches in diameter – and spread a dab of icing in the centre. Place the cake on the board and press gently to fix in position. Spoon all the frosting on top of the cake. With a palette knife, spread the frosting over the top and around the sides of the cake. Either leave smooth or swirl. Keep in a cool place – not in the refrigerator. Decorate before serving.

Fruit and Nut Glazed Christmas Cake

CUTS INTO 18–20 SLICES *Illustrated on Plate Twelve*

1 23 cm/9 inch fruit cake (page 225)
caster sugar
Vanilla Marzipan and Apricot Glaze (page 223)
1 egg white
150 g/5 oz glacé pineapple
150 g/5 oz glacé cherries
100 g/4 oz whole pecan or walnut halves
30 ml/2 level tablespoons granulated sugar

Instead of royal icing, the Christmas cake can look very festive decked with marzipan, glacé fruits and whole nuts all lightly glazed to shine deliciously.

Stand the cake on a silver cake board. Dust the work surface with a little caster sugar and roll the Vanilla Marzipan to a 28 cm/11 inch square. Brush the top of the cake with hot Apricot Glaze and lift the marzipan on top. Gently press on to the cake. Fold the overhanging 2.5 cm/1 inch of marzipan back on to the marzipan topping and pinch with the fingers to form an attractive raised edging. Lightly beat the egg white and brush over the raised edging. Protect the centre of the marzipan with a square of foil. Place the cake under a preheated grill and grill for a few moments only until the edging is golden brown.

Brush the centre of the marzipan with hot apricot glaze. Cut the pineapple into wedges. Arrange the fruits and nuts in an attractive pattern on top of the cake. Dissolve the sugar in 15 ml/1 tablespoon boiling water and gently brush the sugar glaze over the fruits and nuts to make them shine.

THE ULTIMATE CHRISTMAS CAKE

The traditional Christmas cake is dark, mellow and very rich. Made several weeks before it is to be eaten, it may be frequently moistened with brandy, rum or sherry as it matures. Here is just such a cake, but today tastes vary and, for many, a lighter cake with perhaps a fresher flavour of citrus peel or ginger would be preferred. Just follow the basic recipe plus the variation of your choice, for the perfect cake.

We make the basic batter mixture with the help of a food processor or electric mixer, but prefer to fold in the fruits and nuts with a metal spoon to avoid breaking them – they look so much prettier in definite pieces when the cake is cut in slices.

Take time to prepare the cake tin carefully. You will need a 22.5 cm/9 inch square tin. Lightly grease the tin and line the base and sides with a double thickness of baking parchment or greaseproof paper. Tie a double band of brown wrapping paper around the outside of the tin. Cut a double thickness of brown paper large enough to stand the tin on in the oven. Rich fruit cakes take several hours to bake and this will prevent the cake becoming dry. If you have found your oven tends to bake rather dry fruit cakes, try placing a roasting tin of water on the lowest rack of the oven while baking the cake. This provides a little steam, which will help keep the cake moist. Top up the water during baking if needed.

To test whether the cake is cooked, when the baking time is up, gently push a wooden skewer into the centre of the cake – there should be no sign of uncooked cake batter on it.

Fruit cakes can be made ahead – up to a month for dark fruit cakes, 1–2 weeks for the Golden Glacé and the Tropical White cakes. Allow the cake to become completely cold, standing on a wire rack, for 24 hours. Leave the cold cake wrapped in the baking papers. Alternatively, remove the papers, turn the cake upside down, spoon 45–60 ml/3–4 tablespoons sweet sherry or brandy over the soft base crust, and wrap the cake in butter muslin. Slip the cake into a freezer bag and tightly close. Store in a cool dry place.

The Basic Cake Heat the oven to 140°C/275°F/gas mark 1. Beat 275 g/10 oz butter (at room temperature) with 275 g/10 oz soft light brown sugar until light and fluffy. Gradually beat in 5 eggs, 15 ml/1 tablespoon black treacle and 5 ml/1 teaspoon vanilla extract. Don't worry if the mixture curdles, it won't affect the end result. Sift 350 g/12 oz plain flour with 5 ml/1 teaspoon mixed spice and 5 ml/1 teaspoon salt on to a sheet of greaseproof paper (see variations). Using a metal spoon, gradually fold into the creamed mixture until you have a smooth batter. Add the chosen fruits and alcohol. Spoon the mixture into the prepared tin. Spread level, then hollow out the centre slightly so that the baked cake will have a flat top. Bake for 4 hours – the cake should be evenly risen and golden brown. Leave to cool in the tin standing on a wire rack before turning out.

Traditional Rich Fruit Roughly chop 100 g/4 oz stoned dates and 100 g/4 oz dried apricots and place in a large bowl. Rinse the sugar coating from 100 g/4 oz glacé cherries, press dry in absorbent kitchen paper and cut in quarters. Add to the bowl together with 225 g/8 oz sultanas, 225 g/8 oz currants, 225 g/8 oz seedless raisins and 50 g/2 oz chopped almonds. Add 30 ml/2 tablespoons of the sifted flour (see basic recipe) and mix well. Add to the basic batter with 30 ml/2 tablespoons brandy.

Old Fashioned Substitute dark molasses sugar for the light brown in the basic batter. Roughly chop 225 g/8 oz stoned dates, 175 g/6 oz dried figs, 175 g/6 oz tenderized prunes, 225 g/8 oz stoned raisins and 50 g/2 oz chopped toasted almonds. Add 30 ml/2 tablespoons of the sifted flour (see basic recipe) and mix well. Add to the basic batter with 30 ml/2 tablespoons dark rum.

Golden Glacé Use caster sugar instead of light brown sugar in the basic batter. Omit the treacle and the mixed spice. Rinse the sugar coating from 225 g/8 oz glacé cherries (mixed colours), press dry in absorbent kitchen paper and cut in quarters. Roughly chop 225 g/8 oz glacé pineapple, 225 g/8 oz mixed candied peel and 100 g/4 oz walnuts. Add to the glacé cherries with 225 g/8 oz sultanas and the finely grated rind of 1 large lemon. Add 30 ml/2 tablespoons of the sifted flour (see basic recipe) and mix well. Add to the basic batter with 45 ml/3 tablespoons sweet sherry.

Tropical White Use caster sugar instead of light brown sugar in the basic batter. Omit the spices, treacle and vanilla extract. Rinse the sugar coating from 100 g/4 oz yellow glacé cherries, press dry in absorbent kitchen paper and cut in quarters. Roughly chop 350 g/12 oz ready-to-eat apricots and add to the cherries with 350 g/12 oz sultanas, 225 g/8 oz chopped mixed candied peel, 50 g/2 oz finely diced stem ginger and 50 g/2 oz chopped brazil nuts. Add 30 ml/2 tablespoons of the sifted flour (see basic recipe) and mix well. Add to the basic batter with 45 ml/3 tablespoons ginger syrup (from the stem ginger).

Christmas Pudding

MAKES A 900 G/2 LB PUDDING TO SERVE 6–8

For many, Christmas isn't Christmas if they miss out on the pudding. Simple enough to make, the drawback was always the long steaming time required by traditional recipes. We have lightened the recipe and used melted butter instead of suet. In place of steaming over a pan of water, follow the detailed instructions for 'oven steaming' on page 195.

- 100 g/ 4 oz self-raising flour
- 5 ml/1 level teaspoon mixed spice
- pinch salt
- 75 g/3 oz fresh white breadcrumbs
- 175 g/6 oz soft brown sugar
- 1 tart dessert apple
- 100 g/4 oz block dates
- finely grated rind 1 large orange
- 225 g/8 oz mixed dried fruits
- 75 g/3 oz butter
- 2 eggs
- 15 ml/1 tablespoon dark treacle
- 30 ml/2 tablespoons rum

Sift the flour, mixed spice and salt into a large mixing bowl. Add the breadcrumbs and soft brown sugar.

Peel, core and grate the apple. Chop the dates, discarding any stones. Add the grated apple, chopped dates, orange rind and mixed dried fruits to the breadcrumb mix and stir ingredients well.

Melt the butter. Crack the eggs into a small bowl, add the treacle and mix with a fork. Add the melted butter and egg to the pudding mixture and stir with a wooden spoon to blend the ingredients thoroughly. Let the mixture stand for 1 hour, then mix again.

Heat the oven to 190°C/375°F/gas mark 5 (see page 195).

Lightly butter a 900 g/2 lb pudding basin. Spoon the pudding mixture into the bowl and spread level. Lightly butter a square of foil and place over the pudding, tucking the foil securely around the edge of the basin. 'Oven steam' for 2 hours.

When the pudding has cooled, remove the foil covering and spoon over the rum. Re-cover with foil and store in a cool place for up to 1 month. To heat for serving, 'oven-steam' for 1 hour.

Flaming the pudding

This is best done at the table so that everyone can enjoy the fun. Invert the hot pudding on to a warm serving platter but leave covered with the bowl. Make sure you have a lighted candle, a metal soup ladle or large spoon and the brandy bottle on the table. Remove the pudding bowl and bring the hot pudding to the table. Pour about 30 ml/2 tablespoons of brandy into the soup ladle or spoon and hold over the candle flame to warm, then allow the flame of the candle to lick over the edge of the ladle and the warm brandy will flame immediately. Pour it over the hot pudding and it will burn beautifully for a minute or more.

FESTIVE SAUCES

Cream, either lightly whipped or just poured, sinfully rich clotted cream and crème fraîche all deliciously melt into hot Christmas pudding and mince pies. For a lighter, tangy taste try Greek-style yogurt flavoured with a dash of vanilla extract, or simply creamy smetana. True traditionalists will always choose Real Custard Sauce (see page 190) – why not offer a choice? Each sauce serves 6–8.

Whipped Brandy Cream Combine 300 ml/½ pint chilled double cream, 25 g/1 oz sifted icing sugar and 30 ml/2 tablespoons Cognac in a chilled bowl. Whip until thick and light. Turn into a serving bowl and chill until firm – several hours or (covered) overnight. Serves 6–8.

Fromage Frais and Honey Stir 30–45 ml/2–3 tablespoons clear honey into a 500 ml tub of fromage frais and serve well chilled.

Hot Spiced Cream Heat 300 ml/½ pint double cream with 30 ml/2 tablespoons soft brown sugar and 5 ml/1 level teaspoon ground cinnamon until hot but not boiling. Whisk until frothy and serve hot.

Flavoured butters can be made well ahead and frozen. Allow to soften in the refrigerator and serve at room temperature. Packed in small jars, they make very acceptable gifts. Serve with Christmas puddings, hot American-style breakfast muffins or pop a spoonful under the lid of hot apple or mincepies where it will melt into the fruit filling.

Orange Rum Butter In a bowl cream 100 g/4 oz soft butter with 175 g/6 oz light brown sugar until smooth and fluffy. Add the finely grated rind of 1 orange, 30 ml/2 tablespoons rum and 5 ml/1 teaspoon lemon juice and beat until smooth. Chill.

Sherry Hard Sauce Cream 175 g/6 oz soft butter with 225 g/8 oz sifted icing sugar until light and fluffy. Beat in 30 ml/2 tablespoons dry sherry. Chill.

Sugared Fruits in Wine

MAKES 6–8 SERVINGS

A mouthwatering blend of chopped glacé fruits marinated in sweet wine – use marsala, sweet red vermouth or sweet sherry. The fruits need to marinate for at least 2 weeks to allow the glacé fruits to soften and absorb the wine. Spoon the Sugared Fruits over scoops of vanilla ice-cream or poached pears. Make the Strawberry Lemon Layer Cake (page 207) and top the cream with Sugared Fruits instead of the strawberries. Layer the marinated fruits with Amaretti biscuits and Real Custard Sauce (page 190) to make superb trifle. For an iced Christmas pudding stir the fruits into a tub of soft vanilla ice-cream then pack the mixture into a pudding basin lined with clingfilm. Freeze until firm, then briefly dip into hot water and invert on to a chilled serving plate. Lift off the basin, remove the clingfilm and top with a sprig of holly. Sugared Fruits in Wine packed in attractive jars also make very acceptable Christmas gifts.

100 g/4 oz red glacé cherries
100 g/4 oz diced glacé pineapple
100 g/4 oz diced dried papaya
50 g/2 oz angelica
marsala, sweet red vermouth or sweet sherry – about 350 ml/12 fl oz

There is no need to wash the sugary coating from the glacé fruits in this recipe; it will dissolve into the wine during storage. Cut the cherries in half and dice the angelica. Mix all the fruits together and pack in a large lidded jar or polythene storage container. Add sufficient sweet wine to completely cover. Cover and keep in a cool place for up to 2 months, shaking occasionally and topping up the wine if the fruit is exposed. Stir before use.

Fresh Fruit Mincemeat

MAKES 2 KG/$4^1/_2$ LB

This fresh-tasting recipe contains no fat or sugar, which allows the flavour of the dried and fresh fruits really to come through. Cover the prepared mincemeat and refrigerate for 2 weeks to allow the flavours to blend and mature, stirring occasionally. For keeping longer, transfer the mixture to a lidded container and freeze. Thaw overnight before using.

- 225 g/8 oz sultanas
- 225 g/8 oz seedless raisins
- 225 g/8 oz currants
- 225 g/8 oz ready-to-eat dried figs
- 225 g/8 oz ready-to-eat dried apricots
- 450 g/1 lb dessert apples
- 100 g/4 oz blanched almonds
- grated rind and juice of 2 lemons
- juice of 2 large oranges
- 15 ml/1 level tablespoon ground mixed spice
- 10 ml/2 level teaspoons ground cloves
- 150 ml/$^1/_4$ pint clear honey
- 60 ml/4 tablespoons rum or brandy

Place the sultanas, raisins and currants in a large bowl. Quarter the figs and apricots and add to the bowl. Quarter, core and peel (unless you like the skins) the apples and add to the bowl, along with the blanched almonds. Mix well then spoon into a processor (you may need to do this in batches) and buzz until finely chopped. Alternatively, pass the fruits through the coarse blade of a hand mincer.

Either way, return the chopped fruits to the bowl. Combine the grated lemon rind and juice, the orange juice, the spices, honey and rum or brandy and add to the fruit. Mix very thoroughly. Cover and store in the fridge for 2 weeks to mature.

Crumble-topped Mincemeat Cake

SERVES 10–12

This fruity moist cake is just as delicious served cold at teatime as it is served warm with whipped cream or Orange Rum Butter (page 228) for dessert. If you haven't made our Fresh Fruit Mincemeat (page 230), use a 350 g/12 oz jar of traditional mincemeat mixed with 2 dessert apples, peeled and coarsely grated, instead.

- 275 g/10 oz self-raising flour
- 75 g/3 oz chilled butter
- 75 g/3 oz caster sugar
- 25 g/1 oz flaked almonds
- pinch of salt
- 5 ml/1 level teaspoon baking powder
- 100 g/4 oz soft-tub margarine
- 100 g/4 oz soft brown sugar
- 2 eggs
- 2.5 ml/½ teaspoon vanilla extract
- 30 ml/2 tablespoons milk
- 550 g/1¼ lb Fresh Fruit Mincemeat (page 230)
- icing sugar

Heat the oven to 180°C/350°F/gas mark 4.

Butter a 22.5 cm/9 inch spring-release tin.

Start with the topping: sift 100 g/4 oz of the flour, the diced butter and caster sugar in a processor and buzz to coarse crumbs. Tip into a bowl and stir in the almonds. Set aside. (Alternatively, cut the butter into the flour with 2 table knives, using a scissor movement, until the mixture looks like coarse crumbs. Stir in the sugar and almonds and set aside.)

To make the cake: sift the remaining 175 g/6 oz flour, the salt and baking powder into a medium-sized bowl. Add the margarine, soft brown sugar, eggs, vanilla and milk. Stir with a wooden spoon to blend the ingredients, then beat to a soft cake mixture. Spoon into the prepared tin and spread level. Fork the mincemeat evenly over the batter. Sprinkle the topping over the mincemeat. Bake for 45–50 minutes until golden brown. Cool in the tin for 5 minutes before removing the sides. Place the cake on a flat serving plate and sift a little icing sugar around the edge – it looks very pretty if you let a little fall on to the plate itself.

Mincemeat Flan

SERVES 6–8

Quicker to make than individual mince pies, this very fruity flan combines apricots and pineapple with Fresh Fruit Mincemeat (page 230). Alternatively, use a 450 g/1 lb jar of a good-quality mincemeat. The flan shell could be made ahead and frozen unbaked. The flan is at its best served freshly baked.

- Press-in Shortcrust Pastry (page 188)
- 450 g/1 lb Fresh Fruit Mincemeat (page 230)
- 100 g/4 oz ready-to-eat dried apricots
- 4 canned pineapple rings
- 100 g/4 oz icing sugar
- 15 ml/1 tablespoon lemon juice

Make the pastry and press into an ungreased 25 cm/10 inch tart tin, preferably one with a loose bottom. Chill until ready to fill, or overnight.

Heat the oven to 190°C/375°F/gas mark 5. Place a baking tray in the oven to heat up.

Spoon the mincemeat into a bowl. Scissor snip the apricots in half and cut each pineapple ring into 8 pieces. Add to the mincemeat and lightly mix together.

Place the tart shell on the hot baking tray and bake for 10 minutes to set the pastry base. Remove from the oven, spoon in the fruit filling and spread evenly. Return the tart (still on the baking tray) to the oven and bake for 30–40 minutes until the pastry is crisp and golden.

Cool for 5 minutes, then carefully remove the flan from the tart tin. Cool for about 15 minutes on a wire rack.

Meanwhile, sift the icing sugar into a bowl and stir in enough lemon juice to make a thin lemon icing. Drizzle over the mincemeat filling, allowing it to puddle in places. Best served warm.

Chocolate Terrine

SERVES 8

Very rich and creamy, this is the ultimate indulgence – and the perfect ending to a special meal. For stylish serving cut the terrine into 8 slices and then cut each across diagonally into 2 triangles. Arrange on pretty dessert plates and drizzle over a little sauce. The slightly bitter Dark Cocoa Sauce (page 196) contrasts well with the richness. A fruity sauce such as Red Raspberry (use frozen berries) or Black Cherry and Kirsch (page 208) would look very pretty; alternatively, serve quite simply with fresh orange segments.

- 225 g/8 oz plain chocolate
- 2.5 ml/½ level teaspoon instant coffee granules
- 100 g/4 oz soft unsalted butter
- 175 g/6 oz icing sugar
- 3 eggs

Line a 20 × 10 × 5 cm/8 × 4 × 2 inch loaf pan with clingfilm, allowing it to overlap the sides and ends. Break the chocolate into a small bowl, set over a saucepan of hot water (off the heat) until melted (or [M]). Remove the bowl from the saucepan and cool the chocolate slightly.

Dissolve the coffee granules in 5 ml/1 teaspoon boiling water. Place the butter in a large bowl and sift in the icing sugar. Beat until smooth and light. Separate the eggs, beating the yolks into the creamed mixture one at a time. Beat in the dissolved coffee granules. Beat the egg whites until stiff. Fold one-third of the beaten whites into the chocolate mixture to lighten it, then gently fold in the remainder.

Spoon the mixture into the lined pan and level the top. Fold over the ends of the clingfilm and chill until firm, at least 4 hours or overnight.

To serve, uncover the terrine and invert on to a flat serving plate. Lift off the pan and gently peel off the clingfilm.

Apricot Eggnog Trifle

SERVES 10–12

In this 'grown-ups-only' trifle, the chunky marmalade filling for the macaroons makes a tangy contrast with the richness of the rum-flavoured custard. Other fillings could be Sugared Fruits in Wine (page 229) or a good lemon curd. If you haven't time to make Real Custard Sauce (page 190), use a 500 g tub of fresh custard sauce from the chilled cabinet of your supermarket. Add a swirl of whipped cream on top of the trifle if wished.

A festive trifle should be prettily decorated – we like to use shaved (use a swivel potato peeler) or coarsely grated plain chocolate, toasted flaked almonds, crushed caramel, Cape gooseberries with their papery skins folded back to show the brilliant orange fruit, very finely chopped red and green glacé cherries or spoonfuls of Sugared Fruits in Wine.

- 3 (100 g) packets almond macaroons or 1 (250 g) packet Amaretti
- 225 g/8 oz coarse-cut orange marmalade
- 1 (411 g) can apricot halves in juice, drained
- 450 ml/¾ pint Real Custard Sauce, chilled (page 190)
- 1 (500 g) tub Greek-style yogurt
- 60 ml/4 tablespoons rum

Select a pretty serving bowl with a capacity of about 1.7 litres/3 pints. Sandwich the macaroons in pairs with generous teaspoonfuls of the marmalade and arrange in the base of the serving dish, tucking the apricot halves in among them.

Whisk together the custard sauce, yogurt and rum. Spoon the custard mixture over the macaroons. Cover and chill for 24 hours. The macaroons will become deliciously moist. Decorate before serving.

PARTY PUNCHES

Flavouring spices give hot mulls and punches their distinctive aroma and depth of flavour. Mulls are based on wine or cider with the added kick of port, brandy or other spirits. Punches are less alcoholic. Our recipe is based on an infusion of spices and tea which gives it a festive golden colour. Using whole spices instead of the ground variety keeps the liquid clear and sparkling and, if you tie the spices in a loose muslin bag before adding them, it's easy to fork them out before serving. Feeling lazy? Just add a sachet of ready-mixed spices and some soft brown sugar to a bottle of red wine and gently heat.

Each recipe makes 18 glasses.

Mulled Wine Measure 175 g/6 oz soft brown sugar and 300 ml/½ pint water into a large saucepan and stir over low heat to dissolve the sugar. Remove from the heat. Slice 1 lemon and 3 oranges and stud a couple of the orange slices with 6 whole cloves. Add the sliced fruit and 5 cm/2 inches stick cinnamon to the pan and leave to infuse for 10 minutes. Pour in 2 bottles of red wine and ½ bottle ruby port (non-vintage). Heat gently until hot, but keep well below the boil. Draw off the heat. If wished, transfer to a warmed punch bowl. Measure 50 ml/2 fl oz brandy into a small saucepan, warm over a low heat for a few seconds and ignite before stirring into the wine.

Rum Punch Put 15 g/½ oz China tea in a large bowl. Add the thinly pared rind of 1 lemon and 5 cm/2 inches stick cinnamon. Pour over 1.1 litre/2 pints boiling water, stir and leave to stand 10 minutes. Put 225 g/8 oz granulated sugar in a large saucepan, strain in the infused tea and stir over a low heat to dissolve the sugar. Add 300 ml/½ pint dark rum and the squeezed juice from the lemon. Warm gently until thoroughly hot but keep below the boil. Draw off the heat. Thinly slice 3 lemons and place a slice in each glass before pouring in the punch.

Apple Tea Punch Measure 15 g/½ oz Earl Grey tea into a large bowl. Add 5 cm/2 inches stick cinnamon and 6 whole cloves. Pour on 1.1 litres/2 pints boiling water and stir. Add 3–4 pieces pared lemon rind and leave the mixture to infuse for 10 minutes. Pour through a strainer into a large saucepan, add 225 g/8 oz caster sugar and stir over a low heat until the sugar has dissolved. Add 1.1 litres/2 pints pure apple juice and the squeezed juice of 1 lemon. Bring slowly to almost boiling, remove from the heat and add a grating of nutmeg. Ladle into a warmed jug for easy serving. Add a slice of lemon or a red apple wedge to each glass.

Chocolate Marron Cake

MAKES 12 SLICES

Rich chocolate cake layers with a creamy chestnut filling are topped with candied chestnuts called *marrons glacés*. If these are not available, drizzle the vanilla icing over the top of the cake in a zigzag pattern. The Chestnut Cream Filling would be delicious used to fill 2 plain sponge layers. Swirl whipped cream over the top and chill for an hour before sifting over a little cocoa powder just before serving. The Chocolate Sugar Frosting sets softly with a shiny finish and would make any cake special.

- 225 g/8 oz self-raising flour
- 50 g/2 oz cocoa powder
- 5 ml/1 level teaspoon bicarbonate of soda
- 275 g/10 oz caster sugar
- 175 g/6 oz soft-tub margarine
- 3 eggs
- 5 ml/1 teaspoon vanilla extract
- 175 ml/6 oz natural low-fat yogurt
- Chestnut Cream Filling (see page 237)
- Chocolate Sugar Frosting (see page 237)
- 8 *marrons glacés*
- 75 g/3 oz icing sugar
- 2.5 ml/½ teaspoon vanilla extract

Heat the oven to 160°C/325°F/gas mark 3.

Lightly butter a 22.5 cm/9 inch spring-release tin and line the base with baking parchment. Dust the tin with flour and shake out any excess.

Sift the flour, cocoa powder and bicarbonate of soda into a large mixing bowl. Add the sugar, margarine, eggs, vanilla extract and yogurt. Stir with a wooden spoon to blend the ingredients, then beat to a soft cake batter. Spoon into the prepared tin and spread level. Bake for 40–45 minutes. Cool for 5 minutes, loosen the spring clip and remove the sides of the pan. Cool completely on a wire rack before removing the base of the tin.

Slice the cake horizontally to make two layers and sandwich them with Chestnut Cream Filling. Chill the cake for 1 hour to allow the filling to firm up before adding the Chocolate Sugar Frosting.

Place the cake on a wire rack over a large plate. Pour the Chocolate Sugar Frosting on to the top of the cake and, using a knife, quickly smooth it over the top and around the sides. Let the icing set in a cool place but not the refrigerator.

Arrange the *marron glacés* on top of the cake. Sift the icing sugar into a small bowl and add 10 ml/2 teaspoons warm water and the vanilla extract. Stir until quite smooth. Using a teaspoon, drizzle the vanilla icing over each glacé chestnut, allowing it to run down the sides of the cake.

For the Chestnut Cream Filling

Press the chestnut purée and icing sugar through a sieve into a mixing bowl. Add the vanilla extract and unwhipped cream. Beat until very smooth.

- 1 (439 g) can unsweetened chestnut purée
- 90 ml/6 tablespoons icing sugar
- 5 ml/1 teaspoon vanilla extract
- 150 ml/¼ pint double cream

For the Chocolate Sugar Frosting

Spoon the sugar into a small saucepan and add 45 ml/3 tablespoons cold water. Stir over a low heat to dissolve the sugar then bring to a simmer. Draw off the heat and add the chocolate, broken in pieces. Stir gently as the chocolate melts, until the mixture is smooth.

- 50 g/2 oz caster sugar
- 100 g/4 oz plain chocolate

Mixed Nut Florentine

MAKES 12 WEDGES

Packed with toasted nuts and glacé fruits, thin wedges of this impressive confection go well with after-dinner coffee. Wrapped in sparkly cellophane and tied with ribbons, it would make a sweet-toothed friend very happy.

Heat the oven to 180°C/350°F/gas mark 4.

Lightly butter a 22.5 cm/9 inch sponge cake tin and line the base with non-stick baking parchment. Tip the nuts into a large roasting tin and set in the oven until golden brown – about 10 minutes. Leave to cool, then turn into a large bowl.

- 100 g/4 oz whole blanched almonds
- 100 g/4 oz whole skinned hazelnuts
- 100 g/4 oz brazil nuts
- 225 g/8 oz red glacé cherries

100 g/4 oz diced glacé pineapple
50 g/2 oz plain flour
2.5 ml/½ level teaspoon allspice
2.5 ml/½ level teaspoon ground nutmeg
100 g/4 oz caster sugar
100 g/4 oz clear honey
50 g/2 oz plain chocolate

Rinse the cherries of their sugary coating but leave whole. Add both cherries and pineapple to the nuts. Sift the flour and spices over the fruit and nuts and mix. Warm the sugar and honey in a small saucepan over a low heat until the sugar has dissolved. Spoon over the fruit and flour mixture and stir to blend.

Turn the mixture into the prepared tin and spread level. Bake for 25–30 minutes. Allow to cool in the tin for 10 minutes, then loosen around the sides and turn out. Turn the Florentine over so that you have the pretty, uneven surface on the top. Chop the chocolate with a sharp knife and sprinkle over the Florentine – it will melt on the warm surface. Cut into thin wedges when quite cold.

Party Nibbles

Tasty bite-sized finger foods are always welcome served with drink. Don't serve too great a variety – 3 or 4 at the most is plenty – and arrange on flat trays or platters. They can all be assembled ahead of time so that they are served warm and fragrant straight from the oven or grill.

Chicken Satays with Peanut Dip Cut 4 skinned boneless chicken breasts into bite-sized pieces. In a bowl combine 30 ml/2 tablespoons dark soy sauce, 10 ml/2 level teaspoons soft brown sugar, the juice of 1 lemon, 15 ml/1 tablespoon grapeseed oil with a seasoning of salt and pepper, 5 ml/1 teaspoon grated fresh ginger and 1 peeled and crushed clove of garlic. Stir in the chicken pieces, cover, and marinate for at least 4 hours or overnight in the refrigerator. Buzz 1 (220 g) packet dry roasted peanuts in the processor to coarse crumbs and tip into a small bowl. Using a slotted spoon, arrange the chicken pieces in a single layer in a foil-lined grill pan. Grill for about 10 minutes until golden brown on all sides and tender, stirring once or twice. Serve on a flat platter with the crushed peanuts in the centre and cocktail sticks.

Pineapple and Bacon with Mustard Dip Cut well-drained canned pineapple rings into small pieces, wrap in streaky bacon, and secure with a wooden cocktail stick. Whisk together wholegrain mustard and mayonnaise – about 15 ml/1 tablespoon mustard to 150 ml/¼ pint mayonnaise – and spoon into a small bowl. Grill the pineapple and bacon until golden brown on both sides. Serve hot with the dip.

Ham and Cheese Bites Trim the crusts from 8 slices of bread. Spread 4 slices with 100 g/4 oz smoked ham paté and sprinkle with 175 g/6 oz grated mozzarella. Top with the remaining slices of bread and gently press together. Melt 50 g/2 oz butter with 15 ml/1 tbsp olive oil and brush on to both sides of the sandwiches. Bake at 200°C/400°F/gas mark 6 for 8–10 minutes until golden brown and crunchy. Cut each sandwich into 6 and serve hot.

Crostini Cut a baguette in 1.25 cm/½ inch slices, arrange on a baking tray and lightly brush each one with olive oil. Top with one of the following: drain 1 (285 g) jar mixed peppers in oil and cut up any large pieces of pepper. Arrange on top of the bread slices and sprinkle with grated mozzarella. Thinly slice 100 g/4 oz Gouda and arrange on the bread slices. Drain and finely chop 1 (50 g) can anchovies, pile on top of the cheese and drizzle with a little of the anchovy oil. Spread the bread slices with prepared pesto (see page 118) or pesto from a jar. Thinly slice 1 (150 g) log-shaped goat's cheese and place on top of the pesto. Lightly brush with olive oil. Bake the *crostini* for 10 minutes at 200°C/400°F/gas mark 6 for 8–10 minutes. Serve hot.

Crisp Open Sandwiches Cut a baguette in 1.25 cm/½ inch slices, arrange on a baking sheet and lightly brush each one with olive oil. Bake for 5 minutes at 190°C/375°F/gas mark 5 – this can be done 2–3 hours ahead. These baked toast bases can be topped with a variety of attractive ingredients, all from the supermarket shelves or the delicatessen, to make open sandwiches to be served cold. The combination of toppings is endless – those we especially like include black or green olive paste with slices of hard-boiled egg; garlic and herb-flavoured cream cheese with 'fans' of Italian salami; soured cream topped with slivers of pickled herring dusted with paprika; mayonnaise, Parma ham and black olives; ripe Brie topped with kiwi fruit.

Parmesan Shortcake Make ahead. Heat the oven to 160°C/325°F/gas mark 3. Put 150 g/5 oz plain flour, 50 g/2 oz semolina, salt and freshly milled pepper and 50 g/2 oz grated Parmesan into a food processor. Add 100 g/4 oz firm butter, cut in cubes, and buzz until a ball of dough forms. (Or rub the butter into the dry ingredients with the fingertips.) Place the ball of dough on a lightly greased baking tray and, with lightly floured fingers, press out to a circle approximately 18 cm/7 inches in diameter. The dough should be about 1 cm / ½ inch thick. Prick all over with a fork and neatly shape the edges. Coarsely chop 50 g/2 oz roasted peanuts and scatter over the dough, pressing them in slightly. Bake for 35 minutes. Mark into 16 thin wedges while still warm and allow to cool on the baking tray.

TRUFFLES

Handmade truffles are really very special, whether served with a good cup of coffee at the end of a special meal, or packed in a pretty box for a gift. Rum Cream Truffles are the ultimate super-smooth variety, Almond and Ginger Truffles will appeal to those who are not chocolate lovers, while Fruit and Nut Truffles are for peanut butter addicts.

Almond and Ginger Truffles

MAKES 36

Separate the sponge cakes and break into crumbs, or buzz in a processor. Tip into a bowl. Add the ground almonds. Gently warm the jam until it is runny, breaking up any large pieces of fruit. Add to the sponge cake crumbs with the ginger syrup and rum. Mix with a wooden spoon. Finely chop the stem ginger and stir in.

Take walnut-sized pieces of the mixture and roll into balls, then set on a tray and chill for several hours to dry the surface. Sift some icing sugar on to a sheet of greaseproof paper, add 2 or 3 truffle balls and toss gently to coat with the sugar. Place each truffle in an individual *petit four* case. Repeat with the remaining truffles.

8 trifle sponges
100 g/4 oz ground almonds
60 ml/4 tablespoons apricot jam
30 ml/2 tablespoons stem ginger syrup
30 ml/2 tablespoons rum
2–3 pieces stem ginger
icing sugar

Fruit and Nut Truffles

MAKES 24

Sift the icing sugar into a medium-sized bowl. Separate the dates and chop them coarsely; finely chop the walnuts. Add the dates, nuts and peanut butter to the bowl and mix with a wooden spoon to make a chunky mixture.

Shape teaspoonfuls of the mixture into walnut-sized balls on a sheet of waxed paper. Chill until firm. Melt the chocolate in a bowl set over a pan of hot water (off the heat) (or [M]). Stir until smooth. Using a fork, dip each truffle into the chocolate. Return them to the waxed paper, sprinkle with a little grated chocolate and chill until firm. When firm, pack the truffles in individual *petit four* cases. Store in the refrigerator.

100 g/4 oz icing sugar
100 g/4 oz pressed stoned dates
100 g/4 oz walnut pieces
1 (227 g) jar peanut butter
100 g/4 oz plain chocolate
little grated chocolate

Rum Cream Truffles

MAKES 40

350 g/12 oz plain chocolate
50 g/2 oz unsalted butter
150 ml/$^1/_4$ pint double cream
50 ml/2 fl oz rum
cocoa powder for dusting

Break the chocolate into a medium-sized bowl. Add the butter, cream and rum. Set over a pan of hot (not boiling) water until the chocolate and butter have melted. Stir until the mixture is smooth. Remove the bowl from the saucepan. Cool, then refrigerate for at least 4 hours or overnight.

Beat the mixture with a wooden spoon until smooth. Using 2 teaspoons, shape into walnut-sized mounds on waxed paper. Generously dust with cocoa powder and chill until firm. Place each truffle in an individual *petit four* case. Keep in the refrigerator.

CHAPTER FOURTEEN

Good Ideas

Suggestions for seasonal menus

Sunday Family Lunch

Spring

MAIN COURSES	Baked Cajun Spiced Chicken quarters with Garlicky New Potatoes and steamed green beans	74 and 21
	Lamb Steaks with Herbs and Lemon, Minted Butter Rice and stir-fried mangetout	100 and 157
	Spinach with Mushrooms and Feta Cheese Salad, hot rolls with Lemon and Parsley Butter (V)	37 and 31
DESSERTS	Crushed Strawberry Yogurt Ice-cream with Red Raspberry Sauce	217 and 208
	Pineapple with Vanilla Sugar	212
	Fresh Fruit Shortcake	193

Summer

MAIN COURSES	Cold Baked Salmon with Herbed Potato Salad	58 and 49
	Roast Chicken with Courgette and Lemon Stuffing, Green Herb Rice, Baked Tomatoes in Olive Oil and Herbs	78, 80, 157 and 32
	Fragrant Rice with Summer Garden Vegetables, wedges of Cos lettuce with Blue Cheese Dressing (V)	158 and 51
DESSERTS	Banana Fool	215
	Tangy Orange Yogurt Ice-cream with fresh orange slices	217
	Strawberry and Lemon Layer Cake	207

Autumn

MAIN COURSES

Beef Casserole with Chestnuts and Dumplings, mashed potatoes and stir-fried cabbage 112 and 25

Roast Pork with Red Cabbage with Apple and Orange, Sweet Potatoes with Butter and Brown Sugar 102, 33 and 32

Ricotta and Courgette Lasagne, green salad with Honey Mustard Dressing (V) 119 and 50

DESSERTS

Apple and Cheese Tart 189

Pears with Sugared Cream 193

Lemon Cream Pavlova 216

Winter

MAIN COURSES

Steak and Kidney Pudding, Carrots with Orange and Ginger, steamed broccoli 114 and 32

Glazed Roast Gammon, Corn Fritters and Potato and Onion Galette 106, 32 and 33

White Bean and Vegetable Chilli, rice and warm naan bread (V) 26

DESSERTS

Butterscotch Apple Pudding 192

Chocolate Sauce Pudding 197

Spiced Bananas with vanilla ice-cream 194

Simple Suppers

Spring

Summer

Autumn

MAIN COURSES

Ravioli with Grilled Peppers and Sweet Onions, Avocado salad with Tangy Tomato Mayonnaise [V] 121, 13 and 52

Aubergine and Potato Gratin with Corn Fritters [V] 21 and 32

Smoked Tofu and Vegetable Stir-fry ([V]) 28

DESSERTS

Vanilla ice-cream with Fresh Blackberry Sauce 208

Hot Fruit Salad 218

Amaretti Custards 218

Winter

MAIN COURSES

Scalloped Potatoes with Two Cheeses 174

Bombay Crêpes with Paprika Wedges 70 and 20

White Bean and Vegetable Chilli 26

DESSERTS

Pineapple with Vanilla Sugar 212

Brioche and Apple Croûtes 218

Chocolate ice-cream with hot Caramel Sauce 191

Friends for Lunch

Spring

MAIN COURSES	Tortelloni Salad with Artichokes and Broccoli with hot garlic bread (V)	129
	Grilled Avocados with Prawns and Woodland Mushroom Rice	14 and 157
	Courgette and Lemon Risotto with Chive Butter and hot rolls (V)	160
DESSERTS	Raspberry Sundaes	218
	Ginger and Lime Fruit Salad	213
	Cheese board with Sunflower Cheese Crisps	180 and 179

Summer

MAIN COURSES	Salmon Salad Platter with assorted hot breads and Lemon and Parsley Butter	56 and 31
	Courgette Moulds with Mustard Vinaigrette, Herbed Potato Salad and mixed salad greens (V)	29 and 49
	Fusilli Salad with Parma Ham, ciabatta bread and Italian cheeses	128 and 121
DESSERTS	Lemon sorbet with Red Raspberry Sauce	208
	White Chocolate Cream Pots	218
	Sugared Berries	212

Autumn

MAIN COURSES

Penne with Yellow Peppers and Gorgonzola, Baked Tomatoes in Olive Oil and Herbs (V) 123 and 32

Leek, Scallop and Watercress Soup with hot rolls and Anchovy Butter 7 and 31

Cheese and Leek Bake with sliced tomatoes and Fresh Chive Mayonnaise (V) 171 and 52

DESSERTS

Pears with Sugared Cream 193

Hot Fruit Salad 218

Potted Cheese with Walnuts and crisp apples 176

Winter

MAIN COURSES

Spiced Yellow Rice with Chicken Brochettes and lettuce wedges with Blue Cheese Dressing 154 and 50

Bean and Vegetable Broth with garlic bread and Pepper and Apple Slaw (V) 4 and 51

Chicken in Tomato and Pesto Sauce with Speckled Garlic Rice 77 and 157

DESSERTS

Vanilla Pots de Crème 199

Brioche and Apple Croûtes 218

Coffee ice-cream with hot Chocolate Espresso Sauce 196

Dinner Parties to Impress

Spring

STARTERS	Strawberries and Cucumber in Mint Dressing (V)	14
	Chilled Courgette Soup with Tomato Salsa (V)	10
	Asparagus Vinaigrette (V)	15
MAIN COURSES	Salmon and Wild Rice in Filo Pastry, Glazed Courgettes with Lemon	59 and 32
	Grilled lamb chops with Garlic and Herb Butter with Potato and Onion Galette	31 and 33
	Twice Baked Cheese Soufflés with Garlicky New Potatoes (V)	176 and 21
DESSERTS	Fresh Fruit Shortcake	193
	Lemon Cream Tartlets	219
	Berries with Soft Cheese	212

Summer

STARTERS	Iced Avocado Soup with Pepper Salsa (V)	11
	Melon and Berries (V)	15
	Smoked trout fillets with Lemon and Green Mayonnaise	52
MAIN COURSES	Chicken in Gingered Mango Cream, Golden Rice	81 and 157
	Plaice with Anchovy Crumb Stuffing	66
	Pasta Quills with Stir-Fried Asparagus (V)	124

DESSERTS

Cinnamon Toasts with Fresh Raspberry Compote 183

Cheese and Berry Tartlets 219

Lemon Cream Pavlova 216

Autumn

STARTERS

Crunchy Mushrooms with a choice of Dips ([V]) 13

Chestnut and Carrot Soup [V] 3

Pears and Parma Ham 15

MAIN COURSES

Five-spice Duck with Clementines with wild rice 87

Spiced Lamb with Pears and Dates, couscous and wedges of lettuce and red apples topped with Honey Mustard Dressing 97, 133 and 50

Vegetable Ragoût with Toasted Goat's Cheese, Coleslaw Vinaigrette ([V]) 24 and 51

DESSERTS

Sweet Cheese Crêpes 185

Spiced Sugar Plum Cake 198

Coffee Walnut Puddings with Coffee Cream Sauce 200

Winter

STARTERS

Smoked salmon with wedges of pear and avocado 17

Celery and Stilton Soup [V] 10

Mozzarella and Anchovy Croûtes 15

MAIN COURSES	Pheasant with Rich Fruit Gravy, Quilted Potatoes	84 and 20
	Roast venison, Perfect Roast Potatoes and Red Cabbage with Apple and Orange	115, 20 and 33
	Chestnut Mushroom Risotto, hot French bread and Mixed Mustard Butter (V)	159 and 31
DESSERTS	Coffee Crêpes	186
	Apple and Cheese Tart	189
	Marron Mousse	215

Bountiful Buffets

Dishes chosen for a buffet must fulfil several criteria. They should preferably be able to be eaten just with a fork – ingredients should be cut to bite-size. Ideally they should be suitable for preparing ahead, to be cooked just before serving, or ahead of time and then gently reheated. Remember there may well be a vegetarian among the guests. Salads need to retain their freshness for some time. Serve bowls of cherry tomatoes rather than sliced larger varieties. A platter of cucumber sticks and small wedges of Tom Thumb lettuce with a bowl of dressing or crunchy sea salt crystals to dip into will look appetizing far longer than a bowl of dressed salad greens. Pasta, rice, potato and coleslaw salads are a good choice. Go to town with the desserts, several to choose from are always popular. If the weather is hot, keep any desserts containing cream refrigerated up to the last minute.

Index